LEGENDS & LIONS

IRELAND's GREATEST RUGBY PLAYERS

JOHN D. T. WHITE

This edition published 2024

This book is copyright under the Berne Convention. All rights are reserved. Apart from any fair dealing for the purpose of private study, research, criticism or review, as permitted under the Copyright Act, 1956, no part of this publication may be reproduced, stored in a retrieval system, or transmitted, in any form or by any means, electronic, electrical, chemical, mechanical, optical, photocopying, recording or otherwise, without the prior permission of the copyright owner. Enquiries should be sent to the under mentioned address:

© John White 2024

EMPIRE PUBLICATIONS

1 NEWTON STREET, MANCHESTER M1 1HW

ISBN: 9798877434073

Printed in Great Britain

CONTENTS

INTRODUCTION	7
FOREWORD	11
CIARAN FITZGERALD	13
JOHNNY SEXTON	27
TONY WARD	58
RORY BEST	65
JACK KYLE	79
KEITH EARLS	93
MIKE GIBSON	102
BRIAN O'DRISCOLL	113
WILLIE ANDERSON	126
FERGUS SLATTERY	131
RONAN O'GARA	139
JOHN HAYES	151
OLLIE CAMPBELL	168
RICHARD MILLIKEN	184
WILLIE JOHN McBRIDE	190
KEITH WOOD	195
CIAN HEALY	205
DONNCHA O'CALLAGHAN	216
WILLIE DUGGAN	229

Legends & Lions

CONOR MURRAY 235
PAUL O'CONNELL 245
PETER O'MAHONY 262

<u>THE BIG IRELAND RUGBY QUIZ</u>

QUESTIONS 277
ANSWERS 307
    BIBLIOGRAPHY 320
    BOOKS 320
    POEMS 320
    ACKNOWLEDGEMENTS 320

I am dedicating my book to my two sons, Marc & Paul.
I have loved you both from the moment you were born
and I will never stop loving you.
Your Dad

INTRODUCTION

Rugby is not a matter of life or death. It is much more important than that. Well, so one comedian thought when he told the following joke.

Rhys, a Welsh fan, was watching Wales play Ireland in a Six Nations Championship game at Lansdowne Road, Dublin. In the packed stadium, there was only one empty seat and it was directly in front of him. Rhys tapped the man who was sitting beside the empty seat on the shoulder.

"*Who does that seat belong to?*" asked Rhys.

"*I got the ticket for my wife,*" replied the Irish fan.

"*But why isn't she here?*" asked Rhys.

"*I'm afraid she died in an accident,*" replied the Irish fan.

"*So you're keeping the seat vacant as a mark of respect,*" said Rhys.

"*No,*" said the Irish fan, "*I offered it to all of my friends but none of them wanted it.*"

"*So why didn't they take it?*" asked a puzzled Rhys.

"*They've all gone to her funeral today,*" replied the Irish fan.

This is a book about Ireland's Greatest Ever Players and their exploits for their country in the green jersey. Many played their part in Five Nations Championship successes, Six Nations victories, four glorious Grand Slam wins and helping Ireland become the No.1 ranked rugby nation in the world, and not forgetting a few wooden spoons to mix everything together.

And to add a bit of competition to the mix, I have

Legends & Lions

included a Quiz Section at the end of the book for you to test yourself and your friends on just how well you know Irish Rugby Union.

Not every Irish player gets to answer Ireland's call. But the players who do always remember where they were when they first pulled on an Irish jersey and what they achieved wearing it. Ireland's historic four Provinces have all provided us with many national heroes in a game that gets everyone talking.

To paraphrase Al Pacino in the movie *Any Given Sunday*. *"Life is like rugby, it is a game of inches. In either game, life or rugby, the margin for error is small. One half of a step too late or too early and you don't quite make it. A half of a second, too slow, too fast, you don't quite catch it. Either we heal as a team, or we're going to crumble, inch by inch, play by play, until we're finished. The Ireland players fight for that inch. They tear themselves and everyone else around them to pieces for that inch. They claw with their fingernails for that inch because they know that all of those inches are added up, that's going to make the f***ing difference between winning and losing, between living and dying.*

"I'll tell you this, in any fight, it's the guy who's willing to die, who's going to win that inch. And every Irish player knows that if he is going to have any life anymore, it's because he is still willing to fight and die for that inch because that's what playing for Ireland demands, the six inches in front of his face. Now a coach can't make him do it. He has to look at the teammate next to him, and look deep into his eyes. What he will see is a teammate who is willing to go that inch with him. He is going to see a teammate who is willing to sacrifice himself for the team because he knows when it comes down to it, you're going to do the same for him. That's a team, gentlemen. And either the Irish players heal as a team or they will die as individuals. That's rugby, guys. That's all it is. Now, what

are you going to do?"

For us the fans, WE ARE READY TO ANSWER IRELAND's CALL.

John
An Ireland Fan

FOREWORD

Writing a Legends book covering any sport must be a daunting task for any author to do. Inevitably, the entries in it will produce much debate as to whether this player or that player was better than all of the others who played in the same position as him but, John has not gone down that path.

In this book John has written about the players whom he considers to be the Greatest Ever Irish Players.

You may not agree with all of his choices, but he is not saying that any one player was better than the other. His choices are subjective and his own personal choices.

As you journey through the book John takes us on a magical mystery tour with his writing style because not only has he given us an insight into the player's career in the famous green jersey, but he writes with passion about many of the games the player ran out for Ireland in and what makes the player so special to him.

John's choices of players range from some of the heroes of Ireland's first Grand Slam winning side in 1948, a Golden Era for Irish Rugby, many of the players I admired as a young boy including Mike Gibson and the incomparable Willie John McBride, a number of my former teammates and some of the stars of today.

Each player's biography is jam packed with information, facts, figures, appearances, points scored, honours in the game and even a nice little entry at the end of each story entitled *Did You Know That?*

And for a Bonus Point, there is a superb Quiz Section

at the end of John's book which will test your knowledge of the Ireland team since the formation of the Irish Rugby Football Union in 1879 right up to Ireland's 2023 Rugby World Cup matches.

Sit back and enjoy this wonderful read.

Tony Ward
19 Ireland caps (113 points), 1978-87
1 cap for the British and Irish Lions (18 points)

CIARAN FITZGERALD
Where's Your F***Ing Pride?

CIARAN FINTAN FITZGERALD was born on 4 June 1952 in Loughrea, County Galway. At school the young Fitzgerald was an excellent boxer and hurler and could easily have made a career for himself in either sport but chose rugby union for his career path. He won two All-Ireland Boxing Championships and reached the Minor All-Ireland Hurling Championship final with Galway in 1970 where they lost 5-19 to 2-09 to Cork.

He began playing rugby when he attended Saint Joseph's College, Garbally Park situated near Ballinasloe, County Galway. One of his teachers, a priest named Father John Kirby, decided that his pupil possessed all of the attributes of a hooker. When he left Saint Joseph's he continued playing rugby for University College Galway (UCG) and then played senior rugby for St Mary's College, Dublin. In 1973, he graduated from UCG with a Bachelor's Degree.

Many years after he retired, Ciaran was interviewed prior to Ireland's last ever game at Lansdowne Road, Dublin (26 November 2006) before it was demolished to make way for the Aviva Stadium. He was asked about his memories of Lansdowne Road and when he started to play rugby.

"The first game I watched here was in the mid-sixties. I was kind of steeped in GAA tradition in Loughrea. Hurling, football and boxing were the main sports. I came up when the Galway

footballers won the three-in-a-row and as kids, we worked through the three campaigns. And then we said we'd watch a rugby match and it was Ireland-Wales and I remember saying to myself: 'I could do that or I could play that game.' I didn't play the game for another three or four years, it was my last year in college in Garbally when they were stuck for a hooker, it was Fr. Kirby at the time - he's now a Bishop, he's been elevated since for spotting good talent! They were stuck for a hooker and I looked like the previous hooker that was there, same build, same good looks and same speed! So that's when I ended up starting as hooker, I remember that match (Ireland-Wales) left a lasting impression on me."

Fitzgerald combined his amateur playing career with a career in the Irish Army, serving as an aide-de-camp to the President of Ireland, Dr Patrick Hillery.

"No man will make a great leader who wants to do it all himself or get all the credit for doing it."

Andrew Carnegie,
Scottish-born American Industrialist

Fitzgerald was a natural born leader and his displays for St Mary's College earned him international recognition on 3 June 1979. Ireland were on a Tour of Australia and played two Tests against the Wallabies. Ciaran made his debut for Ireland in the First Test which the visitors won 27-12 at Ballymore, Brisbane. Noel Murphy, the Ireland coach, was impressed with how Ciaran handled himself against a very experienced Australia side. Fitzgerald played in the second Test which Ireland won 9-3 to claim a famous 2-0 Test Series victory.

JOHN WHITE

If you can keep your head when all about you
Are losing theirs and blaming it on you,
If you can trust yourself when all men doubt you,
But make allowance for their doubting too

If you can wait and not be tired by waiting
Or being lied about, don't deal in lies,
Or being hated, don't give way to hating,
And yet don't look too good, nor talk too wise

If you can dream - and not make dreams your master;
If you can think - and not make thoughts your aim;
If you can meet with Triumph and Disaster
And treat those two impostors just the same;

If you can bear to hear the truth you've spoken
Twisted by knaves to make a trap for fools,
Or watch the things you gave your life to, broken,
And stoop and build 'em up with worn-out tools

If you can make one heap of all your winnings
And risk it on one turn of pitch-and-toss,
And lose, and start again at your beginnings
And never breathe a word about your loss;

If you can force your heart and nerve and sinew
To serve your turn long after they are gone,
And so hold on when there is nothing in you
Except the will which says to them: 'Hold on!'

If you can talk with crowds and keep your virtue,
Or walk with Kings - nor lose the common touch,
If neither foes nor loving friends can hurt you,
If all men count with you, but none too much;

If you can fill the unforgiving minute
With sixty seconds' worth of distance run,

Legends & Lions

Yours is the Earth and everything that's in it,
And - which is more - you'll be a Man, my son!

If: A Father's Advice to His Son
by Rudyard Kipling

Throughout his career in the army and in the green jersey of Ireland, Ciaran Fitzgerald had the ability to remain calm and keep his composure in the most difficult of situations.

In 1980, Fitzgerald was a mainstay in the Ireland team and played in all four of their Five Nations Championship matches. On 15 March 1980, he scored his first and only try for Ireland when they defeated Wales 21-7 at Lansdowne Road in the tournament. Fergus Slattery was the Ireland captain. He never pulled on the Ireland jersey at all in 1981 due to an injury but he was back to strength in 1982, this time as captain of Ireland, and led them to the Five Nations Championship title and a Triple Crown success. Only a 22-9 loss to France at Parc des Princes, Paris denied the men in green a historic second Grand Slam. Ciaran played in every game for Ireland. 1982 was a watershed year in Irish rugby because it was the first time in 33 years that Ireland had won the Triple Crown, a time when the memory of an embarrassing whitewash in the Five Nations Championship the previous year was still fresh in the minds of fans.

In a documentary made by RTE entitled "*Where's Your Pride?*" Ciaran recalled the 1982 Triple Crown winning campaign and the evening when it was claimed that he snubbed the Taoiseach, Charlie Haughey.

"*I remember after every match, Charlie Haughey used to ring me, saying, 'Well done, keep it going'. I didn't realise he was talking about the nation and keeping spirits up. I remember in Paris after one match, we were out to dinner and I was at the top table and the usher came over and says, 'Mr Fitzgerald, you are wanted by the prime minister'. I got up, but it took me half-a-mile to get to the phone — and he was gone. I was in the Army at the time, and on Monday morning I got a call to say I was wanted up in the CO's office. I went up to the CO and it was all, what was I doing snubbing the Taoiseach?"*

A year later Ireland were co-winners of the 1983 Five Nations Championship with France, Fitzgerald was still the captain and again he played in all four matches of the tournament.

When the British and Irish Lions squad was selected for their tour of New Zealand in 1983, Willie John McBride (Manager) and Jim Telfer (Coach) laid down a number of conditions that they said would be applied to their choice of captain of the team. Former Lions themselves, the duo made it clear that the captain must be sure of his place in the Test team; that he must be capable of fulfilling his many social obligations; that he must have the respect of his fellow players and that his disciplinary record must be exemplary. Fitzgerald's name was not just on the list of players chosen, he was named captain of the side by McBride and Telfer.

However, Fitzgerald was unfairly targeted by the British press when he was named captain of the 1983 Lions' tour as many thought England's Peter Wheeler or Scotland's Colin Deans should have been the Tour Captain. The sports journalists claimed that when it came to playing hooker, Fitzgerald was not a patch on the other two. In fact, a reporter from the *Daily Mirror* described the decision as: *"one of the most sensational omissions in the 73-year history of the British Lions tours."* Clive

Legends & Lions

Woodward, who was a centre for Leicester and England at the time, and who went on the 1983 Tour, was critical of the England set-up for not appointing Wheeler as the captain of England after Bill Beaumont retired in 1982. Steve Smith (Sale) succeeded Beaumont and was also a member of the 1983 Lions squad in New Zealand. But, Big Willie John, always up for a fight on the pitch as many an All Black and Springbok can testify to, was having none of it, saying: *"Ciaran's qualities of leadership not only this year, but for the past two years, made him a pretty foregone conclusion."*

"Lead Me, Follow Me or Get Out of My Way. "

General George S. Patton, US Army

Despite the criticisms, Fitzgerald remained unflappable and concentrated on the job ahead of him and his teammates. *"To win a Series in New Zealand is the ultimate. I have not been there before, but I know enough to say it will be extremely hard, physically and mentally. I see team spirit and teamwork as a crucial element. We must have a unanimity of purpose and must appreciate all the difficulties. There is talent in the squad, but we must use that talent."* Deans went on the Tour but Wheeler didn't.

The Lions played four Test Matches against the All Blacks, Ciaran captained them in all four games but they lost the Test Series, blackwashed 4-0. Ciaran played in 7 of the Lions' other 14 games on the Tour.

Quite spookily, in the year Ciaran was born, one of the most popular songs played on the radio was a song written by Johnnie Ray called *The Little White Cloud That Cried*. New Zealand is known as *The Land of the White Cloud*, but the battle hardened Galway man was not one for crying over spilt beer.

JOHN WHITE

Scotland were Grand Slam winners in 1984, Scotland's 12th Home/Five Nations Championship title and only their second Grand Slam having first won it in 1925. But twelve months later Fitzgerald once more led Ireland to a Five Nations Championship title and Triple Crown success in 1985.

It was during the 1985 Five Nations Championship that Ciaran Fitzgerald's name was engraved in Irish Rugby history. When Ireland went into the 1985 Five Nations Championship, they were seen as the Whipping Boys of the most prestigious Rugby Union tournament in the northern hemisphere. In the 1984 edition of the tournament Ireland played four games and lost them all, thereby being awarded the unwanted Wooden Spoon. They scored 39 points and conceded 87: losing 25-12 away to France, 18-9 to Wales in Dublin, 12-9 versus England at Twickenham Stadium and a demoralising 32-9 hammering by Scotland in the Irish capital. Mick Doyle was the Ireland coach and he was under extreme pressure to turn things around for a proud rugby nation.

First up for Ireland in the 1985 Five Nations Championship was a trip to the Scottish capital, Edinburgh, where they defeated Scotland 18-15 at Murrayfield Stadium. According to most rugby pundits at the time, Ireland had no chance of winning the game against the reigning Champions. It was more a case of by how many points would Ireland lose the match. In their second game of the tournament, Ireland drew 15-15 with France at Lansdowne Road but the Championship title and the Triple Crown was still on. Matchday Three took Ireland to the *Land of my Fathers*, where they beat Wales 21-9 at the National Stadium, Cardiff. On 30 March 1985, Ireland welcomed England to Lansdowne Road for their final game. The Triple Crown was at stake as was the outcome of the Five Nations Championship.

On the day the Irish players delivered, they stepped up to the mark, and won the game 13-10. But, they needed a little encouragement from their captain, Ciaran Fitzgerald. With ten minutes of the game remaining Ireland were trailing 10-7 (Brendan Mullin scored a try and Michael Kiernan scored a penalty) and many of the Ireland players looked like they had nothing more to give for the green jersey, a quagmire of a pitch having sapped their energy. Fitzgerald walked up to his forwards and although the television microphone nearby could not pick up what he said, everyone could read his lips as he uttered: *Where's your f*****g pride?* Many of the fans standing in the decrepit old stands at Lansdowne Road heard their captain's *Call To Arms* and the forwards answered. Michael Kiernan scored a penalty to level the scores before Rob Andrew saw his third penalty attempt sail wide which would have given England a three point advantage once again (Rory Underwood scored a try with Andrew stroking two penalties between the posts).

Cometh the Hour, Cometh the Man and that man was Kiernan who scored a deftly taken drop goal to seal victory for Ireland, win the Triple Crown and claim the 1985 Five Nations Championship. You could have forgiven Ciaran if he had said *Pride F***ing Restored* after winning the match for Ireland but alas he held his emotions well and truly in check. Coach Mick Doyle had a smile on his face wider than the pitch itself.

Winger Trevor Ringland played in the game and some years after it he was asked what effect his captain's words had on the team. Ringland said: "*I'm not sure I actually heard it. But I could see him remonstrating with the forwards and I could certainly understand the message. It was an intervention. And you see in different sports, in many areas of life, at crucial times, an intervention being made that makes a difference. And to me, that was a classic case of one that worked. He inspired the forwards, he made a decision to take a quick throw in, move the ball. And that inspired piece of leadership opened up the game and give Michael the opportunity to kick the points. He knew exactly what he was doing, knew exactly what we needed to do. He had a very clear plan and it worked."*

It was Ireland's sixth Triple Crown win and their tenth overall victory (excluding eight other shared titles) in the Home/Five Nations Championship. Ireland's 1985 Five Nations Championship winning side proved to be their last for 24 years, until their Grand Slam victory in 2009.

Ciaran's rallying call to his teammates was just one example of many moments of inspirational leadership produced by the Irish army man over his career, for Connacht, Ireland and the Lions.

The 1986 Five Nations Championship campaign proved to be the end of the road for Ireland's successful run in the 1980's, they ended up Wooden Spoon winners with no points to their name, and it marked the end of Fitzgerald's international career. On 15 March 1986, he led Ireland out at Lansdowne Road for their Five Nations Championship encounter versus Scotland. It was not the farewell to the Irish fans the Connacht native had hoped for as the visitors spoilt his exit from World Rugby by beating Ireland 10-9. Donal Lenihan who lined out alongside him for the game succeeded Fitzgerald as the captain of Ireland. It was Ciaran's 25th appearance for Ireland in a seven year Test career.

"Leadership is a potent combination of strategy and character. But

Legends & Lions

if you must be without one, be without the strategy."

General Norman Schwarzkopf Jr, US Army

Ciaran Fitzgerald captained Connacht for a decade, representing them for 16 seasons.

In the year of Ciaran's birth, John Ford's magnificent movie *The Quiet Man* was a must-see in the cinema houses up and down the length and breadth of Ireland. Although in the movie Sean Thornton (John Wayne) and Mary Kate Danaher (Maureen O'Hara) get up to all sorts of exploits in Innisfree, County Donegal, the movie was actually filmed in the village of Cong in County Mayo. Cong is situated just 48 miles from Loughrea, and when he was on a rugby pitch, Fitzgerald was most definitely no Quiet Man.

Four years after the leader of the Ireland Rugby Union team wore the green jersey for the last time, he put on a green tracksuit and was the Ireland coach from 1990-92. Under his stewardship Ireland finished fourth in the 1990 Five Nations Championship which was won by Grand Slam winners Scotland. Ireland, jointly captained by Lenihan and Willie Anderson, won just once, 14-8 against Wales, and lost three times. In the 1991 edition of the competition, Fitzgerald chose Rob Saunders as his captain. Many Ireland Rugby sports journalists were scratching their heads at his decision to hand the captaincy to a scrum half who was born in Nottingham, England on 5 August 1968, and who had only made his international debut for Ireland in their opening game of the 1991 Five Nations Championship, a 21-13 loss to France in Dublin. As it turned out, Saunders was no Robin Hood as Ireland could only manage a draw, 21-21 against Wales in Cardiff, and suffered three losses to finish one place above Wales at the foot of the table. Saunders' career in a green jersey was a short lived one as he only made 12 appearances for Ireland, although he did play in all four of Ireland's games at the 1991 Rugby World Cup, when Philip Matthews was Fitzgerald's captain.

At the 1991 Rugby World Cup, Fitzgerald's Ireland side came within minutes of a semi-final place only for Australia's Michael Lynagh to deny them with a try at the death in Lansdowne Road. The Wallabies won the game 19-18 and went on to win the 1991 Rugby World Cup after defeating England 12-6 in the final. To use the title of a song written by Cole Porter for the 1941 movie *You'll Never Get Rich*, it was a case of *So Near and Yet So Far,* for Fitzgerald's army of rugby players.

Ireland endured two extremely embarrassing losses to Namibia away prior to the 1991 Rugby World Cup. In Fitzgerald's last season as the coach of Ireland, they took home another Wooden Spoon having lost all four of their matches in the 1992 Five Nations Championship. The IRFU replaced Ciaran with Gerry Murphy.

The motto of Fitzgerald's birthplace, Loughrea, is *Dia d'ár Stiúrú*, meaning *God our Steerer*. Quite an appropriate motto for one of their sons who steered Ireland to Five Nations Championsip glory in 1983.

> *"I Am a Soldier, I Fight Where I Am Told and I Win Where I Fight."*
>
> General George S. Patton, US Army

Ciaran Fitzgerald may not have played anywhere near the number of internationals for Ireland that the likes of Ronan O'Gara (128), Cian Healy (125), Rory Best (124), John Hayes (105), Keith Earls (101) or Peter Stringer (98) amassed, but then again he was playing in the amateur era and had retired one year before the inaugural Rugby World Cup in 1987 and before the introduction of the annual Autumn Internationals Series. But, none of these players had the leadership qualities which Fitzgerald oozed in abundance: Communication, Courage, Delegation, Empathy, Gratitude, Influence, Integrity, Learning Agility, Respect and Self-Awareness. And when you add up the number of British and Lions caps these six Ireland Legends won during their careers it merely equals the four Ciaran won.

If you could sum Ciaran up in a single song, that song would be *The Champion*, by Carrie Underwood.

I'll be the last one standing
Two hands in the air, I'm a champion
You'll be looking up at me when it's over
I live for the battle, I'm a soldier, yeah
I'm a fighter like Rocky
Put your flag on your back like Ali
Yeah, I'm the greatest, I'm stronger
Paid my dues, can't lose, I'ma own ya, ay
I've been working my whole life
And now it's do or die
I am invincible, unbreakable
Unstoppable, unshakable
They knock me down, I get up again
I am the champion, you're gon' know my name
You can't hurt me now, I can't feel the pain
I was made for this, yeah, I was born to win
I am the champion
When they write my story
They gonna say that I did it for the glory
But don't think that I did it for the fame, yeah

JOHN WHITE

I did it for the love of the game, yeah
And this is my chance I'm taking
All them old records, I'm breaking
All you people watching on the TV
You go ahead and put your bets on me, ay
I've been waiting my whole life
To see my name in lights
I am invincible, unbreakable
Unstoppable, unshakable
They knock me down, I get up again
I am the champion, you're gon' know my name
You can't hurt me now, I can't feel the pain
I was made for this, yeah, I was born to win
I am the champion, oh-oh
Born champion, Luda
The C is for the courage I possess through the trauma (yeah)
H is for the hurt, but it's all for the honor
A is for my attitude working through the patience (hey)
Money comes and goes, so the M is for motivation
Gotta stay consistent, the P is for persevere
The I is for integrity, innovative career (career)
The O is optimistic, open and never shut
And the N is necessary 'cause I'm never givin' up
See, they ask me how I did it, I just did it from the heart
Crushin' the competition, been doing it from the start
They say that every champion is all about his principles
Carrie
I am invincible, unbreakable
Unstoppable, unshakable
They knock me down, I get up again
I am the champion, you're gon' know my name
You can't hurt me now, I can't feel the pain
I was made for this, yeah, I was born to win

Legends & Lions

I am the champion
I'm the champion, yeah, surpassed all rivals
It's all about who wants it the most
I am the champion
Fight for what we believe in
That's what champions are made of
I am the champion (yeah, champion)

Ciaran Fitzgerald was a true Champion, a soldier and a fighter on and off the field, and every time he pulled on a green jersey he showed his *F***ing Pride*.

Did You Know That?

When Captain Ciaran Fitzgerald retired from the army in 1986, the soldiers at his Barracks held a whip round and bought him a Hi-Fi system as a going away present.

JOHNNY SEXTON

The Impossible Dream Made Possible

"Before I formed you in the womb I knew you, before you were born I set you apart; I appointed you as a prophet to the nations."

Jeremiah 1:5

Jonathan Jeremiah Sexton was born on 11 July 1985, in Rathgar, Dublin but his family ties stretch out to North Kerry and West Clare. His uncle, William Sexton, played flanker for Garryowen, Munster and was capped three times by Ireland, winning his first cap on 10 November 1984, in a 16-9 loss to Australia at Lansdowne Road. The game also saw the Ireland debuts of Willie Anderson, Michael Bradley, Philip Matthews and Brendan Mullin. In his early years Johnny played mini-rugby with Bective Rangers, Donnybrook, Dublin, a club his father has been a member of for many years. Sexton attended Saint Mary's College, Rathmines, Dublin and in 2002, he helped the team win the Leinster Senior Schools Cup. It was their fifth, and to date last, victory in the competition (1961, 1966, 1969 & 1994). They defeated Belvedere College 10-6 in the final with Johnny scoring a drop goal with only a matter of seconds remaining in the game. Johnny would make the drop goal attempt a big part of his armoury as France found out in Paris in 2018 when Johnny landed one from 45 metres out in the 83rd minute of the game to give Ireland a 15-13 win in their opening match of the 2018 Six Nations Championship.

In the year Johnny was born, *The Jewel of the Nile*, was a very popular movie to go to the cinema to watch. In

2002, Leinster had found their very own jewel, an emerald, in the shape of a 17-year old Sexton and added him to their squad. But, Johnny had to be patient and bide his time to be able to show what he could do out on the pitch as the Leinster squad in season 2002-03 was packed with talent including Victor Costello, Leo Cullen, Gordon D'Arcy, Girvan Dempsey, Denis Hickie, Shane Horgan, Brian O'Driscoll, Malcolm O'Kelly and a young fly-half named Andy Dunne who Johnny had to usurp from the side. However, Dunne proved to be the least of Johnny's concerns when Leinster signed the sublime Argentinian fly-half, Felipe Contepomi, from Bristol Bears in 2003.

In season 2005-06, Johnny's superb displays for Saint Mary's College resulted in him getting one game for Leinster, a substitute appearance versus the Border Reivers in the Celtic League. The following season he played three times for Leinster, scoring his first points for the team when he converted a try versus Ospreys in the first of these, a 45-22 win at Donnybrook Stadium, Dublin on 6 January 2007, in the Celtic League. Johnny followed this up by scoring three penalties in his other two matches, versus Ulster and Munster. Leinster won the Celtic League in season 2007-08, Johnny's first winners' medal with the side, scoring 73 points overall that season.

Johnny received a call-up from the Ireland coach, Eddie O'Sullivan, to join his 2008 Six Nations Championship squad but had to withdraw from it after fracturing a thumb playing for Leinster prior to the tournament. He was part of the Ireland squad that won the 2009 Six Nations Championship, Triple Crown and Grand Slam, but did not feature in any of their five matches.

First released in 1988, Whitney Houston's power ballad, *One Moment In Time*, was a very popular song which was still being played on the radio in 2009. The song was written for the 1988 Olympic Games hosted by Seoul, South Korea and has since been an inspiration to many athletes and sports stars with lines from it including:

> *Each day I live*
> *I want to be*
> *A day to give*
> *The best of me*
> *I'm only one*
> *But not alone*
> *My finest day*
> *Is yet unknown*
> *I broke my heart*
> *Fought every gain*
> *To taste the sweet*
> *I face the pain*
> *I rise and fall*
> *Yet through it all*
> *This much remains*
> *I want one moment in time*
> *When I'm more than I thought I could be*
> *When all of my dreams are a heartbeat away*
> *And the answers are all up to me*
> *Give me one moment in time*
> *When I'm racing with destiny*
> *Then in that one moment of time*
> *I will feel*
> *I will feel eternity"*

On 2 May 2009, Johnny's *One Moment In Time* came

when he replaced the injured Contepomi in Leinster's Heineken Cup semi-final match against their bitterest of rivals, Munster, the reigning holders of the Heineken Cup, at Croke Park, Dublin. In the 25th minute of the game, Johnny stepped on to the pitch in front of 82,208 fans and his first duty was to kick a penalty to restore his team's lead (the score was 3-3). For Johnny, it must have felt like a footballer coming on as a substitute in the final of the Champions League and being handed the ball by his captain and asked to score an important penalty kick with his first touch of the ball. He was racing with destiny and Johnny seized his big moment in a Leinster shirt and slotted over the penalty and then added two conversions to tries scored in the second half by Luke Fitzgerald and O'Driscoll, although he did miss his first conversion attempt when D'Arcy scored a try in the first half. The attendance was a world record crowd for a club rugby Union match. He then started in Leinster's home match against the Scarlets in the Celtic League, scoring 15 points (including a try) to win the Man of the Match award. On 23 May 2009, life had come full circle for him when he starred in Leinster's 19-16 victory against Leicester Tigers in the 2009 Heineken Cup final played at Murrayfield Stadium. Once again Johnny gave the best of himself scoring 11 of his side's points, converting Jamie Heaslip's try, kicking over two penalties (missed one) and landing a drop goal. O'Driscoll also got in on the action with a well taken drop goal even Johnny would have been proud of. It was Leinster's first triumph in the competition.

On 12 March 2009, it was announced that Contepomi would be leaving Leinster at the end of the season, and that he had signed a 4-year deal to join French side, RC

JOHN WHITE

Toulon. He was 32-years old at the time but he would have realised that his time was up at Leinster as Johnny, aged 23, had not just been constantly knocking on the manager's office door with his performances in the side when he was presented with them, he practically had kicked the hinges off Michael Chieka's door. Indeed, Johnny's consistency in scoring points in matches saw him play for Ireland A in the 2009 Churchill Cup, 6-16 June 2009, in Colorado, USA. Declan Kidney's Ireland A defeated England Saxons 49-22 in the final with Johnny scoring three penalties and three conversions, and he managed this despite being sin binned in a game which saw tempers flare on both sides.

Five months later, 21 November 2009, another step on his path of destiny which saw voted the greatest player in the world by his peers in 2018, presented itself. Johnny was awarded his first Ireland cap when Declan Kidney selected his to start at fly-half versus Fiji at the RDS Arena, Dublin. Kidney had named Johnny in his squad for the 2009 Six Nations Championship but never used him, the ever reliable Ronan O'Gara was Ireland's one-man kicking machine at the time. Ireland beat Fiji 41-6 and Johnny was at the heart of the Irish action, as if he knew that his time had come and now he had to show the world just how good he really was. The weather was atrocious in the Irish capital with the wind swirling around the pitch, but Johnny kept his composure and scored 16 of Ireland's points, converting all five of their tries and kicking over two penalties which earned him the Man of the Match award. It was a hugely impressive debut for the boy from the Southside of Dublin.

No doubt if the famous Irish novelist, James Joyce (1882-1941), who was born in Brighton Square, Rathgar not far from the Sexton family home, had been alive and writing about Sexton's debut in a green jersey he would have likened Johnny to Daedalus from Greek mythology. Joyce's first novel was *A Portrait of a Young Man*, published in 1916. The story traces the religious and intellectual awakening of young Stephen Daedalus, Joyce's fictional alter ego, whose surname alludes to Greek mythology's consummate architect and craftsman, who was considered a symbol of knowledge, power and wisdom. Johnny possessed all of these attributes in rugby terms, a master craftsman with a rugby ball in his hands or at his feet.

Kidney was clearly very impressed with his young charge and picked him ahead of the 33-year old O'Gara to face South Africa at Croke Park a week later. The Springboks were the reigning World Champions having defeated England 15-6 in the 2007 Rugby World Cup final at Stade de France, Paris. South Africa were also the reigning Tri-Nations Champions. It was a huge leap of faith for Kidney to play Johnny ahead of the much vastly more experienced O'Gara but sometimes a coach just knows when the time is right to test a player who up until that time had been a prodigious talent and a novice in the international arena of rugby union. The Ireland coach was not one for letting his sense of morals prevent him from doing what he felt was right.

"The will to win, the desire to succeed, the urge to reach your full potential. These are the keys that will unlock the door to personal excellence."

Confucius

Ireland beat the World Champions 15-10 and not even the legendary Joyce who wrote about the exploits of Leopold Bloom, his character in his masterpiece *Ulysses*, over the course of one day in Dublin, would have believed the exploits of Johnny Sexton over the course of 80 minutes in a green jersey that day. Sexton scored all 15 of Ireland's points from five penalties (10 mins, 30 mins, 48 mins, 52 mins, 68 mins) in what was a masterclass of a performance in a game during which he totally outshined his opposite No.1o, Morne Steyn. The Springbok fly-half, who scored a penalty in the 2007 Rugby World Cup final, could only manage to score a conversion and a drop goal before being replaced by Ruan Pienaar.

Post the match it was announced that Johnny played out the final stages of the game with a broken hand. Confucius knew what he was talking about when it came to Sexton. Ironically, the B side to *One Moment In Time* is *Love Is A Contact Sport*. The Irish fans had found a new love to admire for many years to come. There was no way back for Johnny after Ireland's thrilling victory against South Africa and he played in four of Ireland's five games (missed the Italy game) in the 2010 Six Nations Championship. He was named in Ireland's squad for the 2010 Summer Tests when they toured Australia and New Zealand. He came off the bench to replace O'Gara against the All Blacks in a 66-28 loss in New Plymouth, New Zealand, scoring a conversion in the 76th minute after D'Arcy crossed over the line for a try. He then started against New Zealand Maori and kicked 23 points in a 31-28 loss, and kept his place in the team against Australia, kicking all of Ireland's 15 points in the game. However, the Wallabies ran out 22-15 winners in Brisbane, Australia. Johnny rounded off a successful 2010 for him personally by playing in three of Ireland's

Legends & Lions

four Autumn Tests in their brand new home, the Aviva Stadium, Dublin. Ireland lost 23-21 to the Springboks and 38-18 to the All Blacks but defeated Argentina 29-9, scoring 34 points in the three Tests. Ireland also defeated Samoa 20-10 when Johnny was an unused replacement.

Johnny played 19 times for Leinster in season 2010-11, scoring 237 points, and helped them to win the Heineken Cup when he scored 28 of his team's 33 points to defeat Northampton Saints 33-22 in the final played at the Millennium Stadium, Cardiff. Sexton scored two tries which he converted, converted a try scored by Nathan Hines, and successfully booted over four of his five penalty kick attempts. Remarkably, the Saints led 22-6 at the interval but in the second half, Bram Stoker who wrote *Dracula* and lived in Orwell Park, Rathgar for a time, would have been proud of Johnny's display as he went straight for the jugular of his opponents and drew blood time and time again. The American singer-songwriter, Billy Joel, once famously said that *"I'd rather laugh with the sinners than cry with the Saints. The sinners are much more fun."* Johnny was most definitely a sinner in the eyes of the Northampton Saints for what he did to them over the course of a blistering 40 minute attack on them after the interval, but Johnny didn't care as he was too busy celebrating and laughing with his teammates as they paraded the trophy before a big Irish contingent in the Principality. His 28 points in the match makes him the second-highest scorer in one game in Heineken Cup history. Ireland's David Humphrey's holds the record after scoring 37 points for Ulster versus Wasps in 2002. Johnny stated that his career-defining performance was dedicated to his late grandfather, John Sexton, who had died just a few months earlier.

JOHN WHITE

Billy Joel released his *River of Dreams* album in 1993. Johnny Sexton delivered a performance against the Northampton Saints that could have turned the River Taff, which runs alongside the Millennium Stadium, into a *River of Blood* of his opponents.

A week after they broke the hearts of 15 Saints, Leinster faced their nemesis, Munster, in the final of the Celtic League. The match was played on 28 May 2011 at Thomond Park, Limerick. A unique, indeed unprecedented, Double was there for the taking but a victory was not going to be taken for granted or going to be easy at the home of Munster rugby. This would be a battle of Titanic proportions with two tribes going to war. Leinster were favourites to win but when you faced a side captained by Paul O'Connell, nothing was a certainty. It was also going to be a battle between two of Ireland's precious gems, O'Gara v Sexton, rugby union's equivalent of Borg v McEnroe. Perhaps Ronan did have a bit of the Bjorn Borg about him, the elder of the two fly-halves, a serial winner and as cool a customer you could find yourself facing on a tennis court. When Borg met John McEnroe in the final of the 1981 Wimbledon Men's Singles Championship, Bjorn had already won 11 Tennis Grand Slam Singles titles compared to McEnroe's two. McEnroe was known for his shot-making and volleying skills and Johnny knew a thing or two about taking shots at the goal posts. But, more importantly, O'Gara was himself a Grand Slam winner with Ireland in 2009 when all Johnny could do was sit in the stands with the Ireland replacements cheering their teammates on in the 2009 Six Nations Championship.

In the final, before a crowd of 26,100 fans, it was Johnny who won the head-to-head points scoring war with O'Gara, scoring 9 to Ronan's 4, but it was the Munster fly-half who had the last laugh as his side won the game 19-9. Unlike the 2011 Heineken Cup final there was no Man of the Match award and bottle of champagne for Sexton in the 2011 Celtic League final. Instead, Johnny and his teammates had to settle for a few bottles of cider to drown their sorrows courtesy of the tournament's sponsors, Magners. Sexton started Ireland's first two Pool C matches in the 2011 Rugby World Cup hosted by New Zealand and came off the bench in their last two Pool matches, replacing O'Gara in the 67th minute in both matches. Ireland topped Pool C with four wins from four including a 15-6 win versus the Wallabies, with all of Ireland's points scored by Sexton and O'Gara. Johnny could only manage to score 2/5 penalties whilst O'Gara, who came on as a substitute in the 50th minute for D'Arcy, scored 2/2 penalty attempts. Johnny also scored a drop goal. O'Gara was Ireland coach Kidney's preferred No.10 for their quarter-final game against Wales which they lost 22-10.

In 2012, he played in all of Ireland's Six Nations Championship matches and collected a third Heineken Cup winners' medal following Leinster's 42-14 defeat of Ulster at Twickenham Stadium. He made 3/3 conversion attempts and scored 3/4 penalty kicks. Leinster were narrowly beaten 31-20 by Ospreys in the final of the 2012 Pro 12 which was played at Leinster's own RDS Arena, with Johnny notching-up 15 points in the game.

Season 2012-13 was a hugely successful one for Johnny at club level. He helped Leinster win their first Pro 12 title since 2008, when it was known as the Celtic League, having been runners-up in the previous three seasons. Leinster defeated Ulster 24-18 in the final which was played at the RDS Arena. The Ulster side's talisman was the South African scrum-half, Ruan Pienaar, a truly exquisite player who like Sexton, could win a game for his team on his own. Pienaar, who was born in Bloemfontein, the capital city of the Free State Province of South Africa, was Ulster's Lethal Weapon, and unleashed and in form, his kicking game could destroy opponents without the necessity of his forwards crossing the goal line to score a try. Bloemfontein is known as the country's *Judicial Capital*, and Pienaar was Ulster's law maker, Judge, Jury and all too often, Executioner. Ruan scored all 18 points for Ulster in the game, a perfect six from six penalties. Shane Jennings and Jamie Heaslip scored a try each in the final, Johnny missed one of the conversions, but successfully landed 4/5 penalty opportunities. Sexton was a Weapon of Mass Destruction. Many sports stars have their boots and shoes inscribed with their shirt number or the name of one of their children. Johnny's right boot should have not only included his sponsor's logo but a warning to opposing players that read: "*Exocet Missile Loaded. In-coming attack. Take shelter.*" Johnny also helped Leinster win their first Amlin Cup Challenge (European Challenge Cup) in season 2012-13, beating Stade Francais 34-13 at the RDS Arena. If Johnny had been performing on a gymnastics mat that afternoon in the Men's Floor Gymnastics final at an Olympic Games, the Score Judges would have all given him a Perfect 10. Leinster scored four tries which Johnny converted and he made 2/2 from penalty kicks. However, many fans believed that it would be the last time they would see Johnny play on home turf wearing Leinster blue as he had already announced in January 2013, that he would

Legends & Lions

be joining Racing 92 (France) for season 2013-14. He spent a portion of the 2012-13 season side-lined due to injury, making only two appearances in the 2013 Six Nations Championship which allowed his understudy Ian Madigan to fill in for him for club and country.

"Goodbyes make you think. They make you realise what you've had, what you've lost, and what you've taken for granted."

Ritu Ghatourey, Indian Actress and Singer

The Leinster fans gave Johnny a standing ovation when the game ended, and as if one voice, you could hear them say:

"How can I put into words how wonderful it has been to watch you play for Leinster and for the wonderful memories you have given me? Through all the ups and downs, twists and turns, it has been one interesting ride. But now it has come to an end, and it is time to say goodbye. This has been an experience I will cherish forever. Thank you for everything you did for Leinster. This may be goodbye but it is not the last time we will see each other again, as we look forward to welcoming you back to Dublin, your home, in a green jersey. Bon Voyage."

Johnny played 110 times for Leinster and scored 1,027 points. His former adversary for the Ireland No.10 jersey, O'Gara, was appointed by Racing 92 as a coach in July 2013.

"I'm always looking for a new challenge. There are lots of mountains to climb out there. When I run out of mountains, I'll build a new one.

Sylvester Stallone

Sexton's first season in French Rugby was most certainly

going to be a challenge, a rugby equivalent of scaling peaks never seen before for his new club based in Nanterre, suburban Paris. They had not been crowned French Top 14 Champions since 1990 (winners in 1892, 1900, 1902 and 1959), and had never won, or even reached the final of, the European Rugby Champions Cup (Heineken Cup). But, the French outfit spent big in an attempt to bring success back to the club by also signing Sexton's British and Irish Lions' teammates Danny Lydiate (Wales) and Jamie Roberts (Wales). Three marquee signings for the team nicknamed Les Racingmen who hoped would increase the heartbeat of their fans at their home ground, Paris La Defense Arena. When asked about his decision to leave Leinster, Johnny cited the Parisian club's ambitious new project and impressive training facilities as factors in choosing them over traditionally more successful European clubs outside Ireland. And, he had many suitors chasing his signature to join their club.

"Every season is a new challenge to me, and I always set out to improve in terms of games, goals, assists."

Cristiano Ronaldo

Ronaldo left Manchester United at the end of the 2008-09 season after helping the team win the Premier League Championship title. A year earlier, he scored for United in the 2008 Champions League final, defeating Chelsea on penalties. Johnny left Leinster having played a key role for them winning the 2012-13 Pro 12 Championship and claiming their first ever European Challenge Cup. Ronaldo was to World football what Johnny was to World Rugby. But, crucially, both players were their team's Superstar, their Go To Player, the one player his manager and his teammates

Legends & Lions

depended on to secure a win for the team. Five months and three days may have separated these two Sporting Icons at birth, CR7 was born on 5 February 1985, but you could place a sheet of paper between the pair when measuring the importance they brought on to the field of play with them. Ironically, both stand 6 feet, 2 inches tall but in reality they are towering Giants in their respective sports. "Doing the difficult things again and again have built the giants, the legends, the icons and the superstars."

Hiral Nagda, Author & Motivational Speaker

In 2013, Johnny toured Australia with the British & Irish Lions, starting in all three Tests against the Wallabies, with the Lions winning the Test Series 2-1. Leigh Halfpenny (Wales) was coach Warren Gatland's preferred kicker but Johnny did score a try in their 41-16 win over the Wallabies. Sexton then played in all five games of Ireland's 2014 Six Nations Championship winning campaign.

In Sexton's first year as a Racing 92 player, the team struggled to impose itself as a force in Europe, as they failed to qualify from the group stages of the Heineken Cup. Had Johnny made the wrong step on the ladder of his career? Johnny's sabbatical from his homeland only lasted two seasons, and like the Italian Explorer, Christopher Columbus, searching for the New World in 1492, he decided to return home. In the summer of 2014, Johnny announced that he would be returning to his spiritual home, the RDS Arena, for the start of the 2015-16 season. He said:

"I am pleased to be re-joining Leinster, the club where I started my professional career. I grew up playing my rugby in Leinster and always wanting to pull on the blue jersey so I am delighted to be able to return to play my club rugby in Ireland. I get along

JOHN WHITE

with everyone here and it was a tough decision to take but I had to make a choice for my family and my Test career."

Johnny was one of the players nominated for World Rugby Player of the Year in 2014 but lost out to New Zealand' Brodie Retallick. In the 2015 Six Nations Championship he played in four of Ireland's five games, missing the win over Italy.

During his two year French odyssey he played 40 times for Racing 92, whose home shirt is very similar to the Argentina rugby home jersey, nicknamed *The Pumas*, with light blue and white stripes, and scored 350 points. He just missed home, and just maybe, he missed home cooking. France is famous for some of the best culinary dishes in the world including Bourguignon, Coq au Vin and Ratatouille, but perhaps Sexton just missed his home comforts in the kitchen of soda bread and all that Dublin Bay brought forth for the city's Fishermen, including Coalfish, Ling Pallack, Wrasse over the seas and Codling, Conger, Dogfish, Ray, Spurdog and Whiting caught over mixed ground and sand. And, for Johnny, not forgetting Boxty, Dublin Coddle and Irish Stew. L'Escargot (snails) is another hugely popular delicacy in France, but Johnny's play was a Galaxy away from being pedestrian, slow paced. His game was High Tempo, and watching him play was like booking a ticket to ride on "*The Steel Vengeance*," taking your seat on the only Rollercoaster Ride in the world to score 100% for the thrill factor. Johnny wasn't a Puma, he was a Lion.

"A career is a series of ups and downs, of comebacks."

Steve Guttenberg, American Actor

The parable of the *Prodigal Son*, recounted in Luke 15:11-32, is one of the most famous parables from the New

Legends & Lions

Testament. A man had two sons. The younger son asked his father to give him the money that he had promised him when he passed away, and his father obliged. The younger son then left home and went to live in a "far country" where he squandered his entire inheritance, before returning home much to the joy of his father who had missed him so very dearly. Leinster's Prodigal Son had returned home and was keen to repay the fans for welcoming him back to Dublin.

An injury prevented Johnny from making his second debut for Leinster until 1 November 2015. True to form he scored a conversion in their 27-3 Pro12 victory over Benetton Rugby at Stadio Comunale di Monigo, Treviso, Italy. In his first season back at Leinster (2015–16), Johnny played 16 times, scoring two tries and scored a total of 103 points. Despite his comeback, Leinster finished the season without a trophy, losing 20-12 to Connacht in the Guinness Pro12 final played at Murrayfield Stadium. Connacht had never reached the final before whilst Leinster, coached by Leo Cullen, were seeking a record fifth win in the competition. Johnny scored a conversion and a penalty in the game. In the 2015-16 European Rugby Champions Cup Leinster finished rock bottom of Pool 5 with only one win from their six games played.

"I pay no attention whatever to anybody's praise or blame. I simply follow my own feelings."

Wolfgang Amadeus Mozart

Johnny's mind-set was not too dissimilar to the great Austrian composer's, in that he never got upset if the press criticised his performance for club or country and likewise, he never got carried away with the constant adulation heaped upon him. He just got on with his own game as normal, no changes or re-wiring of his approach to games was required.

Sexton played in all of Ireland's games in the 2016 Six Nations Championship and on 5 November 2016, he enjoyed one of the highlights of his career in a green jersey scoring two conversions and two penalties in a historic first ever win over New Zealand. Ireland defeated the All Blacks 40-29 at Soldier Field, Chicago, USA.

Johnny only managed to make 10 appearances for Leinster in season 2016-17, scoring one try and 87 points in total. Once again it was a trophy-less season for the Dublin side.

In 2017, Johnny was again selected to tour with the British and Irish Lions, this time to New Zealand for three Test Matches against the all-conquering All Blacks, back-to-back Rugby World Cup winners (2011 & 2015). Johnny played in all three games but failed to score any points with Owen Farrell (England) in charge of kicking duties. The Lions won one, lost one and drew one.

In season 2017-18 he became Leinster's all-time record points scorer after scoring 127 points (includes 5 tries) in his 10 games for the Province. More importantly he had helped re-establish Leinster as the powerhouse of domestic and European rugby with Leinster beating Racing 92 in the European Rugby Champions Cup final played at San Mames Stadium, Bilbao, Spain on 12 May 2018. Johnny scored three penalties in their 15-12 victory. Sixteen days later Leinster beat Scarlets 40-32 in the Pro14 final at the Aviva Stadium, with Johnny scoring two conversions and three penalties. It was a record fifth win in the competition for Leinster. The old San Mames Stadium (1913-2013) was nicknamed "*The Cathedral*." The prayers of the Leinster fans for their players to start winning trophies again had well and truly been answered.

Leinster became only the second team to win the Cup four times (Toulouse were winners in 1996, 2003, 2005, 2010) and became the first Pro14 side to win such a double of trophies. It was the fourth European Cup win for Sexton, joining an elite group of players who have won the competition four times, including teammates Isa Nacewa, Devin Toner and Cian Healy.

Leinster's 2018 European Rugby Champions Cup triumph was remarkable as they overcame the *Pool of Death* comprising Glasgow Warriors (who finished the 2017–18 season top of the Pro14), Montpellier (who finished the 2017–18 season top of the TOP 14) and Exeter (who finished the 2017–18 season top of the English Premiership). Leinster defeated all three of their Pool 3 opponents home and away. A perfect six wins from six games played, 176 points for, 93 against. Leinster then faced Saracens, back-to-back defending Champions, in the quarter-finals. Leinster dispatched them 30-19 with the flawless Sexton at the top of his game scoring 2/2 conversions and 3/3 penalties at the Aviva Stadium. Next up for the Dublin crew was an encounter with Scarlets who just happened to be the reigning Pro12 Champions. If Johnny was sensational in the quarter-final win over Saracens, then his performance against Scarlets at the Aviva Stadium in the semi-final was exquisite. He was pure poetry in motion, never put a foot wrong, and everything he kicked turned to gold whether it was an up-field sidewinder looking for touch deep in the opposition half or an attempt on goal. Indeed, his points tally of 18 would have been enough to have beaten Scarlets had no other Leinster player scored in the game. Leinster won the encounter 38-15. He scored a try, was 5/5 for conversions and 1/1 from penalty attempts. A *Five Star* Man of the Match performance from the 33-year old fly-half.

"Efficiency is doing the thing right. Effectiveness is doing the right thing."

Peter F. Drucker,
Management Consultant

Johnny was both efficient and effective and played a pivotal role in Ireland's 2018 Six Nations Championship campaign which saw them win the title, secure the Triple Crown and claim a third Grand Slam title. He scored all 15 of Ireland's points in their quite breath taking, sensational last gasp 15-13 win over France in Paris, successfully landing a drop goal in the 83rd minute of play. Ireland beat Italy 56-19 in Dublin, Johnny was 5/5 from conversion attempts. When Ireland saw off Wales 37-27 at the Aviva Stadium he scored two conversions and a penalty. Another 8 points followed for him in a 28-8 victory against Scotland in Dublin, 4/4 conversions. On Saint Patrick's Day, 17 March 2018, northern hemisphere rugby belonged to Ireland as they defeated England 24-15 at Twickenham Stadium to wrap-up their domination of the 2018 Six Nations Championship. Johnny was 2/2 for conversion attempts. Sexton contributed 44 total points to Ireland's overall tally of 160 and was named as one of six nominees for the 2018 Six Nations Player of the Tournament award. The award went to his teammate, Jacob Stockdale who was the tournament's top try scorer with 7.

Johnny was a member of the Ireland squad that toured Australia in June 2018, and played in all three Test Matches. He was on the bench for the opening Test at Suncorp Stadium, Brisbane which the Wallabies won 18-9, replacing Joey Carberry, who had scored all of Ireland's points in the game from three penalty kicks, in the 56th minute. The Ireland coach, Joe Schmidt, started him in the second Test played at AAMI Park, Melbourne. Johnny had an outstanding game, coolness personified in the face of constant pressure from the Wallabies and scored 2/2 conversions and 4/5 penalties to help Ireland to a 26-21 victory. The outcome of the Series came down to the third and final Test and Schmidt kept his faith in Sexton. The Ireland coach knew that the atmosphere inside the Allianz Stadium, Sydney would be intense, a powder keg waiting to explode, and that he needed two generals on the field, his captain Peter O'Mahony who he knew would not back down in any challenge and Sexton who was more than capable of sending the Australia fans home to cry in their beer when he was being relied upon to put points on the score board. Sydney is nicknamed "*The Emerald City*" and it was Ireland's precious gemstone, Johnny, who glittered throughout the game, slotting over 5/5 penalty kicks to add to a try scored by CJ Stander to help Ireland to a 20-16 win, a 2-1 Test Series victory, and Ireland's first Test Series win in Australia.

When Johnny made his debut for Ireland in 2009, Black Eyed Peas had their second UK No.1 hit single, *Boom Boom Pow*. The Wallabies certainly knew the meaning of the song title as they could only stand and watch Johnny boom the ball over their crossbar time and time again with ruthless accuracy and efficiency.

At the start of the 2018–19 season, Sexton was announced as the new Leinster club captain replacing Nacewa. It was an excellent choice by their coach Leo Cullen who had captained both Leinster and Ireland during his playing career. He knew what Johnny would bring to the role. He knew when things were going against them in games, he could rely on Johnny to change things for the better and lift his teammates around him.

"We rise by lifting others."

Robert Ingersoll,
American Author, Lawyer and Narrator

Johnny finished the 2017–18 season undefeated as a starter for Ireland and, just when Johnny thought things could not get any better for him, to use a phrase from The Who song *You Better You Bet*, they did.

"When I say, "I love you," you say, you better
You better you better you bet
When I say, "I need you," you say, you better
You better you better you bet
You better bet your life
Or love will cut you like a knife"

On 25 November 2018, Sexton rounded the year off in perfect style at a lavish dinner held in Monte Carlo. The gambling paradise played host to the 2018 World Rugby Player of the Year awards ceremony. Johnny was one of the nominees to win the Men'15 Player of the Year award along with New Zealand fly-half Beauden Barrett (winner in the last two years), winger Rieko Ioane (New Zealand) and the South Africa pair, scrum-half Faf de

Klerk and hooker Malcolm Marx. Barrett may well have been the bookies' favourite to scoop the award for a unique treble, but the smart chips were laid on Sexton's name. Johnny became the first Irish player to win the award since Keith Wood claimed the inaugural accolade in 2001.

Johnny couldn't speak when he was presented with the award. He wasn't lost for words, he had lost his voice and in a statement read out by the Ireland captain, Rory Best, he said:

"Thank you to my team-mates and coaches. If a No.10 wins an award like this, it is due to the team around him and his coaches making his job easier. We have some of the best coaches in the world and are led superbly by Rory Best. I'd also like to thank my wife Laura who has been with me from the start. We've three young kids and she does absolutely everything to allow me to concentrate on the day job. I wouldn't have been able to have the season I've had without her. Thank you so much, it is an incredible honour. I look at the other nominees and I admire all of them. Any of them would have been a worthy winner."

Perfect words from a perfect player.

When Johnny was playing it was almost as if the pitch was his very own State of Independence, his own playground to play the game he wanted to play. His ability to score conversions from the most acute of angles was unerring, not even Pythagoras could have worked them out. His success rate at scoring penalties was second to none, the sharpest of sharpshooters. Somehow he managed to see the trajectory of the ball in his mind seconds before he took the kick, the route had been clearly mapped out, wind conditions were quickly calculated into the equation and the final execution was as swift as Michael van Gerwen throwing three darts at the Treble 20 bed on a dartboard and scoring 180. In many ways it was similar to the bigger picture Sherlock Holmes, played by Robert Downey Jr in the 2009 Guy Ritchie movie of the same name, saw in his mind with varying degrees of slow motion, before the very same incident actually took place in real time. So time becomes relative rather than absolute, adrenaline plays games with you in your mind as to how long an experience takes. And, of course there was really no advantage in having a thunderous kick if you couldn't be consistently accurate when attempting a kick at goal.

The tennis player, Roscoe Tanner, was famous for his big left-handed serve which was clocked at 153 miles per hour (246 km/h) during a match in February 1978. The American's unorthodox, but very powerful left-handed serve was tossed into the air very low and struck with a lunge involving his entire body, and earning him the nickname "*The Rocket.*" His booming 153mph serve was the fastest ever recorded in a professional tennis tournament from February 1978 until September 2004 when his fellow countryman, Andy Rodrick, smashed one at 155mph. Tanner faced Bjorn Borg in the 1979 Men's Wimbledon Singles Championship final but a missile of a serve was no match against the guile of Borg, a player who possessed the ability of being able to juxtapose small shots with big shots, as well as quick shots with slow shots. Perhaps Guy Ritchie took his inspiration for his slow motion scenes from watching Borg perform on a tennis court.

On 3 October 2019, Sexton became the 106th player to captain Ireland when he led the team out for their 2019 Rugby World Cup Pool A match versus Russia at the Kobe Misaki Stadium, Kobe, Japan. He was winning his 92nd cap. Ireland cruised to a 35-0 victory with Johnny scoring three conversions in the game before being replaced at half-time by Jack Carty by coach Schmidt. It proved to be a hugely disappointing Rugby World Cup for Sexton and Ireland, finishing runners-up in Pool A to the host nation who beat Ireland 19-12 at Shizuoka Stadium Ecopa, Fukuroi, and losing 46-14 to the All Blacks in the quarter-finals at Tokyo Stadium, Chofu, Tokyo. However, had it not been for several very poor refereeing decisions by Angus Gardner (Australia) in the loss to Japan, subsequently acknowledged by World Rugby, things may have turned out differently for Ireland. As Pool A winners they would have met South Africa in the quarter-finals, who defeated Japan 26-3. Johnny did not feature in the Japan game and was not even named as a replacement for it, Carty started and scored a conversion after Rob Kearney scored a try in the 21st minute (he missed a conversion attempt when Garry Ringrose scored Ireland's first try in the 14th minute) but he was replaced just after the hour mark by Joey Carberry.

Johnny was 2/2 in wins in his last two matches against the Springboks in a green jersey: 29-15 on 8 November 2014 scoring 16 points and 38-3 on 11 November 2017 scoring 14 points. Both games were played in Dublin. South Africa beat England 32-12 in the 2019 Rugby World Cup final played at the International Stadium, Yokohama. On 15 January 2020, the boy who grew up in Dublin dreaming of playing for his homeland was named the captain of Ireland for their forthcoming 2020 Six Nations Championship campaign following the retirement of their Legendary captain, Rory Best, who decided to bring the curtain down on his esteemed journey in an Ireland jersey. Schmidt had left his role as coach and was succeeded by Andy Farrell. In their first two Six Nations Championship campaigns with Farrell in charge, 2020 and 2021, Ireland could only manage third place in the table in both.

On 6 November 2021, Sexton received his 100th cap playing for Ireland, playing Japan in the Autumn International series. In the 48th minute, he celebrated this landmark achievement by scoring a try, his 16th for his country. He also scored four conversions and a penalty in Ireland's 60-5 defeat of Japan at the Aviva Stadium. A week later, 13 November 2021, Ireland welcomed the All Blacks to Dublin. Sexton led the men in green to a 29-20 victory in front of a raucous crow, the first full house at the Aviva since the COVID-19 restrictions at sporting venues in Ireland had been lifted. Johnny scored a conversion and scored 1/3 penalties to make it seven straight Test wins for Ireland.

Ireland finished runners-up to France, Grand Slam winners, in the 2022 Six Nations Championship with four wins from their five matches and only missed out on winning the title and Grand Slam by losing 30-24 to France in Paris, a match Johnny missed through injury. However, Johnny did captain Ireland to their 12th Triple Crown.

In July 2022, Ireland embarked on a three Test Series tour of New Zealand. Farrell knew that with the 2023 Rugby World Cup only 14 months away, and the 2023 Six Nations Championship in between, he had to test the mettle of his players, including his captain, Sexton, who would be celebrating his 37th birthday away from home. But, Farrell did not need to worry about Johnny,

Legends & Lions

a consummate professional, who knew that the game was played with the mind as well as the body. And, Johnny had a mind that a NASA scientist would envy and a mental resolve that a mountaineer needs to climb past the "*Death Zone*" on Mount Everest. In this area, the bodies of climbers who have ascended higher than 26,000 feet feel the oxygen being vacuumed out of them as their blood cells start to die and judgment becomes impaired. Climbers can also experience heart attacks, strokes, or severe altitude sickness.

In the year of Johnny's birth, 1985, the pop duo *Wham!* were celebrating their third UK hit No.1 single with *I'm Your Man*" Johnny was most definitely Andy's Man. Spookily George Michael's fellow *Wham!* band member was called Andy, Andrew Ridgley.

In the first Test, played at Auckland's Eden Park, the All Blacks cruised to victory, 42-19. But neither Farrell nor his trustworthy Lieutenant panicked. Johnny had seen it all before with Leinster and in the green jersey. Johnny had all the attributes to overcome the highest of summits of the sport. He took personal responsibility, he had tremendous pride, he was a dedicated trainer who looked after his body and he was always pushing, testing himself and his teammates. The formula wasn't a Sexton cocktail for success, it had been instilled in him at Leinster by coaches such as Chelka, Schmidt and Cullen. The second Test was played on 16 July 2022, five days after Johnny's birthday, in Dunedin and Johnny put in a performance that rolled back the years. He shone like a diamond converting Ireland's two tries scored by Andrew Porter and was 3/3 from penalties in Ireland's 23-12 victory. A High Fives performance to match his five faultless kicks at goal. Having never previously beaten the All Blacks prior to 2016, Ireland had now won four of the last seven meetings between the sides, with this win sending a message to World Rugby that Ireland were ready to conquer the death zone and plant the Irish tricolour on the sport's highest peak, the World Rankings. It was Ireland's first win against New Zealand in their own back yard and three days later they claimed their first ever win over the Māori All Blacks, a 30-24 victory in Wellington.

The Third Test was the Series decider and all of Ireland and New Zealand wanted to see the best team in the southern hemisphere take on the best side the northern hemisphere had to offer and arguably one of the greatest ever sides Ireland has ever produced. The game was played at Wellington Regional Stadium, Wellington which is the country's third largest, but windiest city. Between 1807 and 1837, Wellington was caught up in "*The Musket Wars*," a series of approximately 3,000 fierce battles, and now the residents of Wellington were about to experience its' biggest ever battle, Rugby union's *Star Wars* battle contested by the biggest Galácticos of the sport. Ireland defeated the All Blacks 32-22 (Johnny scored 3/4 conversions and 2/3 penalty attempts) to win the Test Series 2-1 (they won one and lost one versus the Maori All Blacks) to become only the fifth Touring side to beat New Zealand on their home turf.

"Mountains are not stadiums where I satisfy my ambition to achieve, they are the Cathedrals where I practice my religion."

Anatoli Boukreev, a Soviet and Kazakh Mountaineer

The great thing about reaching the top of a mountain is realising that there's space up there for more than one person. And that you're now in the prime position to help others up, pulling on their ropes to stand above the clouds with you. Johnny Sexton was Ireland's Expedition Leader in New Zealand, he was the first person to scale their summit of victory over the All Blacks. He was Ireland's Preacher of the Gospel of Rugby according to Sexton: Verse 10 in the Book of Remarkable Achievements.

"A lion has come out of his lair; a destroyer of nations has set out. He has left his place to lay waste your land. Your towns will lie in ruins without inhabitant."

Jeremiah 4:7

Johnny Sexton joined an elite group of only five players to have captained their side to a Test Series victory in New Zealand: Philip J. Noel (South Africa, 1937), Trevor Allan (Australia, 1949), John Dawes (British and Irish Lions, 1971), Andrew Slack (Australia, 1986) and Philip Saint-Andre (France, 1994). The sprinkling on the cake for Sexton and Ireland was that their Test Series win meant that they replaced France as the No.1 ranked team in the world. It was the second time Ireland had attained the No.1 World Rugby ranking, having occupied the lofty position for two weeks in September 2019. Ireland had not just taken strides under the Farrell/Sexton partnership, they had hopped, skipped and jumped their way to rugby union's summit top.

Johnny captained Ireland to Grand Slam glory in the 2023 Six Nations Championship, only the fourth time Ireland had achieved this feat. In their final game of the tournament, Johnny overtook O'Gara's record for scoring the most number of points in the history of the competition in all of its' formats including Home Nations Championship and Five Nations Championship. Ronan had 557 points, Johnny 566 points.

JOHN WHITE

At the 2023 Rugby World Cup in France, he became Ireland's oldest international rugby union player aged 38 and broke Ronan O'Gara's points scoring record for Ireland. Johnny played in all four of Ireland's Pool B games, winning them all, and in the 28-24 loss to New Zealand in the Stade de France, Paris in the quarter-finals. It was the fourth time Johnny exited a Rugby World Cup with Ireland whilst the loss to the All Blacks was his 119th and last ever game for his country. After 14 distinguishing years wearing the green jersey of Ireland, Sexton headed into retirement as arguably Ireland's greatest ever player. He scored a total of 1,108 points in an Irish jersey as well as 5 points from the six caps he won as a British and Irish Lion.

Johnny Sexton has been an Ambassador with Make-A-Wish Ireland since September 2009. Johnny helps grant wishes to children with life-threatening medical conditions and launches various fundraising campaigns.

If the IRFU had a Pantheon in Dublin to celebrate the Legendary internationals who spilled blood for their country in a green jersey, a fitting tribute as it where for loyalty and service to the cause of the hundreds of players to answer Ireland's Call, whether they won silver trophies or wooden ones, a statue of Johnny Sexton would adorn he entrance. Greek Mythology has many Gods: Poseidon (God of the Sea, Earthquakes and Horses), Zeus (God of the Sky and Thunder), Apollo (God of the Light and Sun). Hermes (Messenger of the Gods) and Ares, their God of War. Ireland has a mere handful, but Sexton is one of them.

Johnny Sexton is Ireland's Ares, who on his own was unbeatable in hand to hand combat. He was a bloodthirsty savage when fighting and is considered to be a picture perfect soldier and was worshipped by the Spartans, the most skilled soldiers in history. Ares could not be controlled, he wasn't the most powerful, but he was awesome. And according to Greek Mythology Ares had power, he did not need personality, but when it came down to performances in the Ancient Olympic Games, he was by far the strongest Olympian.

When the Nepalese mountaineer, Nimsdai Purja, was told scaling the world's 14 highest mountains in less than seven months couldn't be done, he decided to prove the doubters wrong. In order to prove his point he had his attempt filmed and named the challenge *Project Possible*. And then, he did it. In eight months, Johnny Sexton proved his own doubters wrong by captaining Ireland to a first ever Test Series victory in New Zealand, helped Ireland back to the summit of the World Rankings and guided his country to the pinnacle of northern hemisphere rugby, the Grand Slam. Johnny's made rugby's *Project Impossible* a reality, and to quote some of the lines from the Andy William's song, *The Impossible Dream (The Quest)*.

> *"To dream the impossible dream*
> *To fight the unbeatable foe*
> *To bear with unbearable sorrow*
> *And to run where the brave dare not go*
>
> *To right the unrightable wrong*
> *And to love pure and chaste from afar*
> *To try when your arms are too weary*
> *To reach the unreachable star*
>
> *This is my quest*
> *To follow that star*
> *No matter how hopeless*

JOHN WHITE

No matter how far

To fight for the right
Without question or pause
To be willing to march, march into hell
For that heavenly cause"

For Irish rugby, Johnny made the impossible dream possible.

Did You Know That?

Johnny scored more than 100 career points against five different nations who all happen to be Ireland's Six Nations Championship opponents: Italy 120, France 121, England 123, Wales 137 and Scotland 138.

TONY WARD
Lord Of The Fly-Halves

ANTHONY JOSEPH PAUL TONY WARD was born on 9 October 1954, in Dublin, Ireland, the same year *Lord of the Flies*, written by William Golding was published.

Football was his first love and he played as a schoolboy for Rangers Association Football Club in Dublin and for the Ireland Under-15 side. For the first five years of his life he grew up in Leeds, Yorkshire, England until the premature death of his father meant the family having to return home to Dublin. Tony was educated at Saint Mary's College, Rathmines where his rugby career began. In 1974, he moved to Limerick and attended Thomond College of Education where he studied for a Bachelor of the Arts Degree in Physical Education, graduating in 1978. Thomond College of Education was integrated into the University of Limerick in 1991. Tony once said that the four years he spent on the Plassey Campus at Thomond College of Education were: *"Without fear of contradiction, those were the best 4 years of my life!"*

Tony played fly-half for Garryowen (1975-82), St Mary's (1982-85), Greystones (1985-89), Munster (1975-84), Leinster (1986-88), the Barbarians, the British and Irish Lions and Ireland (1978-87) during his career. He was handed his first Irish cap on 21 January 1978, a 12-9 win over Scotland at Lansdowne Road in the Five Nations Championship. He marked his international debut by scoring a conversion and two penalties. During the

JOHN WHITE

1978 Five Nations Championship the 23-year old scored 38 points, a record for a debutant in the tournament which Ireland finished fourth in. Some sportswriters at the time questioned whether or not Ward was ready to make the leap from club games to international matches. Ward knew he was ready, there was no need for him to remind the Selectors at the IRFU of the ABBA song entitled *Take A Chance On Me*, which was popular at the time from the Swedish Super Group. The men wearing blazers at the IRFU Headquarters did not need to turn the radio on, Ward's outstanding displays game after game for Munster, was the only evidence they needed to realise they had an uncut diamond which was ready to be polished and placed on display, not in a cabinet, but in an Ireland green jersey.

It is the mark of an educated mind to be able to entertain a thought without accepting it."

Aristotle

Thankfully, for Irish rugby the IRFU's Men of Wisdom, discarded the negative sportswriters and allowed the Irish fans to make their own minds up about Tony. But, as the Garryowen and Munster fans would have told the blazers at the time, it did not need an Ancient Greek Philosopher to tell you that the Dublin boy was more than ready to announce himself on the world stage of rugby union.

The following year he toured Australia with Ireland and was named 1979 European Rugby Player of the Year when he had an outstanding season for Ireland in the 1979 Five Nations Championship. Ireland finished in third place and Ward scored 8 penalties, 3 conversions and a drop goal (33 points). But Ollie Campbell proved

LEGENDS & LIONS

to be Tony's nemesis and kept Ward out of the team when he was fit to start.

It would have come as no surprise to anyone attending a rugby union international at Lansdowne Road in 1981, had they heard the No.1 song in the Music Charts being belted out across the PA system as soon as Tony crossed the white line. The song was 'Prince Charming', sung by Adam and the Ants. The other 14 players wearing green jerseys were certainly not ants but Tony was most definitely, Ireland's Prince Charming.

Ollie Campbell took the decision to retire on 4 February 1984 after he played his last ever game for Ireland, an 18-9 loss to Wales at Lansdowne Road and he bowed out of international rugby scoring all 9 points for his country. Tony took over the baton for Ireland in their remaining two matches of the 1984 Five Nations Championship. However, not even the stylish Ward could prevent Ireland from losing both, 12-9 away to England when he scored all of Ireland's points from three penalties and a 32-9 defeat to Scotland in Dublin (he didn't score in the game) as Ireland were awarded another wooden spoon.

Tony was not selected for coach Mick Doyle's 1985 Five Nations Championship squad, 24-year old Michael Kiernan from Dolphin Rugby Football Club was the new big thing in Irish rugby, and he helped Ireland win the title, claim a Triple Crown and was the leading points scorer with 46 to his credit. Just as one door opened for Ward when Ollie left the scene, another was slammed in his face in the shape of Kiernan. Tony must have felt like the person depicted in the masterpiece of a painting by the Norwegian artist Edvard Munch called The Scream. The agonised face in the painting with the person holding each side of their face and mouth open wide, has become one of the most iconic images of art, seen as symbolising the anxiety of the human mind. However, Tony did not give up hope on representing his country again, a bit like the Tony Manero character who refused to give up his dreams of becoming a professional dancer and reappeared on the silver screen in 1983 in Staying Alive. Tony Ward was staying alive in the race to be Ireland's first choice No.1o but it is very unlikely that he ever took his Ireland jersey off and waved it around above his head before tossing it into a corner of the Irish dressing room after a game regardless of how well he had performed in it.

"What moves those of genius, what inspires their work, is not new ideas, but their obsession with the idea that what has already been said is still not enough."

Eugene Delacroix, French Actor

Tony went on to play one more time for his country, the green curtain coming down on his own career in a 32-9 win against Tonga in Brisbane, Australia in a 1987 Rugby World Cup Pool 2 game. Ward scored three conversions and two penalties in the win which brought his tally to 19 caps for Ireland scoring 113 points (comprising 29 penalties, 7 conversions and 4 drop goals) added to his solitary Lions' cap when he scored 18 points for the touring side.

During his career Tony inspired Munster to a historic 12-0 win over the touring New Zealand team at Thomond Park, Ireland on 31 October 1978. Munster remain the only Irish Provincial men's team to defeat the All Blacks. In 1980, Ward played in his only ever Test for the British and Irish Lions, scoring 18 points (5 penalties and a drop goal), against South Africa which remains a record number of points scored by a Lions' player in a Test and the most points scored by a player against the Springboks. South Africa defeated the Lions 26-22 at Newlands Stadium, Cape Town in the opening Test of the Lions' 1980 Tour (Wales' Graham Price scored a try in the game).

While playing rugby Ward was a Geography and Physical Education teacher at Saint Andrews Secondary School, Booterstown, Dun Laoghaire, Ireland. During the 1990's Tony passed on his skills to the pupils at the school when he became their Rugby Coach. There were times when he had to leave the room during a team-talk when one of his assistant coaches played footage of Tony scoring for Ireland. The mild-mannered, shy Ward, blushed every time as he left the room much to the amusement of his young players.

"You don't need anybody to tell you who you are or what you are. You are what you are!"

John Lennon

(Tony shares the same birthday as the former Beatle, Lennon was born on 9 October 1940)

Since retiring as a player, Tony has worked as a sports journalist, most notably with the *Irish Independent*, and as a rugby commentator for RTÉ. He also continues his involvement with Schools Rugby through his role as Director of Rugby at St Gerard's School in Bray, County Wicklow. Although not many of his pupils knew it, Tony loved music, particularly songs from the Sixties. And, no doubt as a result of his early years growing up, Tony is an ardent Leeds United Football Club fan and his hobby is collecting English football match programmes.

On 25 February 1965, the No.1 song in the United Kingdom Singles Charts was I'll Never Find Another You, by The Seekers. When Tony Ward left international rugby the IRFU were searching for a new Tony Ward.

In 1993, his biography was published and entitled: The Good, the Bad and the Rugby - The Biography of Tony Ward.

When Tony was born in Dublin in 1954, his parents, and many other Irish cinema goers went to see a Hollywood movie which was very popular in the movie houses across the country at the time. It starred James Mason and Judy Garland and was called A Star Is Born. Little did Tony's mum know it when she gave birth to her son Tony, that a future Ireland rugby star was born.

Tony was Ireland's first true Sports Star playing rugby at a time when social media did not make you a household name. He, like so many others in Ireland, had to perform in his own sphere, whether it was acting, singing or sport, unlike today when millions of followers on a Facebook page or on a Twitter account, can elevate someone to being so much more famous than what they actually are. Tony Ward's drop goals, penalties and tries for club and country would have burst the internet had they been available to download during his playing career.

In 1954, a band named The Stargazers were No.1 in the United Kingdom Music Charts with their song entitled I See The Moon. During his Ireland career, Tony saw the Whole of the Moon (interestingly a similar name of a Waterboys' song entitled The Whole of the Moon), the Stars and the Galaxy.

Tony's zodiac sign is Libra, which is Latin for scales.

Legends & Lions

The Moon was said to be in Libra when Rome was founded and this was based on the historical passage, which states "Ab urbe condita Roma." Everything was balanced under this righteous sign.

In 2012, Tony was honoured by the University of Limerick when he was presented with their Recipient of Outstanding Achievement Alumni Award for Sport.

Tony Ward was elegance on the field, perfectly balanced, he was Ireland's Lord of the Fly-Halves.

Did You Know That?

Tony Ward also played Association Football for Shamrock Rovers (1973-75) and Limerick United (1981-82) in the Football of Association's (FAI) League of Ireland. In season 1974-75, he scored six goals for the Rovers and in season 1981-82, he played for Limerick United in the UEFA Cup. Ward won an FAI Cup winners' medal playing for Limerick United in the 1982 final when they beat Bohemians 1-0 at Dalymount Park, Dublin.

RORY BEST
You've Been Thunderstruck

RORY DAVID BEST was born on 15 August 1982, and brought up in Poyntzpass, County Armagh, Northern Ireland. His mother was born in Middlesbrough, North Yorkshire, England. Rory took up mini-rugby at Banbridge Rugby Football Club which is situated not too far away from his home when he was aged only 6. He showed tremendous promise with the Under-14's and Under-16's at the club. The young Best was educated at Tandragee Junior High School located five miles away from the family home and at Portadown College. He then studied Agriculture at the University of Newcastle, England. In tandem with his studies, Best was a member of the Newcastle Falcons Academy, a Premiership Rugby Club where he learnt his trade on a rugby pitch. But, Best was always destined to not only be a farmer, but also a rugby union player, and widely tipped to surpass the feats of his older brother, Simon, who played 23 times for Ireland and represented Ulster from 1999-2008, making 118 appearances and scoring 25 points. Simon scored a solitary try for Ireland when they beat Japan 44-12 at Nagai Stadium, Osaka on 12 June 2005, during Ireland's Tour of the country. Simon was born on 11 February 1978, and captained Ulster's 2005-06 Celtic League (Pro12) winning team. Simon also represented Ireland at Schoolboy, Under-19, Under-21, Under-25 and A levels. He also studied Agriculture at Newcastle University and played for

Legends & Lions

Newcastle Falcons.

In the year Rory was born, a song by Survivor taken from the soundtrack of the movie Rocky III, Eye of the Tiger, was a huge hit in the Music Charts. Meanwhile, in the cinemas Sylvester Stallone was the major attraction in Rambo – First Blood. Rory certainly possessed the eye of the tiger and who just like Rambo, never gave in.

In 2003, the 21-year old Best returned home and played rugby for Belfast Harlequins. His natural leadership qualities were fully recognised by Andre Bester, the coach of the Belfast side, who made the young hooker his captain. The eye brows of rugby union pundits covering Ulster rugby were heightened when Bester, how appropriate is it that Best was made captain by someone named Bester? chose Rory to captain Belfast Harlequins in Division One of the All Ireland League (AIL). When Rory arrived at Deramore Park, Belfast from Newcastle University he was one of the youngest skippers in the AIL. Rory was a member of the Ireland squad for the 2003 Under-21 Rugby World Cup, before making his bow for Ulster in the 2004-05 season. During the 2005-06 season he scored five tries in Ulster's Heineken Cup campaign which brought him to the attention of the Ireland coach, Eddie O'Sullivan, who was assembling a squad for the Autumn Internationals in November 2005.

In 2005, Steve Brookstein, the winner of the X Factor, went to No.1 in the UK Singles Charts with Against All Odds, and Nicholas Cage starred in the movie Lord of War.

Rory made his debut for Ireland on 12 November 2005, and it proved to be a baptism of fire for the Ulsterman. Ireland welcomed New Zealand to

Lansdowne Road and the 42,000 fans who attended the game witnessed two dances. After performing their ritual Haka prior to kick-off, the All Blacks then led Ireland a merry dance winning the match 45-7, scoring five tries. Rory came on as a replacement for Shay Byrne with Simon Easterby captaining Ireland in the game. Sitting on the substitutes' bench beside him was his brother Simon and a third Best, Neil. All three Bests played in the game.

A week later O'Sullivan used him as a replacement for Byrne when Ireland lost 30-14 to Australia, Rugby World Cup runners-up in 2003, in Dublin. The Ireland coach was either unsure of his new young hooker's abilities or else he was just bedding him in, knowing that over time he would soon blossom as Best only played once for Ireland in the 2006 Six Nations Championship. His maiden appearance in the competition brought with it a first taste of victory for the 23-year old boy from Poyntzpass wearing the green of Ireland, a 31-5 victory against Wales at Lansdowne Road. Rory had beaten all odds to finally become an international rugby player and went on to become one of the sport's Lords of War.

Andre Bester, a hooker of notable reputation during his playing days in South Africa, always knew that his protégé had the ability and self determination to succeed at the highest levels of the game.

"Rory is one of the most committed young players I have ever worked with. During the early days he spent more time in my office watching videos than he did at home. He was always asking questions and when you have a hunger to get to the top in

Legends & Lions

life nothing will stop you, Rory lives and breathes rugby. He has tremendous leadership qualities and that is why at 21 years old I made him captain at Quins although a lot of people were against it. He is the best captain I have worked with and I believe he will be a future Ulster skipper. He has a great attitude and for me it is something special to see him get international recognition."

Andre Bester

On 24 June 2006, Rory played in Ireland's 37-15 loss versus the Wallabies in Perth, Australia, and played in all three of Ireland's home 2006 Autumn Internationals which saw them defeat South Africa 32-15, Australia 21-6 and a 61-7 mauling of the Pacific Islanders. Rory made his first start for his country in the game against the Springboks and scored the first of his 12 tries for his country in the victory over the Pacific Islanders. The following year he played in all five of Ireland's matches in the 2007 Six Nations Championship, Ireland finished runners-up to France, but won the Triple Crown (their eighth). Best had quickly established himself on the international stage with 10/10 match performances against the best sides in World Rugby. Rory wasn't one for standing on ceremony, he was exactly what it said on the tin! You either liked *Marmite* or you didn't. Never a dirty player, he didn't have to be, he commanded the respect of his opponents regardless of their stature in the game, by playing by the rules and this is an attribute he expected his teammates to follow. As far as Rory was concerned the word *"Team,"* contained only two vowels, and one of them was most definitely not an *"I."* He very rarely won the Man of the Match award in a Test Match, and to his credit he couldn't care who was handed a piece of silverware or a bottle of champagne at the end of a game, so long as the team won. For Rory winning was everything, individual accolades and prizes were too glitzy for his style of rugby.

So long as Rory played at his maximum, knowing he had completely emptied his tank of fuel out on the pitch, he was at ease with his performance, win or lose. But, whether he was on the winning side or the losing side there was one thing Rory made sure was a continuous thread of his game. And, that was that anyone who dared to dip their shoulder and run at him either risked hospital food for six weeks with a dislocated shoulder, or ended up laid flat out on their back on the turf. *Ils ne passeront pas* (French for *They Shall Not Pass*) should have been embroidered into the Ulster and Ireland shirt above the No.2 on his jersey. Or to help out those who dared to take him on in a one-on-one battle, the motto would be better served beneath the No.2 as it would be more visible looking up when you were laid out on your back on the grass as Rory just nonchalantly walked away from the carnage he created. The French saying was notably used by the army of France during the First World War (1914-18) to express a determination to defend a position against the enemy, the German Empire (the Second Reich).

Rory scored his first try in a Six Nations Championship campaign when they beat Wales 19-9 at the Millennium Stadium, Cardiff on 4 February 2007. At long last his patience and perseverance at swapping the green No.2 jersey with Frank Sheahan when Ireland's first choice hooker, Jerry Flannery was unavailable, had finally produced the rewards he had hoped for as he was beginning to establish his position at hooker in the side. He may have worn the No.2 jersey on his back, but for many Irish fans, Rory was their No.1. A player who would run through a brick wall for his country without any fear whatsoever. He was *Mr Ireland*.

For Rory, leadership and learning were indispensable to each other. He was given the captaincy of Ulster during the 2007-08 season, a post he held until he retired in 2019, and was selected for Ireland's 2007 Rugby World Cup squad in France. He played three matches (Namibia, Georgia & Argentina) during the tournament as Ireland crashed out at the Group Stages. In the 2008 Six Nations Championship he started in three of Ireland's games (Italy, Wales & England) but O'Sullivan used Bernard Jackman in the other two (France & Scotland). In 2009, he captained the Ireland team that toured North America, while many of his Ireland teammates were away on duty with the British and Irish Lions who were touring South Africa at the same time. Under his captaincy, Ireland beat Canada 25-6 in Vancouver and then defeated the United States of America 27-10 in Santa Clara, California. Surely, it was only a matter of time before Best swapped his coveted green jersey for the world famous red shirt that a Lion wore. But, he missed the entire 2009-10 season due to surgery on a chronic disc problem. In seasons 2010-11 and 2011-12 he scored two tries for Ulster and he was a part of the Ulster side, captained by Johann Muller, that was defeated 42-14 by Leinster in the 2012 Heineken Cup final. The Leinster side were an exceptional band of brothers which included Rory's Ireland teammates; Sean Cronin, Gordon D'Arcy. Cian Healy, Jamie Heaslip, Rob Kearney, Sean O'Brien, Brian O'Driscoll, Rona O'Gara, Mike Ross, Johnny Sexton and Richardt Strauss. The Leinster team attracted the same media attention as the Irish Boy bands, Boyzone and Westlife. They were pin-up rugby stars.

"If you can't swallow your pride, you can't lead. Even the highest mountain had animals that step on it."

Jack Weatherford

Rory was a player that any nation in the world would have been privileged to have play for them. He was a proud Ulsterman, a proud Irishman and he was very proud to play for the British and Irish Lions. Ireland has been divided for many centuries because of religion and has two international football sides, Northern Ireland and the Republic of Ireland, but their Rugby Union side is *One*. The Irish Rock Band, U2, have a song called *One*, and one of the verses from this hit song helps to sum up the state of Irish Rugby:

"Well, it's too late tonight
To drag the past out into the light
We're one, but we're not the same
We get to carry each other, carry each other
One"

Rory embraced his teammates from the country's other three Provinces, Connacht, Leinster and Munster as a teammate and then as their leader, the player they could look up to when things did not exactly go to plan in matches. As far as Rory was concerned, his religion was rugby and his place of worship was whatever blades of grass Ireland stepped on.

U2's song also included the lines:

"Did I disappoint you?
Did I leave a bad taste in your mouth?"

Legends & Lions

Clearly when Bono from U2, was singing this song, he did not have Rory Best's name in his mind or mouth, but the boy from Ponytzpass had established himself as Ireland's *One*.

Best was a member of the British and Irish Lions squad which toured Australia in 2013, but was not capped on the Tour with the Lions winning the Test Series 2-1. The following year he helped Ireland win the Six Nations Championship, his second winners' medal in the competition. Following the retirement of Paul O'Connell in 2015, Rory became the captain of Ireland and on 5 November 2016, came perhaps his greatest ever moment in an Ireland jersey when they beat New Zealand for the first time in their history. Rory had the honour of captaining Ireland in the game which they won 40-29 at Soldier Field, Chicago, USA. On 26 November 2016, Rory became Ireland' fifth centurion. He won his 100th cap in a 27-24 victory over Australia at the Aviva Stadium. After captaining Ireland in the 2017 Six Nations Championship, Rory was once again called-up by the Lions, for their 2017 Tour of New Zealand. However, although he had the distinction of captaining the Lions to a 34–6 win over the Chiefs and a 31–31 draw with the Hurricanes, he never featured in any of the three Tests. The All Blacks won the Series 2-1.

When he was touring New Zealand with the Lions in 2017, Rory was given the news that he was being awarded the Order of the British Empire (OBE) for his services to rugby.

On 28 October 2017, Best played his 200th game for Ulster in the Pro14, a 25-10 loss to Leinster at the Kingspan Stadium, Belfast (previously known simply as Ravenhill). Ulster liked to play a counter attacking game and Best's ability to win turnover ball in the tackle was a key to their success in his time at the club.

If Ireland were playing Wales in the Millennium Stadium on a rainy day with the stadium roof closed, when Rory Best smashed his body into a red shirt the shudder would have reverberated around the stands with such velocity that the roof would have been blown off. Running at Rory Best with or without the ball in your hands, was like listening to the opening lines of the song Danger Zone, sung by Kenny Loggins from the *Top Gun* movies soundtrack.

> *"Revvin' up your engine*
> *Listen to her howlin' roar*
> *Metal under tension*
> *Beggin' you to touch and go"*

You were running into a Danger Zone which just happened to be wearing the Ireland No. 2 jersey. Attackers were better off changing direction if they saw a 6 feet tall Best, weighing 16½ stones, in their path to the goal line. Rory was a beef farmer so not even a raging bull was going to get past him. When he stood in the Irish lineout prior to the playing of the national anthems his massive chest would cast his teammate beside him in the shade. Throughout his playing career, Rory was fully aware that every time he crossed the white line representing his club or country, he had to be at his strongest, even at those times when he was at his weakest. Similarly, throughout his career, sometimes Rory did not know his own strengths until he came face to face with his greatest weaknesses. For Best, his inner strength came through continuous effort and struggle to make himself the best player he could be.

Legends & Lions

"Strength does not come from winning. Your struggles develop your strengths. When you go through hardships and decide not to surrender, that is strength."

Arnold Schwarzenegger

In 2018, Rory Best captained Ireland to a historic Six Nations Championship success which also saw them win the Triple Crown and a Grand Slam for only the third time. It seemed appropriate that Ireland clinched the title and Grand Slam by defeating England 24-15 at Twickenham Stadium on Saint Patrick's Day. Irish eyes were smiling everywhere.

In *The Dark Knight* (2008) directed by Christopher Nolan, Australian actor Heath Ledger delivered the greatest performance of his career as the movie's main protagonist, *Joker*. Joker ran amok around the crime-infested alleyways of Gotham City, and left a Joker playing card at the scenes of his crimes to taunt the police. If Rugby players were permitted to leave a calling card then surely Rory's would have been a black card with a large yellow thunderbolt in the centre of it. When Rory hit an opponent full on in a tackle it must have been similar to a boxer being hit square on the chin by James *"Bonecrusher"* Smith, the WBA World Heavyweight Boxing Champion from 1986-87. The force of the impact would have left a silhouette of the Ireland crest on Rory's jersey on the *victim's* jersey as he lay flat out on his back on the ground. The stadium announcer could have played the second verse from the AC/DC song *Thunderstruck*, to sum up what had just happened:

"I was caught
In the middle of a railroad track (Thunder)
I looked 'round

And I knew there was no turning back ('Thunder)
My mind raced
And I thought, what could I do? (Thunder)
And I knew
There was no help, no help from you (Thunder)
Sound of the drums
Beating in my heart
The thunder of guns
Tore me apart
You've been
Thunderstruck"

The TV camera could then have focused in on Rory as he took the card from his pocket and tossed it on to the player's chest with Rory looking down at him saying: "*You've Been Thunderstruck.*"

Rory missed Ireland's Tour of Australia in June 2018, with Peter O'Mahony captaining the side to a 2-1 Test Series victory down under. But he bounced back and played against Argentina and New Zealand in the 2018 Autumn Internationals, and captained the team to a 28-17 win over The Pumas and a 16-9 victory against the All Blacks, both games were played at the Aviva Stadium. The defeat of New Zealand cemented Rory's place as one of the most successful captains in Irish rugby history with Ireland recording nine wins during 2018.

On 18 April 2019, Best announced that he would retire from professional rugby after the 2019 Rugby World Cup in Japan.

"It is with mixed feelings that I announce my retirement from Ulster Rugby as of the end of this season. This feels like the right time for me to go out on my terms, a luxury for which I feel very privileged."

Legends & Lions

Rory played his final game for Ulster on 17 May 2019, but it wasn't the ending he had dreamed of as they were beaten 50-20 by Glasgow Warriors at Scotstoun Stadium, Glasgow in the quarter-finals of the 2018-19 Pro14. Between 2004 and 2019, Rory made 218 appearances for Ulster and scored 115 points.

Rory captained Ireland in Japan, playing in three of Ireland's four Pool A games to help them into the quarter-finals of the tournament. But that is where Rory's journey, his love affair, with Ireland came to an end. On 19 October 2019, Rory pulled on the green jersey for the 124th time, puffed out his chest and led the team out at Tokyo Stadium to face New Zealand. The All Blacks won the match 46-14 to bring Rory's rugby Odyssey to an end which began 14 years earlier when he made his Ireland debut against the same opponents. Best was replaced by Niall Scannell in the 63rd minute of the match and received a standing ovation to thunderous applause from the crowd as he left the field. When the final whistle was blown, Rory walked back out on to the pitch with his three children and wiped a tear from his left eye to acknowledge the huge Irish contingent in the crowd.

After book ending his career with matches against New Zealand Rory said: *"I'm unbelievably upset with the thought that I'll never pull on a green jersey again, except to support. We're incredibly disappointed, we had a lot of big characters in that team. Big men were in tears in that dressing room and that's what happens when you put your heart and soul into everything."*

Rugby World Cup tweeted:

"Amazing moment as Rory Best brings the kids onto the pitch after

his last match in an Irish rugby shirt. A Legend of the game, who gave it all for the jersey. Thanks for the memories Rory."

In November 2019, Rory had not quite finished with the game just yet and played his last two professional rugby matches for the Barbarians. On 16 November 2019, he captained the Baa-Baas in their Killic Cup match against a Fiji XV and they won the game 33–31 at Twickenham Stadium. He then captained the Baa-Baas on 30 November 2019, when they were beaten 43-33 by Wales at the Millennium Stadium. When he was substituted in the 51st minute, Rory received a standing ovation from the crowd, paying tribute to him and marking the end of what had been a most illustrious career.

"At 37 years of age Rory has been a tremendous servant to Ulster and Ireland. He has always done and said all the right things as a captain."

Willie John McBride

When starting out on his career, just like the words from the Eminem song *Lose Yourself*, Rory took his one shot, his one opportunity and ended his playing career as an Ireland Legend, with 124 caps (102 starts), 38 as captain of his country, scoring 60 points. He was Ireland's third most capped player at the time he retired and won 4 Six Nations Championships with Ireland (2009, 2014, 2015 & 2018), 4 Triple Crowns (2006, 2007, 2009 & 2018) and 2 Grand Slams (2009 & 2018).

The name Best is woven into the Red Hand of the Ulster crest and the Shamrock at the centre of the Ireland rugby crest.

Not very far from where Rory grew up lies Lough Neagh. According to Irish mythology, the lake was formed when Ireland's legendary giant, Fionn mac Cumhaill

(Finn McCool) tore up a huge piece of ground and tossed it at a Scottish rival. The story goes that the large chunk of earth fell short of its' intended target and landed in the Irish Sea, forming the Isle of Man, whilst the hole in the ground filled up with water to form Lough Neagh. Rory Best was no myth, he was a real life giant of Irish rugby and when he set his sight on a target he didn't miss.

The opponents who dared to face Rory one on one during his playing days are still carrying the aftershock from being a little *Thunderstruck*!

Did You Know That?

Rory Best is the only Irish captain to have a win over Australia, New Zealand and South Africa and he is one of just a few captains to achieve this unique treble.

JACK KYLE
Flying Without Wings

Who is the Greatest Ever player in the history of Irish Rugby? That is a question which has transcended generations of Irish fans and there are, according to the various fan's polls conducted, several contenders for the mantle. Names such as Mike Gibson, Willie John McBride, Brian O'Driscoll, Ronan O'Gara and Johnny Sexton are to quote the title of the 1995 classic movie, *The Usual Suspects*, as the always come to the fore. But again, it comes down to a generational thing and when these polls are published they become a major topic of discussion in the pubs of Belfast, Dublin and every crack, nook and cranny of the Emerald Isle.

To ask an Ireland rugby fan today to name the Top 5 players in the famous green jersey without having seen all of the leading contenders play for their country, is a bit like asking a Manchester United fan to name an equivalent Quintet. Not many of them will have seen Duncan Edwards, the most iconic Busby Babe of them all, Bobby Charlton, Denis Law, Bryan Robson, Eric Cantona or the Genius, who was, the incomparable Belfast Boy himself, George Best, wear the famous red jersey of Manchester United. And yet, the name of Duncan Edwards is always effervescent.

Manchester United's *Usual Suspects* rarely change when fans are polled, but one Ireland rugby union star was his country's *Sirius* (the name of the brightest star in the sky). He is the equivalent to *The Usual Suspects'* main character portrayed by Kevin Spacey, Keyser Söze, John "*Jack*" Kyle.

JOHN WILSON "JACK" KYLE was born in Belfast on 10 February 1926, and was educated at Belfast Royal Academy. He was one of five children who were born to John and Elizabeth, nee Warren, Kyle. His father was an only child born to a Master Baker from Derry, who later worked as a manager for the Edinburgh-based North British Rubber Company. Jack's Dad was in charge of the company's operations in Ireland. Rugby was not part of the Kyle or Warren family history until Jack's older brother, Eric played for Ulster and was given a trial by Ireland. At school Jack was inspired to play rugby by his headmaster, Alexander Roulston Foster, who captained Ireland winning 17 caps between 1910 and 1921, and who was also capped twice by the British Isles (later became the British and Irish Lions) on their Tour of South Africa in 1910. The pupil hung on his teacher's every word. Jack played for the Ulster Schools at fullback but it was on entering Queen's University Belfast to read medicine in October 1944, that he came to senior prominence after a rival for the out-half position, Derek Monteith, broke a leg.

He played for Queen's University First XV, North of Ireland Rugby Football Club and his home province, Ulster. His first appearance for Ireland came during the Second World War in a friendly versus a British Army XV, but no caps were awarded to the men in green for this game.

In 1947, post the aftermath of World War II (1939-45), the Five Nations Championship was resurrected. Despite his young age, 20, Kyle was given his Test debut by the IRFU Selection Committee. Twenty years of age was very young for a rugby union player in 1947, today's

JOHN WHITE

equivalent would probably be 17. He was one of 14 debutants for Ireland in the game, with captain, Con Murphy, the only player in the side to have played an international before the onset of war in Europe, which then spread to other parts of the world. But, it was not the start the Belfast born Kyle had dreamed of, as Ireland lost 12-8 to France at Lansdowne Road. But, someone at the IRFU was orbiting the same planet as Jack, because he played in all of Ireland's three games in the 1947 Five Nations Championship.

"*I Think I Have Found You A Genius.*" These immortal words were sent on a telegram by Manchester United's Chief Scout in Northern Ireland, Bob Bishop, to Matt Busby, the Manchester United manager, after Bishop had stood on the side-lines watching a 15-year-old Belfast boy named George Best weave his magic on the pitch, scoring twice for Cregagh Boys Under-16 team in a 4-2 win against the much bigger and stronger boys from Boyland Football Club, Belfast. In Jack Kyle, the IRFU had found their very own genius.

On 6 December 1947, Ireland welcomed Australia to Dublin for an international friendly. Kyle was naturally selected at fly-half in a team that comprised Bill McKay, Karl Mullen and the captain, Ernest Strathdee. However, the IRFU tinkered with the side that had played in the 1947 Five Nations Championship, and awarded eight new caps: Jimmy Corcoran, Albert McConnell, Desmond McCourt, William McKee, Jimmy Nelson, Kevin O'Flanagan, Paddy Reid and Richard Wilkinson. Perhaps the IRFU Selection Committee had one eye on the forthcoming 1948 Five Nations Championship campaign because Ireland were no match for the experienced Wallabies, their XV did not contain any debutants, winning the encounter against Ireland with relative ease, 16-3.

Ireland won the 1948 Five Nations Championship and with it, the Triple Crown and their first ever Grand Slam title. It was the beginning of a Golden Age for Irish rugby and Kyle, who scored a try in the wins over England and Scotland, would go on to play a significant role in this renaissance period for the Boys in Green. Kyle, McKay, Mullen (captain) et al helped Ireland defend their title by winning the 1949 Five Nations Championship, only a loss versus France in their opening game deprived Ireland of winning back-to-back Grand Slams. Kyle may not have scored during the Championship but he was pivotal in the three games Ireland won, forever looking to receive the ball, slaloming his way was through defences and passing the ball to a teammate who was in a better scoring position than he was with pinpoint accuracy.

Mullen may well have been Ireland's leader on the pitch, a superb tactician, but it was Kyle who masterminded Ireland's successes. He was surgical and explosive on the field, forever making an exquisite nuisance of himself, sucking defenders towards a final spiral as he launched himself forward refusing to look back over his shoulder, knowing that he possessed the nerve and nous to escape a tackle.

When Kyle had the ball in his arms it was as though the players before him were moving in slow motion as he navigated his way through opposing defences, seeing everything unravel before him in high definition.

In 1950, after Ireland finished joint-third in the Five Nations Championship, Jackie was selected to tour Australia and New Zealand with the British and Irish

Lions. His name, and that of his fellow Doctor and Ireland teammate, Karl Mullen were among the first placed on the squad list made up by the Lions' selection Committee and coach Leslie B. Osborne. Mullen captained the side. Kyle was playing for Queen's University Belfast at the time of his selection and postponed his medical studies to go on the four month long Tour to the southern hemisphere, much to the annoyance of his parents.

"It was a huge honour getting picked, of course. But it wasn't without its difficulties. I was studying medicine at University in Belfast and going on Tour by ship for months meant postponing my exams for a long time. My father certainly wasn't happy about me going. I just had to reassure him that I would study extra hard on the ship. The joy of those Tours was the time you got to spend making friends with players from all over the British Isles you had never met on a personal level and reaching places you had only read about in the encyclopaedia."

The Tour involved six Test matches, two versus the Wallabies and four against the All Blacks. Kyle was only one of four players to play in all six Test matches, the others were Roy John (Lock, Neath & Wales), Bill McKay (Flanker, Queen's University & Ireland) and Jack Matthews (Centre, Cardiff & Wales). In total he played in 20 of the Lions' 29 Tour matches, the highlight of which saw him score a try in the First Test, a 9-9 draw with New Zealand at Carisbrook, Dunedin, New Zealand. Kyle was the Man of the Match also setting up a try for Ken Jones (Wing, Newport & Wales) and winning a penalty which was scored by John Robins (Prop, Birkenhead Park & Wales). The Lions lost their tour series 3-0, drawing one Test, to the All Blacks but defeated the Wallabies 2-0 with Kyle scoring a try in the Second Test, a 24-3 win at the Sydney Cricket Ground, Sydney, Australia. He

Legends & Lions

also scored a hat-trick of tries versus Buller (a 24-9 win in Westport, New Zealand) and against West Coast (a 32-3 victory in Greymouth, New Zealand). He remains the only Irish fly-half in Lions' history to score a double hat-trick of tries. Indeed, his performances on the Tour were so good he was named one of the six players of the year by the *New Zealand Rugby Almanac*. High praise for the boy from Belfast.

"If your actions inspire others to dream more, learn more, do more, and become more, you are a leader."

John Quincy Adams

Jack Kyle inspired everyone around him by setting a standard his teammates followed. He made them better players. Kyle may not have captained Ireland in every match he played for his country, but there is no question that he was their leader. And, no matter who he played for, club, country or the British and Irish Lions, his performances never dropped below outstanding. In 1951, Kyle once again inspired Ireland to greatness when they won their third Five Nations Championship in just four seasons. To say that Kyle was magnificent in all four games barely pays tribute to the great man. Ireland beat France 9-8 in Dublin, then England 3-0 at Lansdowne Road, Scotland 6-5 at Murrayfield Stadium and only Wales prevented them from claiming a fifth Triple Crown and a second Grand Slam, when the pair drew 3-3 at the Arms Park, Cardiff on Matchday 4.

With his magnetic energy and mesmeric attacking ability, Kyle was a sea of chaos to opposing teams. He made history and art at the same time.

He graduated from Queen's University Belfast in 1951 and went into practice as a General Practitioner in Belfast.

In 1955, he should have been an automatic choice for the British and Irish Lions Tour of South Africa, but for some inexplicable reason the Lions' Selection Committee took the decision not to select him or any player who was aged 30 or over. Kyle was 29 at the time.

On 1 March 1958, there was barely a dry eye inside Lansdowne Road when Jackie played his 46th, and final ever game, in the green jersey of Ireland. Quite fittingly, he got the send-off he so richly deserved for the service he gave his country on a rugby field. Ireland defeated Scotland 12-6 in their Five Nations Championship match. The match was Ireland's first since the tragedy of the Munich Air Disaster when 8 Manchester United players (7 died instantly in the crash, Duncan Edwards lost his battle for life 15 days later) lost their lives in the crash on a snow covered runway at Munich-Riem Airport, West Germany. They were affectionately dubbed *The Busby Babes*, after their manager, Matt Busby who had no hesitation in playing youngsters in his side in the top tier of English Football, Division One. One of those players was Dublin's very own, William Augustine "*Liam*" Whelan, who was six days short of his 20th birthday when Busby handed him the famous red jersey of Manchester United to make his senior debut for the club. Liam's football career began at Home Farm Football Club near his Cabra home in Dublin, less than six miles from where Jackie entered the gladiatorial arena of international rugby for his Test debut in the green jersey. Whelan was already an established star at the time of his death, 43 goals in 79 games for United and 4 international appearances for the Republic of Ireland, the Cristiano Ronaldo of his era. Whelan and Kyle, one born south of the border, one born north of the border, both Irish sportsmen celebrated in equal esteem.

Kyle scored 24 points, including 7 tries, for his country. He was only 32-years old when he called time on his international career, relatively young for a player today to hang-up his boots when you consider that Johnny Sexton was 38-years old when he retired from the sport. But, then again Kyle and Sexton played in eras that were so very different. Some rugby players today have their own personal trainers, a dietician to advise them on how best to fuel their body to prepare for a game, their own physiotherapist, an agent and a manager. When Jackie Kyle made his international debut, professionalism in the sport was 40 years away, he trained at night on his own after long hours working as a doctor during the day, he had nobody to advise him as to what to eat to maximise his performances and if he received an injury that needed treatment by a physio, then he would have to take his place in the queue after a game as Ireland only had one physiotherapist to look after the entire first team squad. But, when it comes down to it, and you take into consideration that when Jack Kyle was the best No.10 in the world, he juggled his playing career with his University classes to fulfil his ambition of becoming a doctor, the sport was not professional and his place of birth was still experiencing food rationing post World War II.

It is extremely difficult to compare players of different generations, even more so when you compare these Legends of the amateur and professional eras. Jack Kyle would have been the David Beckham of rugby union with sponsors knocking on his door (because a Sports Agent was anathema when Jack played for his country) to get him to endorse their products ranging from Brylcreem for your hair to an aftershave product. Kyle was more into his rugby than his public profile, much to the benefit of his club and country.

When he retired, his 52 international caps (46 for Ireland and 6 for the British and Irish Lions) was a world record at the time. But, he continued playing the game he loved and was a regular for the North of Ireland Rugby Football Club, Belfast. Fans who paid to see him play clutched their match tickets as if it was a winning ticket in a National Lottery Rollover, just to have the proof that they saw him play, watching him glide over the grass beneath his magical feet like Torvill and Dean skating over the ice on their way to winning a gold medal in the Figure Skating Pairs discipline at the 1984 Winter Olympic Games hosted by Sarajevo, Yugoslavia.

Kyle made eight appearances for Barbarian Football Club between 1948 and 1954, scoring three points in total.

"He was so beautifully balanced and had this gift of lulling opposition into a false sense of security. You'd think he was doing nothing, and yet in an instant he'd pull the ball back, and there he was in a position to score or make a try."

Cliff Morgan

The legendary Wales and Lions out-half, and a playing contemporary of Jackie's, speaking after one of the games Kyle starred n for the Baa-Bas

Jack Kyle was awarded an OBE in 1959, and in 1962 he went to work on a humanitarian project in Indonesia. He then returned home but could not resist helping others less fortunate than himself, and in 1966, he moved to Chingola, Zambia, Africa where he worked as a doctor until his retirement from the medical profession in 2000. His work in Zambia was honoured with an honorary doctorate from Queen's University in 1991, and a lifetime achievement award by the Irish Journal of Medical Science and the Royal Academy of Medicine of Ireland.

"I was not a great tackler. If I'd had to play rugby as a forward, I would have never played the game! Our back row of Jim McCarthy, Bill McKay and Des O'Brien was so strong that I didn't have to bother too much with the normal defensive duties of a fly-half."

Jack Kyle

In 2002 he was voted the Greatest Ever Irish Player in a poll conducted by the IRFU and in 2008, he was inducted into the International Rugby Board Hall of Fame. In 2009, when Ireland ended a 61-year drought of winning a second Grand Slam, Jackie was in Cardiff to watch the game and was the first person to congratulate Brian O'Driscoll, the Ireland captain, on the team's achievement. At long last, Jackie was able to pass on the torch of greatness to a future Irish Legend of the sportt.

Aside from how he masterminded the Grand Slam season of 1948, Kyle's career in the Irish jersey was like the epic stage ridden by Ireland's Stephen Roche, born in Dundrum, Dublin, at the 1987 Tour de France. The date was 22 July 1987, and it was the day that would define Roche, winner of the Giro d'Italia a few weeks before the Tour commenced, at the 1987 Tour de France, the world's most gruelling, and most prestigious bicycle race. This single 115-mile stage through the French part of the Alps from Le Bourg-d'Oisans to La

Plagne, was the moment when the Dubliner raised his cycling to a new level and proved he was more than just a cut above the rest. He was struggling on the climbs through the mountains but then found an inner strength, his Olympic moment – *Faster, Higher, Stronger* – to reduce the time deficit on Spain's Pedro Delgado who was in the *Maillot Jaune* (the yellow leader's jersey of the race) to claw back valuable seconds which would ultimately prove decisive in the Tour's General Classifications. Roche won the 1987 Tour de France in a time of 115 hours, 27 minutes and 42 seconds, just 40 seconds ahead of the Spanish rider.

Kyle's other highlights in the Ireland jersey included his outstanding individual try against France in the 1953 Five Nations Championship, a game Ireland won 16-3 at Ravenhill; his drop goal from the touchline to beat Wales 11-3 in Dublin in the 1956 Five Nations Championship; and his tactical kicking was vital in the 9-6 defeat of Australia at Lansdowne Road on 18 January 1958. Apart from his attacking prowess, Kyle was a shield to his team as a defender at a time when the Laws of the game permitted the flanker to stand very close to the opposing No.10. Kyle could read a game like a child could read a comic book story, as he persistently covered cross-field advances by the opposition towards the corner flag and made many of the last-ditch tackles that today's game rarely sees anyone other than the full-back commit to. In many ways, Jackie Kyle, was over courageous, but as far as the Irish fans were concerned, he was brave to a fault. And, on a windy day in the Irish capital on 11 January 1958, Australia were in the ascendency and sought to blow away Ireland who were fighting the wind in the second half. But, up stepped the unflappable Kyle to make courageous marks into touch to deny the Wallabies using the wind factor to their advantage as Ireland *blew* them away 9-6.

"They couldn't touch him. He'd play games and he wouldn't need his shorts laundered afterwards. Jack was just the best."

Jim McCarthy, Ireland 1948-55

In 1964, Cassius Clay Jr. (he later changed his name to Muhammad Ali) was 22 years old when he fought Sonny Liston for the World Heavyweight Boxing Championship. Liston was the reigning World Champion having won the belt two years previously. Just before he entered the ring Clay was asked how he would cope with the onslaught that Liston was about to offload on him. Clay smiled and said: "*I am going to float like a butterfly and sting like a bee. The hands can't hit what the eyes can't see.*" Clay won the contest by technical knockout. The young man from Louisville, Kentucky, USA must have seen footage of Kyle playing for Ireland because, for 11 years Jackie Kyle floated around a rugby pitch and stung his opponents with his ability to shift his bodyweight from one leg to the other, torturously twisting and turning, leaving them standing like a human corkscrew as he weaved his way up-field cutting through hapless defences like a hot knife going through butter. Little wonder then that he enjoyed two quite apt nicknames: *Ghost* and *Scarlet Pimpernel*.

Watching Jack Kyle play was like watching the Maverick leading the dance. No matter the opposition, he never panicked, he simply stalked his prey and then struck them with venom.

Sadly, Jackie passed away aged 88 on 28 November 2014. And, quite possibly the greatest ever tribute paid to Jackie was paid to him by another Irish Legend, the

JOHN WHITE

greatest ever Lion, Willie John McBride who said this of Jackie: *"We talk about gentleman, I could not sum that word up any better than saying - give me Jack Kyle."*

Without question we will never see his like again. If the Ireland fans had been asked to place one word on his tombstone, it would have been *"Immortal."*

The one thing that stood out about him more than anything else was his humility. Speaking about himself, he once said: *"When you think of models, they have to look a certain way. They will be 6ft tall and beautiful. With rugby, it's the same. I just happened to be born with something that meant I could go for a gap and just hope for the best."*

In 1948 and 1949, Humphrey Bogart had massive Box Office appeal starring in *The Treasure of the Sierra Madre* and *Tokyo Joe*. Movie goers flocked to their local cinema to see him. Jack Kyle did his acting on a rugby pitch and thousands paid into rugby stadia in Cardiff, Dublin, Edinburgh, London and Paris to see him play.

In the Pantheon of Irish Sporting Legends, regardless of the sport, Jack Kyle unquestionably occupies the top step. In 1520, Robert Whittington wrote *Vulagria*, which contains the following line: *"A Man For All Seasons."* John Wilson *"Jack"* Kyle was Ireland's main man for eleven seasons.

Jack Kyle reached heights that high on a rugby pitch, that only angels could call them home. He reached peaks no eagle could pass. He could fly without wings.

Did You Know That?

Interestingly, in the year of his birth the following all occurred: *The Great Miami Hurricane*, *Winnie The Pooh* was published by author A. A. Milne, John Logie Baird conducted the first public demonstration of a television and Hirohito was crowned Emperor of Japan. Jack Kyle was a whirlwind in a green jersey but his was not a story of fiction, he was Ireland's Rugby Emperor, he was made for TV audiences to enjoy and for sports writers to try and explain in their match report just how superb a game he had.

KEITH EARLS
Ireland's Running Man

KEITH GERALD EARLS was born on 2 October 1987 in Moyross, Limerick to Ger and Sandra Earls. He has a younger sister. The young Earls began playing underage rugby for Thomond as an open side flanker. His father is a well-known figure in Thomond having played for the club and winning an All-Ireland League Championship title with Young Munster in season 1992-93. On 21 October 1992, Ger was a member of the Munster team that famously defeated Australia, the reigning Rugby World Cup holders, 22-19 at Musgrave Park, Cork. The Wallabies were touring Europe.

Keith attended St Munchian's College in Corbally, Limerick before switching schools to St Nessan's Community College, Limerick which was closer to his home. At St Nessan's his rugby coach moved him into midfield, a move which coincided with him returning to St Munchian's where he won the Munster Schools Rugby Senior Cup in 2006. Conor Murray was one of his teammates in the final when they beat Presentation Brothers College 7-3. His future Ireland teammate, and captain of Munster, Peter O'Mahony, was on the opposing side.

Keith's natural ability attracted the attention of the selectors of the Ireland Schools side and Keith was capped by them. Earls then joined the Munster Academy and played for the Ireland Under-19's, Ireland

Legends & Lions

Under 20's winning a Grand Slam in the 2007 Six Nations Under 20's Championship, Ireland's Under-21's and Munster A. In 2007, he signed as a professional for Munster and played for Garryowen. On 7 April 2007, the Munster coach, Declan Kidney, gave him his Munster debut in a 20-12 away defeat to Ospreys in the Celtic League. The 19-year old who grew up on a Housing Estate in Moyross, came on as a replacement in the 65th minute for Anthony Horgan at the Liberty Stadium, Swansea, Wales. A match report read:

"Earls, so impressive this year with the Ireland Under 21s, really didn't have enough time or opportunity to make an impression at this level but nevertheless it can only be good news for Munster to be able to blood the likes of the Thomond RFC youngster and it is likely we will get to see more him in the final games of this season's Celtic League."

On the day after he was born M/A/R/R/S went to No.1 in the UK Singles Charts with *Pump Up The Volume*, a Dance hit. Keith pumped up the volume in every game he played and danced around defenders with ease.

Earls claimed his first professional winners' medal when Munster defeated Toulouse 16-13 in the 2007-08 Heineken Cup final at the Millennium Stadium. The following season he quickly began to establish himself in the Munster team, scoring ten tries and won his first international cap for Ireland. On 8 November 2008, he pulled on the green jersey for the first time when a Canadian touring side visited Thomond Park. One of the popular songs being played on the radio at the time was a collaboration between Madonna and Justin

JOHN WHITE

Timberlake called *4 Minutes*. It didn't take the young Earls that amount of time to make a big impression at international level scoring a try with his first touch of the ball when Ireland beat Canada 55-0. He crossed over the line in the second minute of the match. However, he did not feature for Ireland in their 2009 Six Nations Championship Grand Slam winning campaign, but his displays were rewarded with a place in the British & Irish Lions squad for their tour to South Africa in 2009 and despite impressing in the midweek fixtures, he did not play in any of the Tests. Keith played in five midweek matches and scored two tries. In season 2008-09, Keith won the United Rugby Championship with Munster.

Keith was selected to play for Ireland in their 2009 November Tests: he came on as a replacement for Luke Fitzgerald in the 20-20 draw versus Australia at Croke Park; started in Ireland's 41-6 win over Fiji at the RDS Arena scoring two tries and played in the 15-10 victory against South Africa at Croke Park.

Earls won the Munster Academy Player of the Year and Young Player of the Year in 2007 and 2009 respectively.

In the red jersey of Munster he played his part in their historic 15-6 win against Australia on 16 November 2010 at Thomond Park. In season 2010-11, he won the Magners League Grand Final with Munster when they recorded a 19-9 victory over their fiercest enemy, Leinster, at Thomond Park with Earls scoring a try. It was his third winners' medal in the competition, also known as the United Rugby Championship. Keith played in all five of Ireland's matches during the 2011 Six Nations Championship, four outings on the left wing and the other at fullback. In preparation for the 2011 Rugby World Cup, hosted by New Zealand, he played in both of Ireland's warm-up games versus France. When Ireland's 30-man squad was announced for the 2011 Rugby World Cup, his former coach at Munster, Declan Kidney, who was now the coach of Ireland, had no hesitation in naming the 23-year old Earls as part of his party. Ireland were drawn in Pool C and he started on the wing against the United States of America (won 22-10) and was on the wing again when they beat Australia 15-6. In their third game in Pool C, Kidney switched Keith to outside-centre and it reaped dividends for the pair as he scored two tries in an emphatic 62-12 win over Russia. When Ireland faced Italy in their final Pool C match, he was back on the wing and celebrated his 24th birthday with two tries in Ireland's 36-6 victory. With four wins from four, Ireland topped Pool C and met Pool D runners-up Wales (to South Africa) in the quarter-finals. Despite scoring his fifth try to become Ireland's leading try scorer in the tournament, Wales defeated Ireland 22-10 in Wellington.

Keith was selected in Ireland's 24-man squad for the 2012 Six Nations Championship by Kidney. He had to withdraw from Ireland's opening game against Wales (lost 23-21 at the Aviva Stadium) as his recently born daughter became unwell but he returned to the squad for the fixture versus Italy and scored a try in Ireland's 42-10 win in Dublin. He also played in a 17-17 draw with France at Stade de France, Paris and in Ireland's 32-14 victory over Scotland in Dublin and a 30-9 loss away to England.

JOHN WHITE

In June 2012, Ireland toured New Zealand and played the All Blacks in three Test Matches. In the first Test he played at inside centre as part of Kidney's new centre-combination alongside Brian O'Driscoll. Ireland lost the game 42-10. A pectoral injury ruled him out of the second Test, a 22-19 defeat, but he played on the wing in the third Test which the All Blacks won at a canter, 60-0. In the 2012 Autumn internationals, Keith played in Ireland's 16-12 defeat to South Africa at the Aviva Stadium and in their 46-24 win versus Argentina in Dublin.

Keith played in all five of Ireland's matches in the 2013 Six Nations Championship but a knee injury meant he missed Ireland's 2014 and 2015 Six Nations Championship campaigns. He returned to action for Ireland's two warm-up games against Wales in preparation for the 2015 Rugby World Cup which was hosted by Wales. On 8 August 2015, Ireland beat Wales 35-21 at the Millennium Stadium with Keith among the try scorers in a Man of the Match performance and on 29 August 2015, Ireland lost 16-10 in Dublin. Earls played in all four of Ireland's 2015 Rugby World Cup Pool D matches and helped himself to two tries when Ireland beat Romania 44-10 at Wembley Stadium, London (used for Pool games during the tournament). Alas, Argentina ended Keith's dreams of winning the Webb Ellis Cup when they defeated Ireland 43-20 in the quarter-finals at the Millennium Stadium.

Keith only missed one game of the 2016 Six Nations Championship, their 10-9 loss to France in Paris, and his form was good enough to be included in the Ireland squad selected by coach Joe Schmidt that toured South Africa later that year. Keith played in the first Test Match which Ireland won 26-20 in Cape Town: missed the 32-26 loss to the Springboks in Johannesburg and played in the Third Test which Ireland lost 19-13 in Port Elizabeth to give South Africa a 2-1 Test Series victory.

On 7 January 2017, Earls won his 50th cap in the European Cup during Munster's 32–7 away win against Racing 92 and was an ever present for Ireland in the 2017 Six Nations Championship. In 2018, Keith played in all five of Ireland's Six Nations Championship games, winning all five, and became a Grand Slam winner, Ireland's third Grand Slam (1948 & 2009). He won his 150th cap for Munster in the Province's 27–22 Champions Cup semi-final defeat at the hands of Racing 92 on 22 April 2018. Having previously been nominated for the Munster Player of the Year Award in 2010, Keith finally landed the prestigious honour by winning the award in 2018. Having won the Munster Academy Player of the Year and Young Player of the Year in 2007 and 2009 respectively, the 2018 award made Keith the first Munster player to win all three awards. To cap a hugely successful season for him, in May 2018, he won the Players' Player of the Year award at the 2018 Rugby Players' Ireland Awards ceremony to become the fourth Munster player in succession to win the award following Paul O'Connell (2015), CJ Stander (2016) and Conor Murray in 2017. But, 2018 brought even more accolades when he started in all three of Ireland's Tests versus Australia in June 2018, with Ireland claiming a historic 2-1 Test Series win over the Wallabies down under. In Ireland's 2018 Autumn Test Matches, Earls started in Ireland's 28–17 win against Argentina on 10 November 2018 in Dublin and in their 16–9 win versus New Zealand on 17 November 2018, his first success against the All

Blacks and Ireland's first ever win in Dublin against New Zealand.

After playing in all of Ireland's matches in the 2019 Six Nations Championship, and despite carrying an injury, Keith was selected in the Ireland squad for the 2019 Rugby World Cup hosted by Japan. During the tournament he played in the host nation's shock 19-12 win over the men in green, Ireland's 35-0 trouncing of Russia and in Ireland's 47-5 win against Samoa. However, Ireland packed their bags and flew home after losing 46-14 to the All Blacks in the quarter-finals. In 2020, Ireland had a new coach, Andy Farrell, who included Keith in his squad for the Six Nations Championship that year which was suspended due to the COVID-19 pandemic. When the final games were eventually played in October 2020, Ireland secured a third-place finish in the competition.

Once again, he was an ever-present for Ireland in the 2021 Six Nations Championship and on 13 November 2021, he played in Ireland's famous 29-20 victory over the All Blacks at the Aviva Stadium. A thigh injury forced him to miss the 2022 Six Nations Championship and following his recovery he was back playing again for his Province. Farrell named Keith in his Ireland squad for their 2022 Tour of New Zealand. On 29 June 2022, he started in Ireland's 32-17 loss against the Māori All Blacks and three days later, 2 July 2022, he was a starter in the first Test against New Zealand scoring a try in Ireland's 42–19 defeat. He missed the second Test Match against New Zealand on 9 July 2022, when Ireland emerged victorious, 23-12, in a chaotic game to claim their first win over the All Blacks on New Zealand soil to level their three-match series.

Legends & Lions

One of the proudest moments of his career came on 12 July 2022, captaining his country for the first time in their second game against the Māori All Blacks which Ireland won 30–24 to draw their Series with them 1–1. When Ireland faced the All Blacks on 16 July 2022, Keith was on the bench but came off it to help the team to a 33-22 win to claim a historic 2–1 Test Series victory, their first ever in New Zealand. A thigh injury meant he sat out the 2023 Six Nations Championship when Ireland won a fourth Grand Slam. However, just as he always did previously he recovered and returned to action. In Round 18 of the 2022-23 United Rugby Championship Earls claimed his 200th cap for Munster in their 22–22 draw away to Sharks (South Africa) on 22 April 2023, becoming only the fourteenth player to achieve this feat for the Province. Five weeks later, 27 May 2023, he came on as a replacement in Munster's 19-14 victory over the Stormers in the final of the 2022-23 United Rugby Championship at DHL Stadium, Cape Town, South Africa. Munster claimed their fourth title at the Stormers' home stadium. He made his Ireland return in their 33–17 win against Italy in Dublin on 5 August 2023, Ireland's first warm-up game in preparation for the 2023 Rugby World Cup in France. A fortnight later Earls won his 100th cap for Ireland and celebrated his milestone in a green jersey scoring a try, his 36th for Ireland, in their 29-10 victory over England at the Aviva Stadium, coming on for James Lowe in the second half. Keith was selected by Andy Farrell in Ireland's 33-man squad for the 2023 Rugby World Cup and started in their opening 82–8 win against Romania in Pool B on 9 September 2023.

In 1987, *The Running Man* starring Arnold Schwarzenegger was a film many movie goers went to see up and down the length of Ireland. Ever since he first picked up a rugby ball, Keith has been his club's and his country's *Running Man*.

Did You Know That?

In October 2021, Keith released his autobiography entitled: *Fight or Flight: My Life, My Choices*. That same month, during an appearance on RTE's *The Late Late Show*, he revealed that he had been diagnosed with Bipolar II disorder back in 2003 and openly discussed his mental health struggles. His coach at Munster at the time, Johann van Graan, was one of the first to praise his player for being so brave and honest. His autobiography won the Sports Book of the Year at the 2021 Irish Book Awards.

MIKE GIBSON
Poetry In Motion

CAMERON MICHAEL HENDERSON GIBSON was born on 3 December 1942 in Belfast, Northern Ireland. Gibson was educated at Campbell College, Belfast, and went on to study law at Queen's College, Cambridge, England. He played for the Cambridge University XV and helped them win the Varsity Match versus Oxford in December 1963. He also won Varsity Blues in 1964 when Oxford were the victors and in their 1965 drawn game, captaining the team in 1965. It was his outstanding performance for Cambridge University in the 1963 game that proved to be the pivotal point in his career. His free flowing style of play attracted the attention of the IRFU Selection Committee, with several members of the Committee enthusing about this 21-year old who every time he took to the field, was a cut above the rest.

Was Gibson ready, indeed, was he worthy enough, of playing for his country on the biggest stage of world rugby at the time, the Five Nations Championship? After all, the 1963 Five Nations Championship was only two months away and 21-years of age was still very much considered to be very young in the upper echelons of international rugby. Looking back the Irish Selectors must have been faced with the same dilemma which fell upon the mind and shoulders of Matt Busby, the manager of Manchester United Football Club (1945-69 & 1970-71), when he sat in his office at Old Trafford, the home of Manchester United on Friday 12 September 1963. Jimmy Murphy, the coach of the famous Busby Babes, told Busby that he had a 17-year old kid from Belfast in the club's junior team who was more than ready to make his debut in the upper echelons of English football. That player was none other than George Best. Busby listened to his trusted right-hand man and gave George his Manchester United debut the next day when he played in United's 1-0 win against West Bromwich Albion at Old Trafford, Manchester in the English First Division. Thankfully, in their infinite wisdom, the IRFU Selection Committee awarded Gibson the first of his 69 international caps for his country on 8 February 1964. The opposition were England at Twickenham Stadium in Ireland's opening game of the 1964 Five Nations Championship. It was a very experienced Irish side he burst into comprising Tom Kiernan, Patrick Casey, Jerry Walsh, Kevin Flynn, John Fortune, James Kelly, Mick O'Callaghan, Ronnie Dawson, Ray McLoughlin, Willie John McBride, Eamonn McGuire, Noel Murphy, Gerry Culliton and skippered by Bill Mulcahy. Gibson played his part in Ireland's 18-5 victory and was involved in all four of Ireland's tries scored by Flynn (2), Casey and Murphy, three of which were converted by Kiernan. Best played for United the same day, but unlike his fellow Belfast man, his side lost 3-2 to Leicester City away in the English First Division. The Irish Selection Committee liked what they saw from their new fly-half and picked Gibson for Ireland's remaining three matches in the tournament. Despite their good start against England, Ireland ended up with the wooden spoon after losing to Scotland, Wales and France. But in Gibson, a star was born.

Legends & Lions

"I would play games only using my left foot or my right foot and develop a strength in each area and then concentrate on getting the basic things right such as taking a pass or making a pass. Then there was the thinking bit which is all about making decisions. I believe that facet separates players."

Mike Gibson (interestingly George Best did a similar thing when he practised his ball skills by kicking a tennis ball, using both feet. along the streets of east Belfast on his way to Primary School)

Mike played in all four games in the 1965 and 1966 Five Nations Championship sandwiched by an appearance versus South Africa at Lansdowne Road on 10 April 1965, a game the Irish won 9-6, a try from Paddy McGrath and two penalties from Kiernan. Ray McLoughlin captained the side that historic day as it was Ireland's first victory over the Springboks since their first meeting in 1906, a case of seventh time lucky for the Boys in Green. In 1966, the British and Irish Lions toured Australia and New Zealand with nine Irish players in their squad: Barry Bresnihan, Ken Kennedy, Ronnie Lamont, Willie John McBride, Ray McLoughlin, Noel Murphy, Jerry Walsh, Roger Young and the 23-year old Gibson who was still studying law at Cambridge University when he received the call-up.

The Tour began in Australia and was a hugely successful one in the country with seven victories from the eight matches played including a 2-0 Test Series win over the Wallabies. Game No.5 in Australia resulted in a 6-6 draw with New South Wales. Gibson did not feature in any of the games. The 1966 squad were the first since 1904 to leave Australia without a defeat to their name. Australia were a good side, with the likes of Ken

JOHN WHITE

Catchpole, one of the Wallabies greatest ever players, and his half-back partner Phil Hawthorne. However, when the touring party crossed the Tasman, they entered a different world in terms of the standard of their opponents. The Lions lost four and drew two of their 21 non-Test fixtures in New Zealand but were whitewashed 4-0 by the All Blacks in the Test Series with Gibson starting all four games. The All Blacks were on an unbeaten journey which would extend to 17 consecutive Tests and were a side packed with brilliance including forwards like prop Ken Gray and Colin Meads, who played alongside his brother during the entire series, Stan at lock, plus flankers Waka Nathan and Kel Tremain and their superbly gifted captain, Brian Lochore.

Gibson played in 19 of the 25 Tour matches in New Zealand including 11 of the Lions' 13 final games. The 1966 Lions were the first to have a coach, the former Welsh international John Robins (11 caps, 1950-53), who was assisted by his team manager, Des O'Brien who won the Grand Slam with Ireland in 1948. Interestingly, every Lions' Tour since has adopted a coach and team manager partnership. On their way home from the Southern Hemisphere, the Lions stopped off in Canada to play two games. Incredibly, they were defeated 8-3 by British Colombia at Empire Stadium, Vancouver on 14 September 1966, but then beat Canada 19-8 on 17 October 1966, with Gibson converting one of the Lions' three tries as well as landing a penalty.

Gibson toured five times with the British and Irish Lions. In 1968, he played in all four Tests in South Africa, losing the Test Series 3-0 with one draw. He made history in the opening Test game of the 1968 Tour

Legends & Lions

by becoming the first replacement in international rugby when he replaced the Welsh fly-half Barry John who received an injury, a broken collar bone. Three years later in New Zealand Mike formed a brilliant midfield partnership with John Dawes (captain) from Wales whilst his combination with Gerald Davies, Gareth Edwards, Barry John and J.P.R. Williams (all Welsh internationals) and England's David Duckham is still revered to this day and for many is arguably the greatest ever back line in Lions' history. The Lions were magnificent in 1971, and to date their 2-1 Test Series win (one game was drawn) remains their sole Series victory over the All Blacks. It was on this tour that the New Zealand sports writers and public hailed Gibson for his work commitment, his exquisite timing and his attacking flair. The young Belfast man attracted admirers, male and female, like moths to a flame.

"Gibson's presence in the Lions back-line was the most frustrating influence of all. I would judge that 80% of All Black back movements came unstuck through Gibson's quickness, skill and courage. As near the perfect rugby player as I have seen in any position."

Colin Meads, All Black captain, 1971

Gibson was selected as a replacement for the second half of the Lions' Tour to South Africa in 1974, but did not feature in any of the four Tests, a Series won 3-0 by the Lions (one game ended in a draw) when the players returned home as "*The Invincibles*" after going unbeaten with a record of 21 wins and the drawn final Test. Mike was an automatic choice for the Lions' 1977 Tour of New Zealand but he did not feature in any of their four Tests, losing three and winning one, because of lower back and hamstring problems for the 34-year old. Nonetheless his selection for the British and Irish Lions in 1977 meant that he equalled his fellow Ireland teammate's record of five Lions Tours, Willie John McBride (1962, 1966, 1968, 1971 & 1974). Mike won 12 Test caps for the Lions, eleven as a starter without scoring (a Test cap was only awarded when a player represented the British and Irish Lions against a Tier 1 rugby nation).

On 16 June 1979, more than fifteen years after pulling on the green jersey for the first time, Mike played for Ireland for the final time. Ireland were touring Australia with eight matches lined-up, including two Tests. Gibson played in both Tests, a 27-12 win over the Wallabies at Ballymore, Brisbane on 3 June 1979 in the first Test. It was fair to say that at the time the 36-year old was not as swift and agile as he once was whilst Ireland had a new fly-half to admire, Ollie Campbell, who scored 19 of Ireland's points in the 27-12 victory. The visitors won the second Test 9-3 at the Sydney Cricket Ground with Gibson standing silently behind Campbell admiring his kicking mastery as he scored all of Ireland's points. It was a fitting venue for Gibson to bring down the curtain on his remarkable Test match career, taking the decision to bowl himself out of international rugby at one of Australia's most hallowed venues for cricket.

It was, for the Ireland fans, a case of – The King is Dead, Long Live the King.

Gibson did not play in great Irish teams. Indeed, Ireland only won a single Five Nations Championship during his international career, 1974, although they were outdone by final-match defeats in the 1965, 1967 and 1969 tournaments and the security concerns that led to the cancellation of Ireland's home matches against

Scotland and Wales after they had already defeated France and England away in the 1972 Five Nations Championship. Many still believe that Ireland would have been Grand Slam Champions in 1972 had it not been for the dark spectre of The Troubles that hung over the nation.

Mike Gibson's 69 caps (56 as a starter) was a record for Ireland which was not surpassed until lock Malcolm O'Kelly won his 70th cap against Scotland in the 2005 Six Nations Championships. It had stood for 26 years. His record of 56 appearances in the Five Nations/Six Nations Championship was not beaten until a fellow countryman, Ronan O'Gara, laced-up his boots for a 57th time for Ireland's final game in 2011. Mike scored 112 Test points (9 tries, 16 penalties, 7 conversions and 6 drop goals), all for his country. On the flip side his longevity also meant that when he retired from the international arena, he was also the most defeated player of all time, with 39 losses and 11 draws.

Mike Gibson was a truly exquisite player despite his humility. He was so versatile he represented Ireland in four different positions and never looked out of place in any of them. Many fans, regardless of their nationality quite rightly claim Gibson to be not only Ireland's greatest ever player, but the finest fly-half regardless of era and one of the best centres ever to play the game after he switched roles.

"Mike Gibson was a world-class outside-half who became a world-class centre."

Willie John McBride

From his early years he was a dedicated fitness fanatic and this reaped rewards for him on the pitch as he

JOHN WHITE

effortlessly dovetailed with his teammates around him to create and score try after try. He possessed deft footwork, impeccable timing, could read an opposing attack like a Chess Grandmaster, had fantastic positional sense, was a courageous forager of the ball, had steely determination and for the vast majority of his career had a rapier like kick. Little wonder then that when he was inducted into the International Rugby Board Hall of Fame in May 2011, his former teammate, Syd Millar, said of him: *"Mike Gibson was one of the finest players of his generation, one of the finest players ever to represent Ireland and the British & Irish Lions and a man who epitomised the very ethos of the game and its values."* Fitting words from a player who himself won 37 caps as a prop, was the coach of Ireland from 1973-75 and coached the British and Irish Lions in 1974 on their Tour of South Africa.

"At times when Irish rugby wasn't successful Mike was always the shining light. He played international rugby for 15 years and that speaks volumes about him. He was a magnificent player and a true ambassador for the game."

Brian O'Driscoll speaking in 2011

Anyone who saw Mike Gibson play will recall how he played with a swagger, not borne out of arrogance, because there was no need for him to show arrogance, it simply was not entwined in his DNA, but because he commanded the respect of every opponent who lined-up against him. He was a player with incredible perception which made him equally dangerous in defence as he was when he was running with the ball. He had a sidestep parallel with that of George Best, and like the Manchester United Legend, he was a Genius. Gibson embraced a distinguished career which he fully enjoyed

Legends & Lions

until he was 42 years of age.

In 1964, the movie *Goldfinger* was a huge success in the Box Offices around the world. The movie, produced on the screen from the novels written by Ian Fleming, was the third instalment of the James Bond *007* Series. Gibson may not have made his debut appearance for Ireland at No.7, but everything he touched, turned to gold on a rugby pitch. In 1964, Fred Astaire's dancing career in Hollywood movies was coming to an end when Gibson first pulled on an Irish jersey. Astaire was an accomplished dancer who was seldom seen without his female partner, Ginger Rogers. The pair glided effortlessly across the dancefloor. Gibson was an accomplished rugby player whose tuxedo was a green jersey, white shorts and green socks and he danced around opponents with the grace and style of Rudolph Nureyev on a ballet stage. Nureyev danced the *Black Swan pas de deux* from Swan Lake in 1964. Mike Gibson danced around 15 Englishmen at Twickenham Stadium when he burst on to the rugby scene that same year. Gibson's Rogers was the ball and he swept it around his teammates with unerring accuracy, a seamless transition from the moment he took possession of it until he released it to a player in a better position. Mike Gibson could dance on air and he oozed that much class it would not have been a surprise for any Ireland fan if the Irish Rugby Football Union hired the entire Ensemble of the Dublin Philharmonic Orchestra to accompany him every time he represented Ireland at Lansdowne Road.

"Mike Gibson was the most complete footballer I ever saw."

Bill McLaren

Mike Gibson was to Irish rugby what George Best was to

Irish football. The Irish fans adored the two Belfast boys in equal measure despite their polar differences, one who shunned the limelight and avoided having his name plastered on the back pages of the United Kingdom's tabloids for anything other than what he did on the field of play for his country, and George, who could fill an entire edition of a newspaper from the cover story on the first page to the entire sports section at the back of the newspaper over the course of a weekend playing for Manchester United. But, both had Chemistry, both had *Joie de vivre* (a joy of living). If the Irish fans were asked to liken both players to characters who had appeared on the silver screen in a movie, without doubt Gibson would be Sean Thornton portrayed by John Wayne in the 1952 classic, *The Quiet Man*. As for George, well as all Irish fans know he enjoyed his Superstar status to excess, despite being a very shy young boy when he first arrived in Manchester, would surely have to be cast as Dr Frank N. Furter, played by Tim Curry, in the 1975 movie *The Rocky Horror Picture Show*. The character of Dr. Frank N. Furter is portrayed as a heightened version of both femininity and masculinity. George Best was adored by both sexes during those halcyon days of the late 1960's when he was the best footballer in the world with even the Legendary Brazil striker, Pele, saying that George Best, *The Belfast Boy*, was a better footballer than him.

Northern Ireland has produced many world class Sports Superstars including Peter Canavan (Gaelic Football), Joey Dunlop (Motorbike Racing), Alex Higgins (Snooker), Eddie Irvine (Formula One), Pat Jennings (Football), Anthony McCoy (Horseracing), Barry McGuigan (Boxing), Rory McIlroy (Golf), Mary Peters (Athletics). On the very rare occasion, two athletes have stood side-by-side on the top step of the medals' podium at a Summer Olympic Games. The pair could not be separated by the distance, height or time they recorded in their own individual event, and thus, the International Olympic Committee awarded both athletes a gold medal, the pinnacle of their sporting career.

Mike Gibson and George Best never represented their country at an Olympiad, but both men were gold medal winning performers in their respective sports. And, when Northern Irish sports fans are asked to take part in a poll to name the Greatest Northern Ireland Sports Person of all Time, the names of Best and Gibson invariably come to the fore. But, just perhaps they both deserve to stand side-by-side on that winners' podium, unrivalled for what they did for their country in a green jersey.

Mike Gibson was a Player for the Ages, quite simply he was *Poetry In Motion*.

Did You Know That?

Mike Gibson was awarded an MBE for services to the game and was born in the same year as the Irish composer and musician, Phil Coulter (19 February 1942).

BRIAN O'DRISCOLL
A Once In A Lifetime Player

BRIAN GERALD O' DRISCOLL was born on 21 January 1979 in Dublin to Geraldine and Frank O'Driscoll, both physicians. Rugby was in Brian's blood from the moment he entered this world, his dad played twice for Ireland, his Uncle Barry was capped four times in the 1971 Five Nations Championship and his Uncle John was capped 26 times (1978-84) and also played for the British Lions sides which toured South Africa in 1980 and New Zealand in 1983. As a child Brian loved playing Gaelic football before making the switch to the oval ball playing for Blackrock College in the 1996 and 1997 Senior Cup. He played for the Irish Schools Rugby side three times. From an early age each time he played his every move was examined under the microscope.

In 1998, Brian played for the Under-19 side which won the Under-19 Rugby World Championship. He quickly realised that he was about to enter a world without any shade when he would be totally exposed, but it was a challenge he embraced willingly. Brian's motto could quite easily have been: *No Regrets, Everything For Victory*.

Upon leaving school he went to University College Dublin (UCD) where he won the first of his four caps for the Irish Under-21 side (19 February 1999) and on 20 June 1999, aged 20, he won the first of his record 133 international caps for Ireland in a 46-10 defeat to

Legends & Lions

Australia in Brisbane. Amazingly, he had played for his country before making his senior province debut for Leinster. At UCD his coach, John McClean, made a decision which would shape Brian's career moving him from the fly-half position to centre. He graduated from UCD with a Diploma in Sports Management.

Brian made his debut for Leinster aged 20 in 1999 helping his Province to the inaugural Celtic League title in 2001-02 and added three more Celtic League titles in 2007-08, 2012-13 and 2013-14. With Leinster he also won 3 Heineken European Cups in 2008-09 (top try scorer), 2010-11 and 2011-12 and in 2013 he helped the team to Amlin European Challenge Cup success.

The warriors of Celtic Europe were amongst the most distinctive of any fighters in the Ancient World. They were very tall, had long flowing dark hair and moustaches, painted and tattooed bodies, weighed upwards of 300 lbs and they had a penchant for collecting enemy heads in the heat of a battle. They fought on foot, on horseback and in chariots. Brian was a Celtic Warrior but unlike his Ancient Forefathers, he stood 5 feet, 10 inches tall, weighed 205 lbs, wasn't into tattoos, rarely sported a moustache but he did possess a fondness for collecting the scalps of Ireland's enemies on the battlefield. He led his men into battle like Russell Crowe's character, Maximus, in the Blockbuster movie "*Gladiator*." O'Driscoll was more than a General wearing green, he was his country's best, most naturally gifted and greatest player during his international career. Adding to the movie analogy, he was Sean Connery's character, Jim Malone the Irish policeman from New York City, in the hit movie *The Untouchables*. O'Driscoll was untouchable on a rugby pitch but then again very few players in the world could attain the levels of performance he continually displayed.

On 12 June 1999, he was awarded his first international cap when Ireland toured Australia that summer. But, it was a debut to forget, well from the point of view of the result rather than the performance of the Dublin born centre, as Australia thumped Ireland 46-10 at Ballymore Stadium, Brisbane. It was the first of two Test Matches for Ireland on the Tour, they also lost the second 32-28 at Subiaco Oval, Perth with O'Driscoll in the side. On 28 August 1999, he won his third cap when Ireland defeated a touring Argentina team 32-24 at Lansdowne Road. His performances at centre in a green jersey were considered to be good enough for him to merit a place in Ireland's squad that went to the 1999 Rugby World Cup. Brian played in all four of Ireland's games in the tournament, scoring his first try for his country in a 53-8 mauling of the USA in Dublin. Wales were the official host nation of the 1999 Rugby World Cup but some matches were played outside the Principality in England, France, Ireland and Scotland.

Brian O'Driscoll had style, he had panache, he was on a different stratosphere to his contemporaries, he soared without wings, he had the X-Factor.

"The one aspect that stands out for me when I think of Brian O'Driscoll is that nobody told him how to be a great player. Nobody told him he had to be a better defender, nobody said he had to develop all these outside breaks. Brian drove himself and created a position all by himself. You can only coach a guy to a certain level, after that, it's up to the player and that's what sets Brian apart. He made the No 13 jersey his own, he always looked to improve his skills, he never sat back and thought he was the finished article and that's why he is a brilliant defender. It's not

LEGENDS & LIONS

because he got slower, it's because Brian has developed this ability to smash guys in the tackle, read defences and just be in the right place at the right time."

Malcolm O'Kelly
92 caps for Ireland, 1997-2008

Brian was one of those players who was quite simply a threat all over the field, brilliant in defence coupled with mesmerising attacking skills that left opponents shaking their heads in disbelief. When he played it was as though a Tornado had swept the pitch such was his brilliance. This was never more evident than his display versus France in the 2000 Six Nations Championship, the first time Italy had joined the northern hemisphere competition. He scored a hat-trick of tries against France at Stade de France to help Ireland to their first win in Paris in 28 years, Ireland winning 27-25. During the competition he had the calmness to elevate himself above all others on the field. Some players have moments others have momentum and once Brian achieved both, he was unstoppable. His performances propelled him to a first British and Irish Lions Tour when they toured Australia in 2001. The Leinster No.13 played in all three Tests with the Wallabies winning two and the Lions winning one for a 2-1 Series defeat.

The rugby pitch was his greatest stage, his time, his place, his match but he knew that is where the challenge starts.

"The greatest leader is not necessarily the one who does the greatest things. He is the one that gets the people to do the greatest things."

Ronald Reagan

Brian was not always the one who did the greatest things in a game. But, he was the one that got his teammates to do the greatest things. In 2002, he was handed the captaincy of Ireland for the first time in Ireland's 18–9 win over Australia at Lansdowne Road, their first win against the Wallabies since 1979. When Ireland's regular captain, Keith Wood, retired from the international scene in 2003, Brian became Ireland's new captain. By this time he was a household name all over the world and in 2003, he captained his country to runners-up spot in the Six Nations Championship, behind Grand Slam winners, England. A year later Ireland went one better when O'Driscoll led them to Triple Crown and Six Nations Championship glory. It was Ireland's first Triple Crown since Ciaran Fitzgerald captained the side in 1985. Such was his popularity at home in Ireland that the Irish fans started to wear t-shirts with "*In BOD We Trust*" emblazoned on them.

He never let time stand still or get caught up in the moment regardless of his rising popularity among Ireland fans. He just simply found a new frontier to turn the spotlight sideways and on 13 November 2004, he captained Ireland to a historic victory when they defeated South Africa 17-12 in Dublin, a first Irish win over the Springboks since 1965. The following year, 2005, he captained the British and Irish Lions on their Tour of New Zealand. The first of three Test Matches was played at Lancaster Park, Christchurch on 25 June 2015, and the All Blacks knew that if they wanted to stop the Lions then they first had to stop O'Driscoll. Less than two minutes into the game Tana Umaga, the New Zealand captain, and Kevin Mealumu carried out a vicious *spear tackle* on O'Driscoll, when at a ruck, the pair each grabbed one of O'Driscoll's legs and drove him into the ground. His shoulder was instantly dislocated, his Tour was over.

"Brian O'Driscoll is as good a centre as Britain and Ireland have ever produced. He had an outstanding tour with the Lions in Australia in 2001. Remember that fabulous try in the first Test? When he came on to the scene he was so quick and sharp but if his career has proven one thing it's just how strong a competitor he is. You need that within a Lions environment and he showed it again when captain in 2005. Unfortunately he was targeted by New Zealand. We'll let what happened to him rest, but it's enough to say they saw him as such a big threat that they definitely targeted him."

Sir Ian McGeechan

In 2006 and again in 2007, he led Ireland to Triple Crown success in the Six Nations Championship. During the 2007 tournament, he broke Wood's captaincy record of 36 Tests. He was also named the Player of the Six Nations Championship in 2006 and 2007.

Injuries then started to take a toll on his body, he was 28, and he missed the 2007 Rugby World Cup hosted by France. On 21 September 2007, France beat Ireland 25-3 at Stade de France in a Pool D game. What Ireland would have given for a fit O'Driscoll, the one who ran Les Bleus ragged seven years earlier in the same stadium when he scared the life out of the French before a partisan crowd, scoring three tries for his country to give notice to the world that here was a mega star in the making. Alas, Ireland did not even make it out of their Pool which was won by the host nation with Argentina runners-up. Ireland finished in a disappointing third place ahead of Georgia and Namibia. But, if you thought his powers were waning then you were effectively writing him off at your peril because what made Brian stand out above all others was his determination. If he had been born in England then without question the city of his birth would have been the Steel City, Sheffield. Although, if you asked Brian he would probably choose Manchester where his favourite football team play and, although he played his club rugby in blue, Brian is a Red, a huge Manchester United fan.

With him there was always something left, that is his Legend finding a way to win with whatever is available to him, broken body or not. And, when he did play it was like his coach had lit the blue touch-paper letting the opposition know to stand clear immediately. Fireworks surrounded his play, a catalyst for the measurement of how those around him performed, as if he had himself been impregnated with nitre. Whether he pulled on the blue of Leinster, the green of Ireland or the red of the British and Irish Lions, and even the black and white of the Barbarians, he precipitated a dramatic change in his side's fortunes. It was as though he was like a bonfire waiting to be ignited.

In his book "*Reggie Corrigan – Leinster In The Beginning*," Corrigan talks a lot about Brian or Drico as he called him with one line stating: "*Shaggy (Shane Horgan) was gregarious and motivated. Drico affable, adept, ambitious and smart.*"

Despite being considered past his peak by some sportswriters, Brian was immense on the field and led Ireland to only their second ever Grand Slam success in the 2009 Six Nations Championship. It was the first time since 1948, that the Boys in Green were invincible in the northern hemisphere's prestigious rugby union tournament. Quite a few journalists, some Irish, dined on a single course for dinner on the final evening of the tournament, a large helping of Humble Pie, but Brian was too much of a professional to ram it down their throats with retaliatory remarks even after he scored a try in Ireland's final game and was named Player of the Tournament for a record third time. Maybe, some sportswriters just no longer liked him, thinking a *Change of the Guard* was needed, as if to discard him, but forgetting he was their Bread & Butter, their staple diet, they had been feeding off for a decade since **BOD** made his international debut in 1999.

If Brian had played *How You Like Me Now?* by the band, The Heavy, before he spoke to the TV commentator during his post-match interview after leading Ireland to the Grand Slam in 2009, it would have been most fitting. The lyrics from the song include:

> *"Now there was a time*
> *When you loved me so*
> *I could have been wrong*
> *But now you needed to know*
> *So how you like me now*
> *How you like me now*
> *How you like me now*
> *Remember the time*
> *When I eat you up*
> *Yeah, I wasn't lyin'*
> *That you can't give up*
> *If I was to cheat*
> *Oh no, would you see right through me*
> *Does that make you love me baby*
> *Does that make you want me baby"*

But, BOD was the consummate professional and put

aside any disregard he held for his newspaper critics because it just gave then an extra inch in their columns. The journalists filled inches whereas Brian enveloped a field with his play. And, Brian ended the campaign as the joint-top try scorer (4) with England's Riki Flutey.

"Experience is the teacher of all things."

Julius Caesar

Not too many of the players from the first Golden Age of Irish rugby were still alive to pay tribute to their modern day fellow internationals. But, Jack Kyle, voted the Greatest Ever Player in the history of Irish rugby, was at the Millennium Stadium on 21 March 2009 when Ireland defeated Wales 17-15 to claim their place in history 61 years after Kyle, Ernest Strathdee, John Daly, Bill McKay, Dudley Higgins, Bertie O'Hanlon, William McKee, Paddy Reid, Barney Mullan, Albert McConnell, Colm Callan, Jimmy Nelson, Jim McCarthy, Des O'Brien and Karl Mullen (captain) beat Wales 6-3 at Ravenhill to win the 1948 Five Nations Championship (11th title), Triple Crown (10th title) and the so very coveted Grand Slam.

"It was wonderful to shake Brian's hand in Cardiff after Ireland won the 2009 Grand Slam. I was delighted to be there and the wonderful photograph taken is a very pleasant memory of a very special occasion. That was the last game I attended. At my age (88), my old immune system isn't all that great so I try to avoid the cold, the wet and the damp. I watch the games on TV now and it's amazing that Brian has managed to survive for so long at the top because I'm told the figures are about 40 per cent of professional players who have to stop because of injury. He has had a few

Legends & Lions

injuries but has managed to survive and keep going. He's been a great servant, a man who has made a tremendous difference to Irish rugby."

Jack Kyle
Winner of the 1948 Grand Slam with Ireland

In 2009, he helped Leinster win the Heineken Cup for the first time, scoring a drop goal in their 19-16 victory against Leicester Tigers. Selection for his third British & Irish Lions Tour followed. His 100th Ireland cap came in the 2010 Six Nations Championship versus Wales but his injuries, particularly his shoulder, were hampering his all-out attacking style. As the saying goes, the mind was willing but the body was struggling to keep up.

He led Ireland into the quarter-finals of the 2011 Rugby World Cup but surgery post the tournament meant he sat out the entire 2012 Six Nations Championship campaign. Brian returned to action for Ireland in 2013 although he was no longer the automatic choice to captain his country. However, his performances in the 2013 Six Nations Championship resulted in a call-up to a Lions' Tour for the fourth time in his illustrious career. He won his eighth Lions' cap in a 16-15 loss to the Wallabies on 29 June 2013 in Melbourne, Australia. The three games Test Series stood at 1-1 but Brian was controversially dropped for the deciding Test which the Lions won 41-16. Not even selected for the bench, he watched his teammates from the stands inside the ANZ Stadium, Sydney and at long last could record being a member of a Lions' Test Series win to his impressive CV.

Putting it quite simply, he was brilliance without an asterisk. That's how good he was. In fact when he played for Leinster or Ireland the stadium announcer should have played Tina Turner's rock anthem, *Simply the Best*, because BOD was Simply the Best.

Ironically, the No.8 best audience attracting movie at the Box Office in 1979, the year of Brian's birth, was a move called *The Life of Brian*.

In September 2013, he announced that he would retire at the end of the season. Brian pulled on the Ireland jersey for the 133rd and final time when they played France at Stade de France in the 2014 Six Nations Championship. Ireland won 26-22 in the *City of Lights* for only the second time in 42 years, a win which crowned them 2014 Six Nations Champions. It was an appropriate venue for Brian to dim the lights of his international career.

"I've worked with Brian for four years now. He's a man I respect immensely and he's a player that I really enjoy coaching, His work ethic is massive – to be talented and have such special attributes, and then to work so hard that you maximize those special attributes, that's the character he demonstrates."

Joe Schmidt, Ireland coach 2013-19

Julius Caesar's letter to the Roman Senate around 47 BC after he had achieved a quick victory in his short war against Zile, the modern day Turkey, included a famous line that for many Irish fans best summed-up Brian's all-conquering career in a green jersey: *Veni, vidi, vici* (translated from Latin it means: "*I came. I saw. I Conquered.*"

Leinster paid a moving tribute to Brian on the big screen at their home ground, the RDS Arena, before his 186th and final appearance for the club (scored 311 points). On 31 May 2014, Leinster defeated Glasgow

Warriors 34-12 in the 2014 Pro12 Grand Final. It wasn't the send-off that Brian had hoped for as he had to leave the pitch in the 9th minute of the game injured. However, he did help his captain, Leo Cullen, lift the trophy after the game ended much to the delight of the Leinster fans who came to pay their respect to a rugby Legend. Fans watched Brian in action for Leinster on the screen covering his 15 years with the club. The action was accompanied with a song from the American rock band, The Killers, entitled *A Shot At The Night*. Some of the lines from the song summed Brian up perfectly.

"Once in a lifetime, the suffering of fools
To find our way home, to break in these palms
Once in a lifetime
Give me a shot at the night
Give me a moment, some kinda mysterious
Once in a lifetime, the breaking of the roof
To find that our home, has long been out grown
Draw me a life line, 'cause honey I got nothing to lose
Once in a lifetime
Look at my reflection in the mirror
Underneath the power of the light
Give me a shot at the night
Give me a moment, some kinda mysterious
Give me a shot at the night"

Once in a lifetime a certain player comes along and lights up a sport. They provide a sparkle of gold dust. They become a player for the ages. For Irish rugby, that person was Brian O'Driscoll.

Did You Know That?

In the RBS Six Nations Championships he is the tournament's all-time try scorer with 26, won the Player of the Tournament award in 2006, 2007 and 2009. Other notable awards include: **IRUPA** Players' Player of the Year 2008-09, **IRB** International Try of the Year 2008 (Australia v Ireland), Texaco Sportstars Rugby Award in 2000, 2002, 2007 and 2009, *Rugby World* magazine's Player of the Decade (2000), also being named in the magazine's Team of the Decade, Dubliner of the Year award in 2008 and in 2014, he was justifiably inducted into the RTE Sport Hall of Fame.

WILLIE ANDERSON

Our Willie Is Bigger Than France's Condom!

WILLIAM "*WILLIE*" ANDERSON was born on 3 April 1955, in Sixmilecross, County Tyrone, Northern Ireland and attended Omagh Academy. Willie made his international bow on 10 November 1984, a 16-9 loss at Lansdowne Road to Australia who were touring Great Britain and Ireland.

Willie was well known to Irish rugby fans long before he pulled on the green jersey for the first time. In 1979 he made his debut for Ulster and the following year, 1980, he went on a Tour of South America with Penguin International Rugby Football Club, an invitational rugby union side based in Britain. During the tour with The Penguins, Big Willie was arrested and imprisoned for three months. Following a game versus Banco Nacion in the Argentine capital, Bueno Aires, The Penguins said farewell to their hosts and left the post-match reception to go into the heart of the city to enjoy whatever nightlife was on offer to tourists. Banco Nacion had the renowned Argentina out-half Hugo Porta in their ranks.

In 1979, Anderson went on a Tour of Canada with Stranmillis College, Belfast and to remember his adventure in North America, he brought home a Canadian national flag as a souvenir. A year later he was making his way into the centre of Buenos Aires and spotted an Argentina flag which was fluttering on a flag pole outside an enormous white building. The flag was easily identifiable as the country's national flag with its two horizontal light blue stripes above and below a white horizontal stripe with an image of the sun in the middle of it. Added to this, the flag had been seen all over Britain and Ireland in 1978 when Argentina won the FIFA Football World Cup at Estadio Monumental, Buenos Aires. So, Willie decided he would take the flag home as a souvenir of his visit to the country. What he didn't know was that the imposing building was in fact a Government building. A coup d'etat occurred in the country in 1976 that resulted in Argentina coming under Military Rule, the Armed Forces of the Argentine Republic ruled the population with an iron fist led by the Junta Generals.

Sometime later when he was asked about the incident of being charged of *"Demeaning a patriotic symbol,"* Willie explained what had happened that fateful evening in South America when he could have lost his life for what he thought was just a playful prank, but which the Argentine authorities took very seriously.

"I was playing for Dungannon at the time, I had just left Stranmillis. I was just coming back from a match to the hotel, we went out again for another beer, but we weren't drunk or anything. Buenos Aires was probably the safest city in the world at that stage because it was under military rule. We just saw a flag and me and another fella took it and went back to the hotel. The next thing there was army and policemen with machine guns coming through the door to try and get the flag back. I was there for three or four months: it was a fairly tough time and you think you mightn't get home at all, you think you have to do jail or even worse, some generals wanted us executed."

Anderson and his co-accused spent time in jail and after the rest of The Penguins flew home, the offending Penguins were placed under house arrest awaiting trial.

Legends & Lions

Willie said: *"I was writing letters home and I felt very guilty about the two or three guys that went down with me all having UK passports. I just ran every day, I would have got up and got a bite to eat then go for a run, go for walk or just write letters. In fairness a lot of the Argentine folk were fairly kind and couldn't believe that I was still there at the end. My lawyer was always being threatened because he was representing a UK citizen; I was glad it wasn't it a year later, but the tension then was high and gathering over the Falklands."*

Anderson was sentenced to two years on conditional release, and one of the people he spent his time writing to back home was a girl named Heather who he ended up marrying. Willie has always said that he will forever be grateful to the people from Dungannon Rugby Football Club who supported him during his unexpected prolonged stay in the *"Fair Winds,"* the Spanish translation of Buenos Aires.

But his infamy for what happened in Argentina pales into significance for what he did in an Irish jersey at Lansdowne Road on 18 November 1989. Ireland were facing New Zealand in an international friendly, or so it was supposed to be, and Anderson was handed the honour of captaining the side for the first time in his career. Jimmy Davidson was the Ireland coach who made Willie his captain for the game and he spoke to Willie about a plan he had in mind which might just upset the touring All Blacks.

"Jimmy Davidson was instrumental in ensuring we got the applause and not the haka. That was significant, and it was one of the greatest atmospheres I've ever played in. Jimmy had it planned most of the week, he told the players that we were going to link arms and move forward and eyeball the player in front of us. I seemed to be pulling a few guys along with me at that stage. It was

a fairly iconic moment in my career, and anybody who was at the game still remembers and reminds me of it."

Anderson's defiant march towards the All Blacks players, who were performing the Haka at the time, is one of the most defining moments in the history of Irish rugby and although Ireland lost the game 23-6 (Brian Smith scored two penalties for Ireland), it paved the way for the Irish side who achieved a first ever victory over their *"Invincible"* nemesis, a 40-29 monumental victory at Soldier Field, Chicago, United Sates of America on 5 November 2016. Fans of the British TV Show *Dad's Army*, would have enjoyed Anderson hauling his 14 teammates towards their opponents in an arrow like movement on the hallowed turf of the home of Irish rugby.

Willie was a key member of the Ulster team that dominated Irish rugby in the 1980's winning 10 consecutive Interprovincial titles from 1985-94, two of which were shared wins. In total, Anderson played 78 times for his Province.

Willie may well have begun his international career more towards the end of his playing career than the beginning of it, he was 29 years old when he won his first cap. But, he played in all four games of the 1985 Five Nations Championship, when Ireland won the title and Triple Crown.

On 2 March 1985, Ireland played France at Lansdowne Road in the Five Nations Championship, a match that ended 15-15 which prevented Ireland from claiming a feat that would have won the country a second Grand Slam following their first in 1948. The TV cameras spanned the crowd and spotted a banner which an Irish fan had made for the game. The banner read: *"Our Willie's bigger than your Condom!"* Jean Condom played in the game and won 61 caps for France from 1982-90.

Willie was capped 27 times by Ireland between 1984 and 1990 and his place in the upper echelons of Irish Rugby history are well and truly embroidered into the team's emblem and history books.

Willie Anderson's Zodiac birth sign is Aries (Ram) and the boy from Sixmilecross possessed all of a ram's attributes. In nature documentaries the sheer power and strength of rams are often displayed when two rams are seen butting heads in duels of strength. In Mythology the ram is heralded for its' masculinity, strength, great force, power and instinctive reactions. The ram represents the power to penetrate, overcome, and achieve. It reflects the assertion of strength in creative ways to achieve a breakthrough. It is also associated with sacrifice. Battering rams were used in many battles and wars to knock down the gates of enemies. Willie Anderson was Ireland's battering ram.

Did You Know That?

Willie is the father of the fashion designer, Jonathan Anderson, who designed the outfit worn by Rhianna at the Superbowl on 12 February 2023.

FERGUS SLATTERY
The Prince Of Irish Rugby

John Fergus Slattery was born on 12 February 1949 in Dun Laoghaire, Ireland. It was the same day that Ireland faced England in the 1949 Five Nations Championship campaign. Ireland won the Grand Slam the previous season for the first time in the country's history but despite losing 16-9 to France at Lansdowne Road on 29 January 1949, the Triple Crown was still within their grasp. Apparently when later asked about the day she gave birth to Fergus, his mother said that the doctor was in a bit of a hurry: "*Ireland were playing for the Triple Crown in Lansdowne Road and the doctor wanted to be there.*" Ireland beat England 14-5 and went on to retain the Championship and the Triple Crown. Thirty-three years later Fergus was a member of the next Irish side to win the Triple Crown doing so in 1982, also claiming their ninth Championship.

The young Fergus played schools rugby for the famous Blackrock College which spawned so many Irish Rugby Legends. When he left secondary school he played for University College Dublin, yet another famous nursery school for future Irish internationals.

In 1969-70, South Africa embarked on a Tour of Great Britain and Ireland. There were a number of anti-apartheid protests throughout the controversial Tour as it was played at a time when South Africa's apartheid system was in place. Protests took place at most of their 26 games organised by the *Stop the '70 Tour,* led by Peter Hain. Peter Hain was born in Nairobi, a Kenyan colony at the time in southern Africa and went on to serve the British Government as the Secretary of State for Northern Ireland from 6 May 2005 to 28 June 2007, under the leadership of the British Prime Minister, Gordon Brown.

Ronnie Dawson, the first person to be appointed the coach of Ireland (1969-72), selected the 21-year old Slattery to make his first appearance for Ireland versus the Springboks at Lansdowne Road on 10 January 1970. It was a massive step up in class for Slattery, just as it was for two other new Irish debutants, Eric Campbell and William Brown. But, Dawson, who won 27 Ireland caps during his playing career, had the utmost faith in his new maiden Test Match trio. Mind you, the Ireland XV that faced South Africa that day was not exactly short of experience with Tom Kiernan captaining the team which also included Alan Duggan, Barry Bresnihan, Mike Gibson, Barry McGann, Roger Young, Syd Millar, Ken Kennedy, Philo O'Callaghan, Willie John McBride, Ronnie Lamont and Ken Goodall. The match ended in a draw, 8-8, before a crowd of 28,000 in the Irish capital with Duggan scoring a try which was converted by the sure-footed Kiernan who also successfully scored a penalty attempt at goal like an archer's arrow hitting a bullseye from 30 yards out.

Slattery first toured with the British and Irish Lions in 1971 but did not start any of the Test matches as the tourists collected their first, and only, series win in New Zealand. The Lions' back-row berths were claimed by Mervyn Davies (Wales), Peter Dixon (England) and John Taylor (Wales) leaving Slattery as a reserve although he did have a niggling injury. Fergus wore the

JOHN WHITE

British and Irish Lions shirt 25 times and amazingly only ever tasted defeat once in it, and that came in his debut when Queensland beat the tourists 15-11 at Lang Park, Brisbane, Australia on 12 May 1971. Mind you the home side did include 10 capped Wallabies in their starting XV. He then embarked on an incredible run of 23 games unbeaten in a red jersey and a draw in his final appearance on their 1977 Tour of New Zealand. It is a truly remarkable achievement that is unlikely to be ever matched. Speaking about his debut for the Lions he said:

"Before we got to New Zealand on the 1971 Tour we had two games in Australia. We opened the Tour against Queensland and then faced New South Wales. I don't think that if we had played as well as any Lions team could have done we would have won that game in Brisbane. The penalty count against us was 15-3 in Queensland and then 21-3 in New South Wales. It was incredible. We managed to beat New South Wales 14-12, but if we could make that many mistakes in those two games and then go to New Zealand and go unbeaten in all our provincial matches it either says something about our team, or the referees."

Slattery played in 12 winning Lions teams in Provincial matches, including the notorious "Battle of Canterbury," one of the most brutal games in not only the history of the British and Irish Lions, but in world rugby. On 19 June 1971, the Lions played Canterbury at Lancaster Park, Christchurch and won the bruising battle 14-3. It was the eleventh match of a 26 game itinerary. The match itself was a war of attrition with bodies from both teams regularly ending up flat out lying on their back on the turf. The game was played a week before the First Test against the All Blacks and

LEGENDS & LIONS

it has been said that their opponents had strict orders to injure as many players in red as possible. Fergus was one of the Lions who received an injury, suffering concussion and having his front teeth cracked down to the root after receiving a blow at a line-out. It was a nasty assault. "Canterbury just went out to kick the s**t out of us," said Slattery, who had only made his debut for Ireland 18 months earlier after an impressive run of form for Blackrock RFC.

Fergus played for the Barbarians in the famous match against New Zealand at Cardiff Arms Park on 27 January 1973, which is one of the greatest ever games of rugby played. The match was a game of attack and counterattack, with the Barbarians winning 23–11, to deliver a fourth defeat on the All Blacks who were touring Great Britain and Ireland. Gareth Edwards (Wales) scored a try in the game which is widely considered to be the greatest ever in rugby union, but not many fans will recall that Fergus Slattery from Dun Laoghaire got in on the action himself by scoring a try. It was the All Blacks final game of their tour which saw them draw 10-10 with Ireland at Lansdowne Road on 20 January 1973 with Slattery in the Irish side.

"I made the tackle which led to them kicking the ball away, and I could have got the ball passed to me, but it became a very Welsh try, especially the closer it got to the line!" said Fergus in an interview many years later.

When the British and Irish Lions squad was selected for the 1974 tour of South Africa, Fergus was an automatic choice for the team, forming one of the best ever Lions back rows alongside Mervyn Davies and Roger Uttley (England). Quite simply, he was just too good to leave out and aged 25 he was already the best

JOHN WHITE

open-side flanker in the sport. Slattery was a master tactician who unlike most players in his position did not set his sights on the stand-off from the scrum. Using his ability to win possession he utilised his blistering pace to hassle the Springboks from the first whistle in the game to the last. Slattery was so quick off the mark that he was already among the opposition's centres before the ball arrived with them. The tour was a huge success with the Lions, captained by Slattery's Ireland teammate, the colossus that was Willie John McBride, winning three of the four Tests and drawing one, the final one. On this tour McBride introduced his iconic "99" call to his players meaning that every Lion stood his ground at every confrontation with a Springbok and if one Lion was injured by an opponent then it was the duty of every one of his teammates to hit the closest person in green to him. In November 1973, six months before the tour began, the United Nations declared South Africa's apartheid policy as a "Crime Against Humanity." Many "crimes" were committed by the Springboks on the field in the four Tests who could have done with introducing a 999 call to alert the local police to the constant beatings they were given by the Lions who defeated them 12-3, 28-9 and 26-9 plus the 13-13 drawn game. Fergus played in all four Tests. The Lions were so dominant they won 21 of the 22 matches they played but it should have been a perfect clean sweep of victories, a Tour Whitewash, because in the dying minutes of the fourth Test at Ellis Park Stadium, Johannesburg, Fergus crossed over the Springboks' try line and scored. However the referee, who just so happened to be a South African, Max Baise, disallowed the score because he claimed he did not see the ball being grounded. It would have been the perfect ending to Fergus's tour who scored six tries in the twelve games he played. Indeed, Fergus accepted Baise's decision to rule out his try saying: "The referee is always right even if he's wrong." However, it could so easily have been the Perfect Tour as Slattery explained many years later:

"But I don't think that was the reason why we didn't win that final Test. As a side, we played as though we had packed our bags to go home on the Thursday. I certainly felt that and I think we were probably a bit guilty of pushing that fourth Test down the agenda a little bit. We had a couple of injury problems and perhaps we didn't give the game the full attention it deserved at the end of a long, but otherwise successful Tour."

The 1971 and 1974 Tours by the British and Irish Lions resulted in the only back-to-back series victories the Lions have ever enjoyed since they embarked on their inaugural Tour in 1888, with five victories, two draws and one loss in eight Test Matches - New Zealand 2-1-1 & South Africa 3-1-0.

In 1979, Fergus was the No.1 choice as captain of the Ireland side that toured Australia which was selected by the Ireland coach, Noel Murphy. The Irish coach won 48 caps for Ireland from 1958-69 and scored 15 points from his flanker position and was capped 8 times by the Lions (1959-66) scoring 3 points. It was a hugely successful touring side in Australia with Ireland winning seven of eight matches including the two Tests in Brisbane and Sydney against the Wallabies. Then, in 1982, he captained Ireland's Triple Crown and Five Nations Championship winning team, only the fifth time they had beaten England, Scotland and Wales in the same tournament and the ninth time they were crowned

Champions but missed out on the Grand Slam (their first since 1948) after losing to France. On 21 January 1984, he pulled on the Ireland shirt for the final time, having captained the side on 18 occasions, scoring 12 points. It was his 61st appearance for his beloved country but there was no fairy tale ending as France won their 1984 Five Nations encounter 25-12 at Parc des Princes, Paris.

Fergus may have missed out on the professional era and European Cup Rugby but his place among the Legends of Irish rugby lives on.

Post his playing days, Fergus established himself as a successful property developer and was very much in demand as a guest speaker on the after-dinner circuit. In 2007, Fergus was inducted into the International Rugby Hall of Fame, and in 2020, he joined the Lions once again, by joining the board of The British & Irish Lions Charitable Trust.

The surname Slattery is of Irish origin and the coat of arms shows three red submissive lions against a white background indicating a family that are magnanimous in warfare and yet kind and warm in peacetime. Slattery means "*descendant of slatra*" meaning robust, strong, bold. But Fergus was so much more than this.

In Paris, Raphael Nadal is worshipped as the Prince of Roland-Garros having won the French Open Men's Singles Tennis Championship on 14 occasions at the home of French tennis. Fergus possessed an all-court game, renowned for his tireless work ethic around the fringes, superb hand-to eye movement, tremendous balance, agile, pacey, practically flawless in possession, mobile and tenacious in the loose. He had charisma, he played with panache. But, on that 1984 day at Parc des Princes in the heart of the French capital, the Prince of

Irish Rugby said *Au Revoir* to the sport he had graced with eloquence every time he laced-up his boots.

Did You Know That?

Gordon Brown, was the organiser for the Edinburgh, Scotland arm of the "*Stop the '70 Tour,*" and later served as the British Prime Minister from 27 June 2007 to 11 May 2010.

RONAN O'GARA
Ireland's Conductor

RONAN JOHN ROSS O'GARA was born on 7 March 1977 in San Diego, California, United States of America. His father, Fergal, was employed as a post-doctoral fellow in microbiology when Ronan came into the world although his stay across the Big Pond was a short one as his family moved back home to Ireland when he was only six months old. Rugby was in his life from the moment he was born as Fergal had played wing for the University College Galway club in Connacht. His mum was born in County Mayo.

Interestingly, one of one of the biggest selling moves in 1977, was called *The Greatest*.

And home to the O'Gara's in Ireland was Cork city. Ronan attended Scoil an Spioraid Naoimh Primary School and his first year at secondary school was spent at Bishopstown Community School near his home where his mother worked as a school teacher. In the year of his birth, the band Hot Chocolate had a No.1 hit in the UK Singles Charts called *So You Win Again*. From Year 2 onwards he was a pupil at Presentation Brothers College, Cork where he was a winner himself, a Junior Cup medal in 1992 and a Senior Cup medal in 1995. O'Gara also went to University College Cork where he won an All-Ireland Under-20's medal with the team in 1996 and three years later, 1999, he graduated with a Bachelor of Arts and a Master's Degree in Business Economics.

In August 1997, aged 20, he made his Munster debut

LEGENDS & LIONS

against Connacht and scored 19 points in the game alongside his long-time Munster and Ireland teammate, David Wallace. The following month, O'Gara played in his first Heineken Cup game, a 48-40 loss to Harlequins at Twickenham Stoop, London, England. He kicked 15 of the visitors' points that day. Over the course of the next three seasons he earned himself a guaranteed starting position in the Munster side on a regular basis, and in 2000 and 2002, played in a losing Heineken Cup final side. Munster lost 9-8 to Northampton Saints in 2000 (Wallace scored a try and New Zealand's Jason Holland scored a drop goal). In the 2002 final Leicester Tigers won their contest 15-9 with Ronan scoring three penalties.

Ronan won a cap for the Ireland A team on 9 April 1999, against Italy A, and was selected for Ireland's preliminary training squad ahead of that year's Rugby World Cup. However, he missed out on selection for the squad despite being a member of the Munster side that beat the Ireland side in a warm-up game, that went to the tournament as the management decided to take two fly-halves and an extra prop to Wales instead of three fly-halves. Eric Elwood and David Humphreys, the latter being Ronan's nemesis during the early part of his international career at fly-half leaving Ronan to watch the games at his home.

On 19 February 2000, O'Gara was handed his first Ireland cap as one of five debutants in the green jersey when they played Scotland in the newly created Six Nations Championship. The 23-year old had a great game converting two conver Dublin. Simon Easterby, John Hayes, Shane Horgan (scored a try) and Peter Stringer made-up the new pack of five who played in the game. David Humphreys also played in the game, coming on in the 51st minute as a replacement for O'Gara, converting three tries and scoring a penalty, thereby beginning a fierce rivalry between the pair for the coveted No.10 jersey. In 2001, he went on his first Tour with the British and Irish Lions but he did not feature in any of the three Tests against Australia although he did play four times, scoring 26 points. The Lions lost the Test Series 2-1 to the Wallabies. O'Gara scored all of Ireland's points in their 18–9 win over Australia at Lansdowne Road in the Autumn Tests of 2002.

But, Rona did help Munster win the Celtic League in season 2002-03 when they defeated Neath 37-17 in the final played at the Millennium Stadium on 1 February 2003. He scored four penalties in the game.

In March 2003, he was approached by the Miami Dolphins, an American Football team from the National Football League (NFL) to join them as a kicker (the player who attempted a kick over the crossbar for a point after a touchdown was scored, worth six points) but he turned down their advances despite the very lucrative salary on offer. He was a key member of Ireland's 2003 Rugby World Cup squad, playing all four Pool games plus the quarter-final defeat to France, scoring 30 points.

In 2004, Ronan helped Ireland to their first Triple Crown success in 19 years and scored all of Ireland's points in a 17–12 win over South Africa at Lansdowne Road on 13 November 2004. Two weeks after his exploits versus the Springboks, Ronan was in the limelight again, scoring a last minute drop goal in a 21-19 win over Argentina in Dublin. Not surprisingly, Ronan was named the RTE Sports Person of the Year in 2004. A year later, 2005, he was in the Munster team that beat

Legends & Lions

Llanelli Scarlets 27-16 in the Celtic Cup final, scoring 17 points: a try, which he converted as well as converting the tries scored by Anthony Horgan and Mike Mullins, plus a drop goal and a penalty in a Man of the Match virtuoso performance. Anthony Foley captained the side which also included Irish Legends, Paul O'Connell, Peter Stringer and David Wallace.

In 2006, O'Gara was an instrumental figure in the Munster side that won their first ever Heineken Cup title. At long last the bridesmaids had become the bride when they defeated Biarritz from France, 23-19 at the Millennium Stadium before 74,534 fans. The Welsh capital was accustomed to dealing with a Tsunami of red home shirts but on this occasion, Irish men, women and children donned them as they invaded the Principality to watch their team play. It has been claimed that Saint Patrick, the Patron Saint of Ireland, was born in Wales and when he was 16-years old, according to the *Confession of Saint Patrick*, he was captured by a group of Irish pirates, from his family's home at Bannavem Taburniae, Northumberland, England and they took him to Ireland where he was enslaved and held captive for six years. Patrick writes in the *Confession* that the time he spent in captivity was critical to his spiritual development. He explains that the Lord had mercy on his youth and ignorance, and afforded him the opportunity to be forgiven his sins and convert to Christianity.

Saint Patrick recounts that he had a vision a few years after returning home: "*I saw a man coming, as it were from Ireland. His name was Victoricus, and he carried many letters, and he gave me one of them. I read the heading: "The Voice of the Irish.*" During his illustrious playing career in a green jersey, 2000-13, the young boy born in San Diego, was truly Victorious.

Ronan scored 14 of his side's points in the 23-19 victory, two conversions from two (Trevor Alstead & Stringer scored a try) and three penalties. Munster were crowned Champions again in 2008 after winning a tense final 16-13 versus Toulouse (France). And once again it was O'Gara who was the key figure in the victory by scoring three from three penalty attempts and converting Denis Leamy's try.

Ronan toured New Zealand with the Lions in 2005, and faced stiff competition for a starting place from Stephen Jones (Wales) and Jonny Wilkinson (England). O'Gara's Test Match experience was limited to a replacement appearance in the third Test against the All Blacks. The All Blacks won the Series 3-0, their third series clean sweep of the Lions, following the feats of their 1966 and 1983 winning teams. In 2006, he overtook David Humphreys as Ireland's highest points scorer and helped Ireland win the Triple Crown.

On 11 February 2007, O'Gara stamped his name in the Ireland rugby history books when he scored the first Irish international try at Croke Park. Lansdowne Road, the home of Irish rugby since 1878, had been demolished to make way for a new home, the Aviva Stadium. France were the visitors to the spiritual home of GAA sports and defeated Ireland 20-17 in the 2007 Six Nations Championship. An inauspicious start for Ireland under their new landlords, although Ronan did score all of the Irish points that day, his try and four penalties. However, Ireland had already beaten Wales 19-9 on Matchday 1 at the Millennium Stadium with O'Gara scoring a try and converting two of his team's three tries. Matchday 3 brought England to Dublin and they were sent packing, heads bowed low, after O'Gara scored 21 of Ireland's points in an emphatic 43-13 victory (3/3 conversions and 5/5 penalties). O'Gara was flawless in the game and if an Irish fan could have requested a song to be played at the end of the game to rub Ireland's majestic performance into their gaping wounds, then surely the fan would have asked the stadium announcer to play George Michael's 2004 hit, *Flawless*, which includes the line: "*Maybe tonight, they'll see you tonight (flawless, absolutely flawless).*" Well, at Croke Park on 24 February 2007, Ronan O'Gara was absolutely flawless. He was at the peak of his rugby skills. In Round 4 of the 2007 Six Nations Championship, not for the first time, O'Gara scored all of Ireland's points. On this occasion Ireland beat Scotland 19-18 at Murrayfield Stadium to land the Triple Crown with the Irish Superstar scoring a try, which he also converted, and four from four penalty attempts. France won the title. The definition of flawless is "*Without any imperfections or defects; perfect.*" In 2007, it was about time the English dictionary added the name of Ronan O'Gara to that description.

Ireland went to their sixth successive **Rugby World Cup** in 2007, and he played in all four of their Pool games, scoring 19 points. But, it was a disappointing tournament for the Irish who finished third in the table behind Argentina, Pool D winners, and runners-up France. On 15 March 2008, Ronan proudly captained his country for the first time. But, despite scoring a penalty and converting a try scored by **Rob Kearney**, it was a baptism of fire for him as England beat Ireland 33-10 in the Six Nations Championship at Twickenham Stadium. Almost a year to the day later, 14 March 2009, Ronan overtook Wilkinson to become the top points scorer in the history of the Six Nations Championship (including Home International and Five Nations editions of the Championship). Ireland defeated Scotland 22-15 at Murrayfield with Ronan notching-up 17 points to add to a single try from Jamie Heaslip (a conversion, four penalties and a drop goal). Six days later, 20 March 2009, he scored a late drop goal in the 78th minute to beat Wales 17-15 in the Principality and secure for Ireland their first Grand Slam for 61 years.

O'Gara was named in the Lions squad for their 2009 Tour to South Africa. On 27 June 2009, he came off the bench in the second Test Match against the Springboks, winning his second Lions' cap. But, it is a Tour he will want to forget because he conceded a penalty in the 79th minute of the game at Loftus Versfeld, Pretoria when he collided in the air with South African scrum-half, Fourie du Perez. The score was tied at 25-25, and up stepped Morne Steyn who scored the penalty to win the game 28-25 for South Africa, who won the Test Series 2-1. O'Gara played 5 games in total on the 2009 Tour, scoring 49 points. It was a bitter pill for the Munster player to swallow. Ronan started versus Australia in the first match of Ireland's November 2009 Series scoring 10 points. He then lost his place in the starting line-up to Johnny Sexton and did not play in the matches versus against Fiji or South Africa.

Ronan didn't exactly have a great 2010, in and out of the Ireland team despite being lethal when asked to convert a try or score a penalty kick. His battle with Leinster's Johnny Sexton for the Irish fly-halve spot was one of sport's Titanic battles, sometimes a struggle, depending upon who the incumbent was. He began the 2010 Six Nations Championship as coach Declan

Legends & Lions

Kidney's preferred option and played against France and Italy. Yet, despite having a 100% kicking record in those games, he found himself sitting on the bench. Ireland beat Italy 29-11 in Dublin with O'Gara scoring 2/2 conversions and 4/4 penalties; Ireland lost 33-10 to France in Paris, O'Gara converted David Wallace's try and scored the single penalty which Ireland were awarded in the match. Sexton now had a firm grip on Ireland's iconic No.10 jersey.

But, Ronan was selected to tour Australia and New Zealand with Ireland for their 2010 Summer Tour. O'Gara, aged 33, started the First Test versus the All Blacks but left the field at Yarrow Stadium, New Plymouth, New Zealand with his head bowed as Ireland were humiliated, beaten 66-28. It was a crushing loss, although Ronan did successfully kick all three penalties he was presented with. When Ireland played the Wallabies at Suncorp Stadium, Brisbane, Australia a fortnight later, the 24-year old Sexton was given the nod by Kidney to start the Test. Ireland were beaten 22-15 with Sexton scoring all of his side's points, 5/5 penalties.

O'Gara versus Sexton was the biggest sporting rivalry in Ireland if not world rugby.

On 6 November 2010, Ireland welcomed South Africa to the Irish capital for an Autumn Test at the Aviva Stadium. Kidney started the Leinster fly-half against the Springboks. The Ireland fans were quickly realising that O'Gara was playing second fiddle to his greatest adversary, who just happened to be a teammate. But, in the 67th minute of the Test, Kidney replaced Sexton with Ronan, and Ireland's No.21 received a standing ovation from the partisan crowd to celebrate his 100th cap for his country. Sexton scored 3/4 penalty attempts and Ronan's conversion of Tommy Bowe's try with 12 minutes of play remaining was not enough to prevent the Irish Centurion from being on the losing side, 23-21. He became just the third player to win 100 caps for Ireland.

During the 2011 Six Nations Championship, Ronan became the first Irishman to score over 1,000 points in international matches when Ireland lost 19-13 to Wales at the Millennium Stadium. He achieved the milestone after converting Brian O'Driscoll's try. His form for his club, and in the green jersey, merited a place in Ireland's 2011 Rugby World Cup squad. He played in all of Ireland's Pool C matches and became Ireland's highest points corer in the history of the Rugby World Cup (1987-present).

In an interview after Ireland's 15–6 Rugby World Cup Pool C victory over Australia on 17 September 2011, at Eden Park, New Zealand, O'Gara hinted at his possible retirement from international rugby after the conclusion of the tournament, but subsequently said that his words had been misinterpreted.

Following Munster's 16-10 defeat to ASM Clermont Auvergne on 27 April 2013, in the semi-finals of the 2012-13 Heineken Cup he decided it was the right time for him to retire.

"I have ambitions in the years ahead to coach at a high level and, with this in mind, I can confirm now that I will be joining Racing Métro's coaching staff in July. I am trusting my instinct and it is telling me now is the appropriate time to stop (playing). Had I already decided to retire before the (Heineken Cup semi-final) loss in Montpellier last month? I kind of knew. My legs are gone."

Ronan O'Gara

Legends & Lions

"In wishing Ronan the very best in the future, I'd like to acknowledge the immense contribution he has made to Munster Rugby and indeed rugby in general in Ireland over the course of what has been a fabulous career."

Garrett Fitzgerald, Munster Rugby Chief Executive

When he hung-up his boots, he held the record of being the all-time top scorer in both the Heineken Cup (2,065 for Munster from 1997-2013) and for Ireland (1,083), as well as being Ireland's second most-capped player with 128 caps. Truly remarkable accomplishments. In May 2016, Ronan was inducted into the Irish Rugby Union Professionals' Association Hall of Fame and in September 2018, he was inducted into the World Rugby Hall of Fame, the 12th Irish inductee. He was also awarded the Freedom of the City of Cork.

"He had this confidence about him. He was obviously learning, back then (in the late 1990s), and trying to find his way into the professional era, particularly in the international set-up. He had played for Munster before I had played for Ireland, but then I got capped (in 1999) before he did. You knew immediately that he was a competitor and a born winner. Someone that really backed his own ability. You can really see that now, in his coaching. He's guided - with Jono Gibbes last year, obviously - his team to three finals in 13 months, which is no mean feat. He's gone away and done the hard yards - gone to Christchurch, Paris and, now, La Rochelle - and has now earned his coaching stripes. So, he's never been shy of hard work and never been shy of doing things the difficult way to get results. From early on, he was always someone that set a tone."

Brian O'Driscoll

Ronan O'Gara is one of the greatest sportsmen Ireland

has ever produced. He was a magnificent kicker whether the ball was dropped to his feet or placed on the turf. His accuracy from penalty kicks was second to none during the peak of his career, similar to Robin Hood firing an arrow which split the arrow of a competitor that was already lodged deep in the heart of the bullseye. A sublime tactician and reader of the game, for more than a decade he made the out-half position for Munster and Ireland his own. When things were not going particularly well for his team, he took the pressure off them with long kicks up field which were measured to perfection. He had a cool head when the pressure was on.

San Diego, Ronan's place of birth, is Spanish for Saint Didacus, who was venerated by the Roman Catholic Church, when he was canonised on 15 July 1588, at Saint Peter's Basilica, Rome by Pope Sixtus V. San Diego's main economic engines are military and defence-related activities, tourism, international trade, research, and manufacturing. Ronan O'Gara was venerated by Ireland's rugby fans, and because of what he did for his country on a rugby pitch, was also held in high esteem by fans of other sports. He was "*One of their Own,*" and regardless of an individual's religion, or the sport they excelled in, when an Irish sports star represented the country similar to the level Ronan achieved, they received the same adulation. And as for San Diego's military prowess, it pales into insignificance when compared to Ronan's talent as he had the raw born ability and talent to see off waring opponents with his lethal right boot.

Ronan's Zodiac birth sign is Pisces (Fish), not the most apt for a player who was more of a Great White Shark than a mere fish in an Ireland jersey.

Legends & Lions

The name Rónán, anglicised as Ronan, is an Irish male Christian name and is also a surname. The surname is derived from the Gaelic Ó Rónáin *"Descendant of Rónán."* The name has several meanings including: *"Seal," "A Pledge"* and *"A Promising Oath."* The word for seal in Irish Gaelic is *rón*. There is no question that Ronan O'Gara pledged his playing career to Munster and to Ireland which received the seal of approval from the fans.

Every time he pulled on an Ireland jersey he was one of the first players in the faces of the opposition, leading from the front, a player whose kicking ability gave his team so many attacking opportunities. When he had the ball he exuded flair, created excitement in the stands and handed his teammates so many scoring opportunities. His kicking of the ball was done so with grace and equanimity.

When Ireland were in tune, Ronan O'Gara was Ireland's Conductor on the pitch. Ireland were at Peace.

Did You Know That?

Ronan O'Gara made history as the head coach of La Rochelle leading *Les Maritimes* to victory in the 2022 European Rugby Champions Cup, for the first time in the club's history. This made him the first person ever to win the Heineken Champions Cup as a player and as a head coach, for two different teams. He lifted the trophy with Munster in 2006 and 2008. Under O'Gara's leadership, the French club finished runners-up in the tournament in 2021, and successfully defended the title in 2023.

JOHN HAYES
The Bull

JOHN HAYES was born in Dromsally, Cappamore, County Limerick on 2 November 1973. His first love in sport, as it remains today, was hurling and he played for his local team, Cappamore GAA hurling club. He played in the Mackey Cup for East Limerick in 1985 and won the East Limerick Long Kick competition when he was a pupil in Cappamore Boys National School.

Incredibly he didn't start playing rugby until he was 18 years old after some friends suggested to him that he should join Bruff Rugby Football Club in County Limerick.

When he left Bruff RFC he joined Shannon Rugby Football Club and played at Lock before emigrating to New Zealand in 1995 aged 21 to play for Marist Oldboys Rugby Club in Invercargill. It is the southernmost city in New Zealand and one of the southernmost in the world, with a population of approximately 50,000. Up until he packed his bags to move to New Zealand, John Hayes had never set foot on a plane before. When he arrived down under he was still somewhat of a novice who was trying to understand the game. Vin Nally, his coach at Marist, recognised his potential and after he persuaded Hayes to "*bulk up*," he switched him to Prop. Marist has a history of Irish players including former Munster captain Pat Murray, Dave Dineen, Derek Tobin and Seamus Twomey.

Legends & Lions

"John came to the club and we had him playing lock. Eventually, we said he would be better at prop. He went back to Ireland and the rest is history!"

Bill Dowling, Marist President

When he returned to Ireland at the end of the 1995-96 season, he re-signed for Shannon RFC and won a place in the Munster squad before re-joining Bruff RFC after they became a member of the All Ireland League in 2004. John's last appearance for Shannon RFC was the 2002 All-Ireland League final versus Cork Constitution. It was a very special day for the Hayes family as John lined out with his younger brother, Thomas, who played behind him in the second row. The brothers helped Shannon RFC win their fifth league title that day and another Hayes brother, Michael, also claimed a winner's medal as he had also been involved in Shannon's campaign that season. Three brothers winning All-Ireland League medals in the same season is an extremely unique achievement in the history of the All-Ireland League.

In 1973, the year John was born, Peters and Lee enjoyed their only No.1 hit single, *Welcome Home*. No doubt everyone in Limerick were rummaging through boxes in their attics frantically searching for the 45rpm vinyl record of the song to play and celebrate Hayes' homecoming. The chances of them finding a record player to play the single on were slim but the sentiment was there.

On 19 February 2000, his gargantuan performances for Munster were rewarded when Warren Gatland handed him his first Ireland cap. Scotland were the visitors to Lansdowne Road for Ireland's first ever home game in the newly created Six Nations Championship. Ireland were beaten 50-18 by England a fortnight earlier at Twickenham Stadium. Ireland beat Scotland 44-22, and Gatland had discovered his first choice at Prop and selected Hayes for the next three games in the competition. There was no looking back for Hayes and he went on to become a constant presence in the Irish front row for a decade.

He scored his first try for Munster in their famous 31-25 semi-final victory over Toulouse in the 1999-2000 Heineken Cup, the same day Ronan O'Gara scored his first European try. However, they lost the final 9-8 to Northampton Saints at Twickenham Stadium.

Ireland played four Tests after the 2000 Six Nations Championship and Hayes starred in them all: a 34-23 loss away to Argentina in Buenos Aires on 3 June 2000; a 27-27 draw in Canada two weeks later; a 78-9 victory over Japan at Lansdowne Road on 11 November 2000 and a 28-18 loss to a touring South Africa side in Dublin on 19 November 2000. Hayes was a towering figure and influence for Ireland in the 2001 Six Nations Championship when they narrowly lost out on winning the title to England, who like Ireland won four of their five games (England lost 20-14 to Ireland in Dublin and Ireland lost 32-10 away to Scotland), but England had the superior points scored/conceded difference. This was the tournament which was affected by the outbreak of foot-and-mouth in the UK and Ireland which resulted in Ireland having to play their last three games in September 2001 and October 2001. In order to keep the team in good shape for these latter three games,

Legends & Lions

the Ireland coach, Eddie O'Sullivan took the squad to Eastern Europe for a friendly international. On 2 June 2001, Ireland beat Romania 37-3 at Dinamo Stadium in the Romanian capital Bucharest. Romania was part of the Iron Curtain, the military barrier erected by the Soviet Union post World War II to seal itself and their dependent eastern allies off from having any form of open contact with the west and other non-communist countries.

Two years prior to Ireland's trip behind the Iron Curtain, movie goers in Romania went to their local cinemas to see *The Iron Giant*, a 1999 American animated science fiction movie. The plot of the film concerns an object from space crashing into the ocean just off the coast of Maine, USA in October 1957, during the Cold War. The object was a 50 foot tall alien robot that then made his way ashore. Standing 6 foot, 4 inches tall and weighing 19 stone, Hayes must have looked like a green giant to the Romanian players and to their fans as he caused carnage on Ireland's opponents throughout the match.

"Improving my scrummaging was something I just had to do. I knew it was the weakness in my game. The hardest thing to do when I changed from second row to prop was to get to grips with it. Every time you'd come up against a new fella, he'd do something you hadn't come across before and you'd have to keep learning."

John Hayes

John's zodiac birth sign is Scorpio but it really should have been Taurus to match his nickname, *The Bull*. Mind

JOHN WHITE

you, John carried a massive sting in his play. On 11 October 2001, he was part of the Ireland team that beat Samoa 35-8 in Dublin, and the following week he played his first international against New Zealand. The touring All Blacks defeated Ireland 40-29 at Lansdowne Road. During the 2002 Six Nations Championship campaign he appeared in all five of Ireland's games. Later that year the Munster Prop toured New Zealand with Ireland, playing in both Test Matches which were won by the All Blacks. The Bull earned his nickname because he was a world-renowned scrummager and a fierce physical presence in the loose. More adept at preventing points being scored against Ireland than providing assists to teammates to score a try or score himself, Hayes got his name on the scoreboard for the first time in a green jersey on 7 November 2002. The Iron Giant terrorised Romania for a second time scoring a try in Ireland's 39-8 victory in the Irish capital. Transylvania in central Romania is the home of Bram Stoker's *Count Dracula* but once again the boy born in Limerick sucked the blood out of their attack. In the 16th and 17th centuries Limerick was sometimes called the most beautiful city in Ireland. In 1620, Luke Gernon, an English born judge and a resident of the city wrote that when he first saw Limerick it reminded him of Oxford, England with its lofty buildings of marble just like the Colleges and University in Oxford. Hayes wasn't from Oxford but his opponents sometimes thought he was made of marble. The word *"marble"* derives from the Ancient Greek *mármaron* meaning *"crystalline rock, shining stone."* Hayes was the bedrock of Ireland's defence for a decade.

LEGENDS & LIONS

"There is nothing blasé about him (John), he just rolls his sleeves up and he gets on with his work. He is just very understated and a great guy to have in your squad."

Brian O'Driscoll

In 2003, he played in all five games of Ireland's Six Nations Championship campaign and helped Munster win the United Rugby Championship (Pro12/Pro14). He went to the 2003 Rugby World Cup with Ireland and played in every one of their games in Australia. The following year he was an ever present member of Ireland's 2004 Triple Crown winning side. Indeed, he never missed a single Six Nations Championship game for Ireland from 2001-10, ten years of outstanding performances in the green No.3 jersey. Regardless of whoever was in charge of the national side, the name of John Hayes was guaranteed to be on the Ireland team sheet. During the 2005 Six Nations Championship he scored his second, and last, try for Ireland when they beat Scotland 40-13 at Murrayfield, Edinburgh. On 25 May 2005, Hayes won the first of his two caps for the British and Irish Lions when they faced Argentina in a friendly at the Millennium Stadium. Sir Clive Woodward, the head coach of the Lions, wanted to see how his squad members performed ahead of their forthcoming tour of New Zealand (4 June 2005 to 9 July 2005). The Pumas totally surprised the Lions by claiming a famous 25-25 draw in the Principality despite fielding an under strength side as a result of several injured players in their squad.

The Lions played three Test Matches versus the All Blacks. Woodward opted for Julian White (England) ahead of Hayes for the opening Test which the tourists lost 21-3, the infamous game which ended the Lions' captain, Brian O'Driscoll's, tour after being on the end of a double barrelled spear tackle by two All Blacks. Despite the defeat, and Hayes playing and training well, White retained his place in the side for the next two Tests which the tourists lost 48-18 and 38-19. The poor test results, despite Woodward having one of the most experienced playing squads and the largest management team of any Lions tour, led to criticism of Woodward, particularly his selection policy, and prompted commentators to question the future of the Lions. Many sports writers could not fathom many of Woodward's preferred choices in certain positions including Prop. White (Leicester Tigers) was considered to be an aggressive tight head prop, one of the most powerful forwards in world rugby who was best known for his destructive scrummaging ability. But, he was no John Hayes and without the domineering Munster man in the side the Lions were blown away like a feather in the wind of a country known as the Land of the Long White Cloud.

With Munster he lifted the Celtic Cup in season 2004-05 and in 2006, he won a second Triple Crown winners' medal and added a second Heineken Cup winners' medal to his ever bulging medal box.

On 24 February 2007, Hayes was seen by millions of viewers on television crying as he sang the Irish national anthem at Croke Park. England were the visitors to the Irish capital for a Six Nations Championship match being played at the home of the Gaelic Athletic Association. It was Ireland's temporary home until the Aviva Stadium was ready. The atmosphere was very tense, there was something in the air which you could not quite put your finger on. The fact that the match was being played at a ground were an atrocity occurred 87 years earlier was not lost on some of the reporters at the game, or indeed some of the 81,611 fans who turned up to watch two bitter rivals do battle before them. On 21 November 1920, British forces (Auxiliaries, British soldiers and members of the Royal Irish Constabulary, nicknamed "*The Black and Tans*") entered Croke Park on foot and in trucks and armoured vehicles to conduct one of their regular cordon and search operations during the Irish War of Independence, 1919-21. A small crowd of around 5,000 were at Croke Park to see their home side, the Dublin GAA Football Team play Tipperary's GAA Senior Football Team in an All-Ireland Championship match. The monies raised from ticket sales would go to the Republican Prisoners' Dependents' Fund. The game kicked off at 3.15pm, 30 minutes late, and ten minutes into the game the trucks and armoured cars entered the stadium via the southwest gates at the Royal Canal end of Croke Park. As soon as they got through the gates they opened fire on the spectators and players, killing or fatally wounding 14 civilians and wounding at least sixty others. Two of the slain were children. Several Black and Tans claimed they were fired on first and the British authorities believed them. However, every one of the other witnesses said the shooting was unprovoked, and a military inquiry concluded it was indiscriminate and excessive. The massacre further turned Irish public opinion against the British authorities and the massacre became known as "*Bloody Sunday*."

Perhaps John Hayes was aware of Bloody Sunday when he sat in the changing rooms at Croke Park pulling on his green Ireland jersey for the 70th time. The walk from the changing rooms to the tunnel, and then entering what was an amphitheatre for Ireland in comparison to their former home at Lansdowne Road, welcomed by the home partisan audience with a cacophony of cheers that would have been heard in every single one of Dublin's 1,090 townlands from Abbeyville to Yellowmeadows, and beyond the city's boundaries. He had just stepped out on to a pitch where 14 people had lost their lives, not in battle, but playing in or watching a Gaelic Football match. An Ireland versus England match is the highlight of an Ireland or England player's career because of the history of the rivalry, intensity, on occasion hatred, sometimes envy of the opposition but more often than not, the bragging rights to which side is the better team.

Phil Vickery, one of the rocks of England's Rugby World Cup winning side in 2003, playing in every game and scoring his first international try in the tournament, a British and Irish Lion and England's captain for their battle with Ireland, wasn't that far from Hayes when the two teams lined-out for the playing of the national anthems. The words to *"God Save The Queen,"* may not have resonated too well with Hayes, a Cappamore native, and as his eyes welled up with tears, his heart was raging like the Raging Bull inside him, to go head-to-head with his opposing No.3. Ironically, Vickery, a London Wasps player, was given the nickname of *"Raging Bull."* And when two Bulls lock horns, there is only one victor. *The Young Bull* is an oil painting of a Bull by Paulus Potter, a Dutch Artist. His painting challenges the hierarchy of Genres by its almost heroic treatment of an animal.

"You knew how important the game was when that freak was

Legends & Lions

going to be crying."

Brian O'Driscoll,
Ireland captain in the win over England

Vickery was born on 14 March 1976, but Hayes, the older and more experienced leader of his herd, O'Driscoll apart as the Ireland captain, sent the England captain to the abattoir when he made mincemeat of him in Ireland's 43-13 win.

After winning the Triple Crown for a third time in 2007, John attended his second Rugby World Cup with Ireland later that year when France played host to the tournament. Despite playing in all of Ireland's four Pool D games, it was a very disappointing Rugby World Cup for the team as they could only manage a third place finish in the table meaning elimination from the competition

Another European Rugby Champions Cup success came his way with Munster in season 2007-08. Going into the 2008-09 season, John was 35 years old, but the old Bull had not lost any of his strength, although his horns were a little longer. Many young bulls were snapping at his heels to force their way into his position at Munster and seeking to take his place in the Ireland squad. But Hayes had a wise head on his broad shoulders which is reminiscent of the story of the old bull and the young bull.

"The old bull and the young bull were standing at the top of the hill overlooking a paddock of many gorgeous young heifers. The young bull said, "Let's charge down the hill, knock over that fence and service one of those heifers each." The old bull wisely replied, "Why don't we saunter down the hill, open the gate, take a sip at the water trough and then service ALL of those heifers?""

JOHN WHITE

The pretenders to John's throne were becoming increasingly disheartened at not being able to usurp him from his position as Munster's and Ireland's top Prop. To use some lines from the Linkin Park song, *Numb*, they simply could not walk in his shoes.

> *"I'm tired of being what you want me to be*
> *Feeling so faithless, lost under the surface*
> *Don't know what you're expecting of me*
> *Put under the pressure of walking in your shoes*
> *Every step that I take is another mistake to you*
> *(Caught in the undertow, just caught in the undertow)*
> *I've become so numb*
> *I can't feel you there*
> *Become so tired*
> *So much more aware*
> *I'm becoming this*
> *All I want to do*
> *Is be more like me*
> *And be less like you"*

The year 2009 was the zenith of his rugby career, a time when he was at his maximum power and his most successful for both club and country. He won a second United Rugby Championship winners' medal in the red of Munster but he more than exceeded this in the green jersey. Ireland blitzed their way to the 2009 Six Nations Championship title, the Triple Crown and the Grand Slam. Hayes could now take his rightful place as a Legend of Irish rugby and stood on the shoulders of the giants who won Ireland's first Grand Slam in 1948. When Ireland beat Scotland 22-15 at Murrayfield Stadium on Matchday 4 of the 2009 Six Nations Championship,

Legends & Lions

John Hayes became Ireland's most capped player when he pulled on an Ireland jersey for the 94th time. On 18 June 2009, he was called up to the British and Irish Lions squad in South Africa as a replacement for the injured Euan Murray (Scotland). And so, on 4 July 2009, the bull became a Lion again winning his second cap when they defeated the Springboks 28-9 in the Third Test in Johannesburg.

"My power is discombobulating devastating. I could feel his muscle tissues collapse under my force. It's ludicrous these mortals even attempt to enter my realm."

Mike Tyson

Any mortals that were brave enough to enter John's realm on a rugby pitch felt the full force of his tackles. The next year, John became an Irish centurion winning his 100th cap for his country. On 27 February 2010, he captained Ireland to a 20-16 victory over England at Twickenham Stadium in the 2010 Six Nations Championship. When he led the team out on to the pitch the crowd took to their feet and applauded this Irish Legend. In Roman history terms he was more of a Gladiator than a Centurion.

Prior to the game versus England, Declan Kidney, the Ireland coach, was asked to pay his own tribute to Hayes who also played for him when Kidney was the Munster coach.

"I don't know. I am not sure what to say because he is like that. He is a very private man but he enjoys his rugby. He loves it. He can just turn out wearing a t-shirt and shorts when everyone else is wearing tracksuits and tops. He is just a man's man. John Hayes is in probably the toughest position going so to get to 99 caps in one position is a huge testimony to the way the guy looks after

JOHN WHITE

himself. It is not just about turning up for the game with him, it is the whole lifestyle. He would be a good example to young pros coming through as to what you can achieve if you look after yourself but at the same time he does enjoy it. I know that."

Declan Kidney

In season 2010-11, he won a third United Rugby Championship with Munster. He became the fifth Munster player to win 200 caps in the Magners League playing in a semi-final tie against Ospreys on 14 May 2011.

Hayes was selected in Ireland's training squad for the 2011 Rugby World Cup finals hosted by New Zealand and came off the bench for Tony Buckley in Ireland's first warm-up against Scotland. Ireland lost the encounter 10-6 in the Scottish capital. This turned out to be his last appearance for Ireland, 105 games, as he was not selected in the final 30-man squad for the tournament. And so, the curtain was brought down on his international career against the same opponents when he made his debut for Ireland eleven years previously.

On 12 November 2011, Hayes became the first player to achieve 100 caps in the Heineken Cup when he came on as a replacement for his Munster teammate, BJ Botha, in their 23-21 win over Northampton Saints at Thomond Park.

Hayes announced that he would retire after Munster's Pro12 match versus Connacht on 26 December 2011. John was substituted in the 58th minute of the match, walking off the pitch to a huge standing ovation from the crowd. Munster won the match 24–9. When he walked out of the tunnel at Thomond Park there was a banner draped across it which read: *"Go On Bull Tis Your*

Legends & Lions

Field." It was his 217th game for Munster in a 13-year career wearing red, following in the footsteps of Anthony Foley, Alan Quinlan, Peter Stringer and Ronan O'Gara in reaching 200 caps for the Province. Thomond Park was most definitely Hayes' field.

In an interview with the *Irish Independent* he was once asked how he acquired the nickname Bull and replied: *"I have no idea who came up with that nickname. Some people address me as John. Some use the full handle when they're greeting me: 'John Hayes'. The English and Welsh lads on a Lions tour would call me 'Hayesie'. But an awful lot of people call me 'Bull'. Friends, strangers, team-mates. 'Howya, Bull.'*

> *I never minded. I actually liked it, and it became second nature a long time ago now. I didn't have the nickname when I was at Bruff or Shannon. It only started when I moved onto the Munster scene. But I can't for the life of me remember how it started or who started it. It caught on fairly quick anyway, and took on a life of its own. I presume it's farming-related in some way or other. It might have had something to do with my build too. I suppose, realistically, no one was ever going to nickname me 'Greyhound' anyway."*

John Hayes

On 1 April 2000, Melanie C, a former member of the girl band The Spice Girls, went to No.1 in the UK Music Singles Charts with *Never Be The Same Again*. Following John's debut for Ireland six weeks before the song was released, the Prop position in the Munster and Ireland team would never be the same again. He more than added his own spice of life to the position.

"The whole of Ireland can see that he had no interest in attention, that all he ever wanted was to get on with the job. He's very

JOHN WHITE

humble and respectful and all the things most people think he is, but he's very funny too and he'd do anything for you. And I do mean anything. When I had my dislocated shoulder in Australia during the 2003 World Cup, I couldn't reach around to wash my own back. Hayes never blinked - he scrubbed my back for me for the rest of that tournament. Talk about above and beyond the call of duty."

Munster Legend, Alan Quinlan

In September 2012, he released his autobiography "*The Bull: My Story*," which details his sporting life. There are many funny stories in it but one in particular stands out. Hayes was on tour with the Lions in 2005 and Prince William, a keen rugby enthusiast, visited their training camp and was introduced to all of the members of the squad. John wrote:

"William is a big rugby fan and he came into our dressing room after one of the games and went round shaking our hands. I was sitting next to O'Connell. William told him he'd heard of Munster rugby and the legendary Thomond Park. So Paulie said to him he should come over for a game some time. William said he'd love to but it wouldn't be easy; a visit like that to Ireland would take a bit or organising. And quick as a flash O'Connell fires back, 'Some of your ancestors hadn't much problem coming over to Ireland.' He kind of half said it under his breath so I wasn't sure if Prince William had heard it or not. But I had and I nearly fell off my seat laughing."

Taken from "The Bull – My Story" by John Hayes

"I was gonna rip his heart out. I'm the best ever. I'm the most brutal and vicious, the most ruthless champion there has ever

LEGENDS & LIONS

been. No one can stop me. I'm Alexander! I'm the best ever. I'm Sonny Liston. I'm Jack Dempsey. There's never been anyone like me. I'm from their cloth. There is no one who can match me. My style is impetuous, my defense is impregnable, and I'm just ferocious. I want his heart!"

Mike Tyson

In 2015, John was immortalised in his home parish when a bench was erected outside his former school which is now a library. It is known as *"The Bull Bench."*

John Hayes was the perfect professional rugby player. On and off the field of play he epitomised humility and dedication. He was more concerned about the well-being of others than he was about the many plaudits he received. In 2019, John heard that a Limerick man, and a huge fan of Munster and Ireland, was dying of cancer. The big kind hearted Hayes sent the pensioner a signed Munster jersey and tracksuit bottoms. *"John Hayes heard I wasn't well last year and sent me over a signed Munster jersey and tracksuit bottoms. It meant the world to me that a legend like John Hayes did that for me,"* said the Limerick resident.

Anyone who crossed the path of John Hayes respected him, a true gentleman on and off the field.

The famous American boxer, Jake LaMotta, World Middleweight Champion from 1949-51, was nicknamed *"Raging Bull."* Having won three United Rugby Championships, two Heineken Cups and the Celtic League with Munster, 105 Ireland caps (2000-11), four Triple Crown successes (2004, 2006, 2007 & 2009), a Six Nations Championship victory and Grand Slam win in 2009, two British Lions tours (2005 & 2009), there is no question that John Hayes was World Rugby's Bull, and a player who has more than earned his legendary status in

JOHN WHITE

Irish rugby.

Did You Know That?

During his time with Marist, he worked in a tannery named Slinkskins Ltd which was owned by the former All Blacks and Southland RFU Club Legend, Edward John "*Jack*" Hazlett, who was also a Prop, to help pay for his stay in New Zealand. In 2001, John's younger brother, Michael, played for Marist and helped them to their first Galbraith Shield success in 22 years.

OLLIE CAMPBELL
Ireland's Grand Master

SEAMUS OLIVER CAMPBELL was born on 5 March 1954, in Dublin. He was educated at Belvedere College, a famous rugby school in the Irish capital which produced so many wonderful Ireland internationals including: Thomas Crean (de facto captain of the British and Irish Lions Tour of South Africa in 1896), George Morgan (who captained Ireland and went on the Lions tour to South Africa in 1938), Karl Mullen (captain of the British and Irish Lions Tour of Australia and New Zealand in 1950), Tony O'Reilly, whose 38 tries for the Lions on two tours (1955 and 1959) remains a record and Cian Healey (an Ireland Rugby Centurion). Even though they didn't know each other at the time his parents were both in Ravenhill on March 13th 1948 when Karl Mullen led Ireland to their first Grand Slam. It was his mother's 25th birthday that day and Ollie was subsequently raised on the exploits of that famous team, not least the immortal and incomparable Jack Kyle.

Campbell won the Leinster Schools Senior Cup with Belvedere in 1971 and helped them retain the title the following year thus following in the footsteps of his uncle's Seamus and Michael Henry who both captained the school to victory in 1938 and 1946 respectively. Ollie played for Old Belvedere at club level and represented Leinster at Provincial level, prior to the professional era, and toured the United States of America with the club in 1978, where he first met the aforementioned Tony O'Reilly at his home in Pittsburgh, at the end of tour party.

On 17 January 1976, the 21-year old 11 stone Campbell was given his international debut for Ireland by coach Roly Meates when Australia toured Great Britain, Ireland and the United States of America. Ireland lost 20-10 and it was the only team he was ever dropped from in his 21 year playing career and for whatever reason only known to Ireland's coach and the national side's Selection Committee at the Headquarters of the IRFU, the young Belvedere student's next outing in the green jersey of his country did not come about until Ireland played the Wallabies away in Brisbane on 3 June 1979.

In between these years. Anthony Joseph Paul (*Tony*) Ward made his debut against Scotland on 21 January 1978, in the 1978 Five Nations Championship, playing in all four games in the competition, and he also played in the 10-6 loss to New Zealand at Lansdowne Road on 4 November 1978, scoring all of Ireland's points (two penalties). Two weeks after Tony featured for Ireland against the All Blacks, a band which formed in 1975 not too far away from where Tony grew up in Dublin, went to No.1 in the UK Music Singles Charts with their mega hit, *Rat Trap*. It was the first song by a New Wave or Punk Act to top the Hit Parade. Little did Tony know it, but he would soon be caught up in a game of cat and mouse when it came down to the coach of Ireland selecting his No.10 for an international. *A Tale of Two Cities* is a historical novel published in 1859 by Charles Dickens, set in London and Paris before, during and after the French Revolution (5 November 1789 to 9 November 1799). The most famous jersey in Irish rugby, the No.10, was a revolution in Ireland that lasted for six years (1978-84) and became a tale of two fly-halves, Ollie Campbell and Tony Ward.

The 1979 Test Match versus Australia in Brisbane also witnessed the introduction of a future Ireland Legend, Ciaran Fitzgerald. Fergus Slattery captained the men in green to a 27-12 victory with Campbell winning the Man of the Match award after converting the two tries scored by the brilliant Colin Patterson, kicking four penalties and landing a successful drop goal. Ward was on the bench for the game but given Campbell's Master Class kicking tutorial, the pin-up boy of Irish Rugby at the time, just had to watch on in admiration. Ireland won both tests and Campbell set an Irish record by scoring 60 points on the tour, 19 of them in Brisbane which at the time was an Irish record for points in a test match. His selection for that first test was one of the most sensational in the history of Irish rugby, not least because Ward had won the coveted European player of the year in 1978 and 1979.

For many Irish Rugby journalists, Campbell was just walking in the shoes of Ward when Ward was unavailable to play, but as it turned out the shoe, or in this particular case, the boot was soon on the other foot.

"The shoes of leadership have many ways to pinch and blister the feet of those who walk in them. But here's the thing, when we do walk in them despite the difficulties and challenges, our gait gradually changes from an ungainly, self-conscious toddle to a poised, purposeful stride that inspires trust in those who follow."

Jodi Detrick

During the 1980 Five Nations Championship, Campbell was the first choice at fly-half for the Ireland coach,

JOHN WHITE

Tom Kiernan, and he played in all four of the matches during the tournament. A popular song being played on Irish radio stations at the time was *Oliver's Army* sung by Elvis Costello and the Attractions. On the terraces of Lansdowne Road, he was the No.1 attraction for his own Irish army of fans. Ireland won two and lost two matches to finish second in the table behind Grand Slam winners, England. Campbell played exceptionally well in all four games, scoring points in each one of them: all 9 of Ireland's points in their 24-9 loss to England at Twickenham Stadium, 14 when they beat Scotland 22-15 at Lansdowne Road, another 14 came in their 19-18 loss to France in Paris. In the final match he scored 9 points in a 21-7 victory over Wales in Dublin. He was on a roll and there was nothing Ward could do about it.

From 10 May 1980 to 12 June 1980, the British and Irish Lions went on Tour to South Africa with four Test Matches against the Springboks arranged. Ireland's Syd Millar was the Lions' manager and the coach was another former Ireland great, Noel Murphy. The pair had no hesitation whatsoever when naming their captain. For both of them there was only one player as their automatic choice, Bill Beaumont, who was the captain of Fylde Rugby Union Football Club, captain of Lancashire County Rugby Football Union and the man who captained England to their 1980 Grand Slam success. It was as the saying goes, a no-brainer and amazingly he was the first Englishman to captain the Lions for 50 years. However, the Lions' Irish management team were faced with a dilemma as they had to decide which two fly-halves they would select in their 30-man squad. Campbell was Ireland's top scorer in the 1980 Five Nations Championship with 46 points but there was also Gareth Davies the graceful Welsh fly-half. Davies had helped Wales to a Triple Crown win the previous year and he did enough for his country during the 1980 Five Nations Championship to warrant a place on the tour and of course there was also the brilliant Tony Ward too.

Interestingly, Davies injured his knee in the Second Test which ended his Tour early, and after representing the Principality 21 times, captaining his country in five of those games, aged just 29 he retired from international rugby in 1985, after the Welsh No.10 shirt was listed as *A.N. Other* for Wales' 1985 Five Nations Championship game versus England on 20 April 1985 at the Cardiff Arms Park. The No.10 shirt went to Jonathan Davies who made his international debut in the game, scoring a try and a drop goal in the home side's 24-15 victory.

But who would secure the fly-half spots when the plane took off for South Africa. Like Campbell, England's William Henry *"Dusty"* Hare scored in all four games during the 1980 Five Nations Championship and was a serious contender to get a boarding pass on the plane along with Davies given his kicking abilities. Nemesis are not born, they are made and Campbell was Ward's Nemesis and vice versa.

"Good becomes better by playing against better, but better doesn't become the best by playing against good."

Amit Kalantri, an Indian Author

Throughout the 1979-80 season, Ollie was one of Old Belvedere's most consistent players. In the same season, Ward was just Ward, doing what he did best for his club, Garryowen, racking up point after point on the scoreboard for them. Ward scored conversions, penalties and drop goals for his club as consistently as the legendary baseball player, Babe Ruth, smacked home runs at Yankee Stadium for the world famous New York Yankees. And, in 1978, perhaps the crowning moment of his Princely career, Tony inspired Munster to a historic and legendary 12-0 win against a touring New Zealand side at Thomond Park scoring two drop goals and a conversion on 31 October 1978. The game will not only forever be remembered for Munster's unexpected win, but also for the night when a boy born in Leinster (Tony was born in Dublin on 9 October 1954), knocked the mighty All Blacks right off their perch as the best team in the world. It was a David versus Goliath moment with Ward replacing the young David's stone in a sling shot with his venomous right boot. Some years later a very successful play called *Alone it Stands* by John Breen was produced to celebrate that unique and historic occasion in Limerick.

Ironically, sitting in the stand that day was Ollie Campbell, with a leg in a plaster cast and with crutches, due to a serious medial ligament knee injury.

In their wisdom when it finally came down to decision time, the Irish Lions management of Millar and Murphy selected Campbell and Davies as the tour fly halves. As luck would have it though both were injured before the first test, so Tony was flown out, and not only played in the First Test against The Springboks at Newlands in Cape Town but scored a record number of points for a Lion in a test match i.e. 18 (5 penalties and a drop goal). Gavin Hastings and Johnny Wilkinson have since matched this feat, but it has never been beaten. However South Africa won 26-22 with a heartbreaking try in the dying minutes. But the Garryowen player had made a huge statement

Legends & Lions

to his coach that he was the man for the job, or so he thought. Millar opted for Davies in the Second Test, much to the disbelief and disappointment of Ward who had just set that Test record for the Lions. The Second Test was played at Free State Stadium, Bloemfontein with the Springboks taking an early 2-0 lead in the four match Series. Davies scored a conversion and two penalties in the 26-19 loss before being replaced by Campbell during the contest. The fly-half selection carousel continued into the Third Test when Campbell was handed his first start in a Lions Test with Ward on the bench. The Springboks won 12-10 at Boet Erasmus Stadium, Port Elizabeth in horrendous conditions, the day Tony forgot his boots!! In his maiden start in the red of the British and Irish Lions, Campbell scored two penalties. The final Test was played on 12 July 1980, at Loftus Versfeld Stadium, Pretoria, the 18th and last game of what had been a gruelling Tour although the Lions did win all of their other 14 games played against Provincial sides one of the few Lions teams in history to do this. Campbell was given the nod to start and helped the Lions win 17-13, scoring five points. With John Robbie at scrumhalf they were the first Irish half backs to play in a test for the Lions since George Morgan and George Cromey in the final test in Cape Town in 1938.

The Lions arrived in South Africa as Big Game Hunters but never really showed their teeth and left the country with only the scalp of a single Springbok over the four Test Series. They were simply no match for the physicality their hosts brought into every game and every bone shattering tackle, characteristics of every South African team that has ever taken the field.

The player of the series was full back Gysie Pienaar

JOHN WHITE

father of future Springbok and Ulster scrum half Ruan.

Over the course of the next four years Campbell and Ward would go toe-to-toe in the fight for the coveted No.10 jersey of Ireland. They were rugby's equivalent of Sugar Ray Leonard and Roberto Duran, two World Welterweight Boxing Champions who fought each other twice in 1980 with one win each. Ward was more like Leonard, nicknamed Sugar, who every boxing fan seemed to like. Tony was the pin-up boy of Irish rugby with his long flowing black hair and boyish good looks. Irish Sport had not seen anything like him, and bear in mind that this was still the amateur era of the sport, since George Best played in the green jersey of Northern Ireland, and like Ward in a red jersey, only the Belfast Boy's was the red of Manchester United. Duran was as hard as nails, nicknamed *Hands of Stone*, an out and out brawler who was brought up fighting from a very young age when he played on the hard streets of Guarare, Panama. Campbell wasn't a fighter on the pitch, but he was battle ready every time he stepped on to it and had a right boot like a stone hammer as he smashed down defences with his long thunderous penalty kicks.

Campbell played in all four of Ireland's games in the 1981 Five Nations Championship, scoring 17 points. Moss Keane described it as Ireland's best ever whitewash, as Ireland had been ahead at half time in each game, and lost each game by just one score! Campbell played fly-half against France and at centre in the other games with Ward at fly-half-an experiment never tried before or subsequently. Ollie was named in Ireland coach Tom Kiernan's squad to Tour South Africa in May and June

Legends & Lions

1981, but Tony was not included due to his reservations about the apartheid system in South Africa at the time proving forever that he was not just a brilliant sportsman but a man of high principal and substance too. By this time Kiernan knew everything there was to know about his Dynamic Duo anyway, their skill set, their kicking ability, their passing qualities, their dedication to training, their temperament, their integrity, how they bonded with their teammates, their passion in the No.10 jersey, right down to their preferred choice of hair shampoo. No doubt Ollie was a down to earth Vosene man whereas Tony was more of a L'Oreal type of guy (because he was worth it). You can almost picture Tony playing out John Travolta's character, Tony Manero, in the 1977 movie *Saturday Night Fever*, sitting in front of the mirror making sure that there wasn't a single hair on his head out of place before he went out for the evening. In the movie Manero had to deal with social tensions and disillusionment in his working class ethnic neighbourhood in Brooklyn, New York. Ireland's Tony was dealing with his own stresses when it came to whether it would be him or Campbell wearing the Ireland No.10 jersey in their next international fixture. But one thing was certain in the minds of all Ireland fans and that was that both players were head and shoulders above their peers.

Ironically, on 18 November 1978, when the Boomtown Rats performed *Rat Trap* on *Top of the Pops*, as the new UK No.1 hit single, Bob Geldof and his fellow band members began their debut on the BBC TV show by tearing up pictures of John Travolta and Olivia Newton-John as they yawned to emphasise the fact that the pair, who had spent a total of 16 weeks out of the preceding 22 at the top of the charts with songs from the worldwide sensational hit of a movie, *Grease*, had finally been deposed. The Commodores occupied five of those weeks at No.1 with *Three Times A Lady* whilst 10cc enjoyed one week as the biggest selling artist with *Dreadlock Holiday*. On the movie scene, *Magic* was a big attraction for cinema goers in 1978. Ireland fans had their very own two Magic No.10's to go and see at Lansdowne Road. There was never any animosity between the pair, neither one ripped the other's photo up, although having said that photos and posters of Tony were awash in the sports papers and magazines whereas images of Ollie and his bright red hair were not particularly in abundance. The most important thing to Ollie and Tony was that they both wanted Ireland to win regardless of who was wearing the No.10 jersey in the team.

Campbell played at centre in the first of the two Test Series in Newlands, Cape Town in 1981, and despite a brilliant try under the posts by scrum half Robbie McGrath Ireland were beaten 25-13 by the Springboks. This was also the time Ireland played against the great Danie Gerber who scored a wonder try. Ollie did not feature in the second Test through injury when Ireland lost 12-10 at King's Park Stadium, Durban the day the South African fly half Naas Botha kicked three drop goals. Later that year, Ward played fly half when Australia visited Dublin on 21 November 1981. Ward scored all 12 of Ireland's points against the Wallabies, four penalties, but Australia won 16-12.

The year 1982 proved to be a turning point in the fortunes of both players. Campbell scored 46 points in the 1982 Five Nations Championship to help Ireland win the title and claim their first Triple Crown in 33 years, their fifth and the first ever in Lansdowne Road. Ireland were denied a Grand Slam after losing 22-9 to France in their last game but Campbell's play that year inspired the famous journalist Con Houlihan to write a piece on that Triple Crown win entitled: *Ollie Campbell was a conductor who could bring glorious music from a scratch band*.

Many of Ireland's female fans had posters of Simon Le Bon, the lead singer of Duran Duran, on their bedroom walls, some had photographs of Tony Ward. However, good looks were not enough in itself to swing a starting place in the Ireland team, like Duran Duran's 1982 hit song, Tony remained *Hungry Like The Wolf*.

"Success is neither magical nor mysterious. Success is the natural consequence of consistently applying basic fundamentals."

E. James Rohn,
American Author and Motivational Speaker

Twelve months later, in 1983, Ollie was Ireland's Mr Consistency racking up a staggering 56 points for Willie John McBride's Ireland team, finishing the 1983 Five Nations Championship's top points scorer for the second year in a row. He was like an artist drawing lines around his thoughts as placed the ball down to size up a kick at goal. Ireland finished joint winners with France in the tournament. Campbell then went on Ciaran Fitzgerald's team to New Zealand, his second Lions tour. Ollie played in all four Tests which resulted in a black wash, a 4-0 Test Series defeat which was a much closer fought series than that might suggest. However, like two of his great rugby heroes, Jack Kyle in 1950 and Barry John in 1971, Ollie was named as one of the 5 New Zealand players of the year. Tony featured for Ireland in that Five Nations season, as a replacement for Ollie in Ireland's

JOHN WHITE

25-15 victory over England at Lansdowne Road and received a long, memorable and resounding ovation from the crowd when he ran on to the field. You could have forgiven Tony if he had given McBride a copy of Duran Duran's 1983 single entitled *Is There Something I Should Know?*

For Ireland coaches and the fans alike, it seemed that when it came down to Ollie Campbell or Tony Ward as your starting No.10, you were either a Duran Duran fan or a fan of the band's biggest rivals during the New Romantic era in the early 1980's, Spandau Ballet. History showed that too many Kings ruined an army. Kings are like the sun, they rise and they set. Every man is a King so long as he has someone to look down on. But Campbell and Ward did not look down upon each other with disdain, they were sporting adversaries not enemies, they respected one another and Ireland's cause came first and foremost before their own egos or personal ambitions. Egyptology is the study of the language, history, and culture of ancient Egypt, a country ruled by famous Pharaohs. The word *Pharaoh* derives from the Egyptian compound "*great*" or "*high.*" The Pharaohs ruled Egypt for centuries. Campbell and Ward were Ireland's Pharaohs from 1976-87 and have remained great fiends since their playing days.

Ollie was McBride's No.10 in their opening game of the 1984 Five Nations Championship, scoring all of their points (4 penalties) in a 25-12 loss at Parc des Princes. Paul McCartney was at No.1 in the UK Music Singles Charts with *Pipes of Peace*. Hardly, a choice of song for Campbell or Ward whose fight for the jersey was beginning to play out like William Shakespeare's play, *The Two Noble Kinsmen*, both players accepting the decision of their national coach, good or bad. More a case of all is fair in love and war for the two hugely gifted fly-halves than the Bard of Avon's Jacobean tragicomedy, because being overlooked to represent your country was no laughing matter for Ollie or Tony.

"On a battlefield we hear the dying screams
no-one cares; no-one helps.
We all look after number one;
ourselves.
After all; all is fair in love and war.

Dirty tricks;
to get what we want
whether it be a person
or an objective.
All's fair in love and war.

On a battlefield you see the wounded lying there;
who gets up to help them?
Who's brave enough not to put themselves first?
More often than not no-one
After all; all's fair in love and war.

Lies, twisting words and cheating
are our main weapons
with them we cut down our opponents
and leave them broken and ruined.
All's fair in love and war.

On a battlefield weapons so terrible
that they should never see the light of day
are weilded
with deadly accuracy.

JOHN WHITE

After all; all's fair in love and war.

Sneaking around, making deals;
setting other people up for a fall.
To get what we want;
what we need.
After all; all's fair in love and war.

On a battlefield people are thrown away
like lambs to the slaughter.
The generals treat it as a chess game
as they play with peoples lives.
All's fair in love and war.

Cutting down
whomever gets in your way
to get that which you most want.
Showing no mercy.
After all; all's fair in love and war.

But when it happens to you;
when you're the soldier
lying in your own blood.
Dying and hurting.
Is it fair then?

When you're the person
who's been thrown aside
so someone else
can get what they want.
Is it fair then?

When you're left alone

Legends & Lions

crying and hungry or
bleeding and dying
victims of that phrase.
All's fair in love and war.

You ask yourself,
Is it?"

By DarkStatic

On 4 February 1984, Campbell played for Ireland on Matchday 2 of the Five Nations Championship, which was also his last ever game for Ireland. They lost the game 18-9 to Wales at Lansdowne Road and he bowed out of international rugby scoring all 9 points for his country. It was his 22nd appearance for Ireland, scoring 217 points, to add to the 7 Lions' caps he collected during his career, scoring 26 points. Three years of personal battles with niggling hamstring injuries prematurely ended his career when he was just 29 years old and with his best years undoubtedly ahead of him while Tony went on to play for Ireland in the first ever Rugby World Cup in Australia and New Zealand in 1987 and subsequently became a long standing highly respected rugby correspondent with the *Irish Independent*, a rugby commentator with RTE, and an influential and inspiring teacher and coach in St Andrews school in Dublin and St Gerard's school in Wicklow.

The most famous painters in history are known as a Grand Master. The Italian Grand Master Michelangelo painted the ceiling of the Sistine Chapel, Vatican City.

"A man can be an artist... in anything, food, whatever. It depends on how good he is at it. Creasey's art is death. He's about to paint his masterpiece."

JOHN WHITE

From the 2004 movie, Man on Fire

Ollie was a Grand Master whose conversions, drop goals and penalties were a work of art. Alas, for Ollie injury prevented this Master of the Kicking Game from saying more with his right boot and adding to the points he had already painted on his canvas, the Lansdowne Road pitch.

Did You Know That?

Ollie and Tony have both been inducted into the Rugby Writers of Ireland Hall of Fame.

Tony is a Freeman of the City of Limerick and Old Belvedere's ground on Anglesea Road in Dublin was renamed Ollie Campbell Park in Ollie's honour in 2019.

Tony was also a gifted soccer player, played for Shamrock Rovers and Limerick United (with whom he won an FAI cup medal in 1982) and Ollie has been on the IRFU Charitable Trust for over 30 years.

Tony and Ollie are firm friends to this day and are both United fans too -Tony of Leeds and Ollie of Manchester!

RICHARD MILLIKEN
Bangor's Mr Invincible

On 10 February 1973, Bangor Rugby Football Club's RICHARD "DICK" ALEXANDER MILLIKEN made his debut for Ireland and it was a game to remember for Dick and the Ireland fans. The 1972 Five Nations Championship was aborted after two Rounds of games when Scotland and Wales refused to play in Dublin due to the anti-British feeling in Dublin and the ongoing troubles in Northern Ireland. However, to their credit, England honoured their commitment to play Ireland at Lansdowne Road in the 1973 Five Nations Championship. The England players walked out of the tunnel first and the usual boos and whistles of derision they were always welcomed to the ground with, were replaced with cheers and applauding as the home fans gave the visitors a standing ovation. It was a cacophony of noise that no other England side had ever heard before when playing Ireland in Dublin.

Milliken took to the pitch wearing the green No.13 shirt at right centre and stood beside his fellow Northern Ireland man, Mike Gibson No.12 at left centre, when the two national anthems were being played. Dick must have felt a little nervous as he looked down the Irish line-up which also included captain Tom Kiernan, Tom Grace, Ken Kennedy, Arthur McMaster, Barry McGann, Ray McLoughlin, John Maloney, Fergus Slattery and the colossus who was Willie John McBride. But, Milliken took to international rugby union in a seamless fashion and just did what he did at club level, always ready to receive the ball to attack his opponents. And he attacked the England back line all match long and was rewarded for his endeavours by scoring a debut try in Ireland's 18-9 victory. Sweet were one of the most popular bands at the time and were No.1 in the Music Charts with *Blockbuster*. It was a Blockbuster debut to remember for the 22-year old who was born in Bangor, County Down, Northern Ireland on 2 September 1950, and whose rugby talent first came to prominence when he captained Bangor Grammar School in 1969 and led the team to the school's first, and arguably most famous victory, in the Schools Cup over the 18 times Champions, Campbell College at Ravenhill. He was 18-years old at the time of Bangor's 6-3 victory and one of nine players who had won the Medallion Shield three years earlier. McGann also scored a try in the win over England and converted both, kicked a penalty over the bar and landed a delightful drop goal. James Buckley was also given his international bow in the game by the Ireland coach, Syd Millar.

The Ireland coach purred with delight watching Dick run the England defence ragged, regularly fed with pinpoint passes by his sidekick, the exquisite Gibson. Dick quite rightly retained his place in the Starting XV for Ireland's remaining three fixtures in the Championship, a 19-14 away loss to Scotland, a 16-12 defeat by Wales in Cardiff and a 6-4 victory over France in Dublin. Millar remained in charge of the team for the 1974 Five Nations Championship with McBride taking over the captain's role from Kiernan who bid farewell to international rugby in 1973. Along with his captain's name, and that of Gibson, the name Milliken was an automatic selection for the Ireland team sheet.

He played in all four games of the 1974 Five Nations Championship which saw Ireland win two games (England 26-21 away and Scotland 9-6 at home), draw 9-9 with Wales in Dublin and lose 9-6 to France in Paris. The French capital is known as "The City of Lights," and although Ireland tasted defeat, Milliken was starting to light-up Ireland's play. Ireland were crowned Five Nations Champions in 1974. Milliken, a Geography student from Queen's University Belfast was quickly gaining a reputation for himself as a confident ball carrier who was hard tackling, all in all, the ideal foil for the silky hands and feet of Gibson.

From May to July 1974, the British and Irish Lions toured South Africa. Alun Thomas (Wales) was their manager and Millar was their coach. Four centres were selected: Roy Bergiers (Llanelli & Wales), Geoff Evans (Coventry & England), Ian McGeechan (Headingley and Scotland) and Bangor's favourite son, Dick Milliken. Mike Gibson ruled himself out of selection due to business commitments but subsequently joined the squad as a replacement. This was the famous Lions' Tour which is remembered for three things; the brutal violence dished out by both sets of players in the four Test Matches: captain Willie John McBride's infamous "99" call: The Lions' 3-0 Test Series victory which should have been 4-0 had the referee, a South African, had the courage to award the Lions a try in the final minutes of the fourth Test that ended in a 13-13 draw and the Lions going unbeaten, winning 21 of their 22 matches, to earn the title of "Invincibles." Milliken played alongside the coach of the 2009 British and Irish Lions, Ian McGeechan, in all four Tests against the Springboks, scoring a superb try in the Second Test and setting up two tries for the incomparable JJ Williams (Llanelli & Wales). Dick's late score at Loftus Versfeld Stadium, Pretoria gave the Lions a 28-9 win, their biggest Test victory to date.

It is important to remember that when he was called-up to the Lions' squad Dick had only played eight times for Ireland, whereas players such as Phil Bennett, Gareth Edwards, Andy Irvine and Willie John McBride were all established internationals for their countries, household names across Europe. He may not have grabbed the back page headlines in his four Tests and nine other games on the Tour, scoring four more tries, but what he brought to the team should never be forgotten, one of the unsung heroes of the Invincible Lions Tour of South Africa in 1974.

"The Springboks were physical and frightening. But they believed we were invincible."

Dick Milliken

In late 1974, Dick played for Ireland against a Presidents XV and against the mighty All Blacks. Ireland drew 18-18 with the Presidents XV and lost 15-6 to New Zealand with both games taking place at Lansdowne Road. The following year he played in all of Ireland's 1975 Five Nations Championship games, making his 14th and what ultimately proved to be his final appearance for his country, in a 32-4 loss to Wales at the Arms Park on 15 March 1975.

With the rugby world at his feet, Dick suffered a broken ankle which interrupted his international and Lions' progress and by the time he recovered and returned to action in late 1976, he was unable to regain his international place. Ballymena Rugby Football Club's John Alexander McIlrath was Gibson's new partner. The injury was far worse than originally diagnosed and brought a premature end to his senior career, aged just 24, although he never stopped playing the game he loved, regularly turning out for Bangor RFC's Seconds. It seemed quite fitting that when he walked off the pitch in Cardiff he did so for one last time with Gibson, Grace, Kennedy, McLoughlin, McMaster, Maloney, Slattery and his captain, McBride.

And quite spookily, the game in the Principality marked the end of the international careers of three Irish Princes, namely Ken Kennedy, Ray McLoughlin and the iconic Willie John McBride.

The actor who played *Kojak* in the US police series of the same name, Theodore "*Telly*" Savalas, was No.1 in the Music Charts with the song *If* when Ireland lost in Cardiff. There is no question that if the curtain not been forcibly brought down on his career, Richard Milliken could possibly have gone on to give Mike Gibson a run for his money as the greatest ever player to play for Ireland who was born in Northern Ireland.

John Berger's classic text on art entitled *Ways of Seeing*, was one of the most popular books being read when Dick pulled on an Irish jersey for the first time. In the 18 international games he played (12 in the Five Nations, 2 friendlies and 4 Lions' Tests), all from the start, the boy from Bangor had telepathic vision, seeing a way through opposing defences with sublime balance and attacking flair.

Dick Milliken will forever be remembered as *Bangor's Mr Invincible*.

JOHN WHITE
Did You Know That?

Dick Milliken was the first Bangor RFC player to be capped at full international level by Ireland.

WILLIE JOHN McBRIDE
The Greatest Ever Lion

"This patch of grass. This blood stained ground. This cauldron of noise. This maker of Kings. This sanctuary. A fortress built to enthral. Forged to stand against adversaries. Apprentices, testers, against true competitors and those who merely come to compete. This Lion's den. This Lansdowne Road. A world on its own. This journey of ours. Dark nights. Endless dawns. Blood, sweat and tears. Serving as refuge, home and shelter. This arena. This theatre. This battleground. This conquest. Hand me my robe. Put on my crown. I have eternal longings to be King."

WILLIAM JAMES MCBRIDE was born in Toomebridge, County Antrim, Northern Ireland on 6 June 1940. Aged just 4 he lost his father and spent most of his childhood helping out on the family farm. There was no rugby history in the McBride family until he attended Ballymena Academy, County Antrim. Aged 17, a house match at his school would change that and his life forever. *"They came to me and said, you're a big guy. If you play we'll have 15. I hadn't a clue about this game, but I was big and it wasn't a problem to me, I could shake people off. Next week I was picked for the school 3rd XV, and the following week the 2nd XV then the following week the school's first XV,"* recalled Willie about the time the rugby coaches at Ballymena Academy asked him to play for their team.

On 10 February 1962, the 6 feet, 4 inches weighing 16 stones, 1 pound 21-year old McBride won his first cap for Ireland. But, it was a debut to forget as Ireland lost 16-0 to England at Twickenham Stadium in the Five Nations Championship, losing three and drawing one (3-3 with Wales in Dublin) of their four games to end up with the dreaded Wooden Spoon. Later that same year he was selected by the British and Irish Lions for their Tour of South Africa. On 10 April 1965, Willie was a member of the Irish side that defeated the Springboks for the first time in their history, winning 9-6 at Lansdowne Road. Two years later, 13 May 1967, WJ helped Ireland record their first ever win in Australia when they beat the Wallabies 11-5 at Sydney Cricket Ground. It was the first time a Home Nations side had beaten a major southern hemisphere team in their own country. In 1966 (New Zealand) and 1968 (South Africa) he toured with the Lions again.

In the much feted, glorious and illustrious history of Ireland's and the British & Irish Lions' rugby union odyssey, one man, Willie John McBride, stands majestically high above all others, a *King of Kings*. He was a Leader of Men, a rugby Demigod, his teammates happy to be subservient to his every call to arms. Willie is the undisputed Lion King and he donned his red King's Robe 17 times, a record number of Test caps won by a British and Irish Lion. He was the man who conquered rugby union's Mount Everest when he helped the Lions to a first ever Test Series win over New Zealand in 1971. Despite being considered by some rugby commentators to be "*Over The Hill*" in 1971 aged 31, Willie was made *Leader of the Pack* on that historic 1971 Tour to the southern hemisphere. One of the lines from the song *Leader of the Pack*, written by **George "*Shadow*" Morton, Jeff Barry, and Ellie Greenwich,** was a No.1 pop hit in the USA Billboard Charts in 1964 for the American girl group The Shangri-Las, is *"I'll never forget him, the leader of the pack."*

When the Lions toured South Africa in 1974, their manager, Syd Millar, who was also the head coach of Ireland (1973-75) knew only too well who he wanted as his captain. And he did not have to look too far from the Emerald Isle, appointing Big WJ captain of his Lions, which included a few uncapped cubs in the squad. The Lions' 1974 Tour of South Africa was marred by some of the most brutal and violent international matches ever played. But the Ulsterman led his men from the front and attacked the Springboks like an Irish wolfhound, ordering his troops never to take a step backwards. He instigated a policy of *"One In, All In"* meaning that when one Lion retaliated against an opponent his 14 teammates were required to join in the melee or pick a fight with the closest Springbok to him. The plan was known as the *"99"* (as opposed to the *999* a person telephoned in the UK for an emergency) and it worked to great effect as the referee was left bewildered as to which player had actually started the violence that had unfolded on the pitch. The lack of cameras at games at the time meant that the referee was left powerless in terms of handing out punishment to any single instigator and no Lion was sent off during the Tour. The *99* was used a few times on the tour and most memorably in the Third Test at Port Elizabeth when the legendary Wales full-back, JPR Williams, ran half the length of the pitch to knock out Springbok second-row, Johnnes van Heerden.

Willie John led the Lions to a historic, and first Test Series win over South Africa, winning 21 of the 22 matches they played including a clean sweep of *The*

JOHN WHITE

Springboks with a 3-0 Test Series victory. The Lions were held to a draw in the fourth Test, 13-13 at Ellis Park, Stadium, Johannesburg in controversial circumstances. In the dying minutes of the game, Irish flanker Fergus Slattery broke through the South African line and appeared to successfully ground the ball, only for the referee to adjudge it held up. The referee was South African (Max Baise). With the Lions just two metres from the Springboks' line in the 76th minute of the game, Baise, a School Master, blew for the final whistle. It denied the Tourists a whitewash in South Africa, at a time when apartheid was a cancer in the country, but it granted the 1974 British and Irish Lions the legendary moniker of *"The Invincibles."* When he was asked about the decision afterward, Baise is said to have replied: *"Look boys, I have to live here."*

The 1974 British and Irish Lions squad, *"The Invincibles,"* are regarded as the greatest rugby touring side in history and Big Willie John was the leader of their pack. He went to South Africa as a Warrior and left the country a Gladiator.

On 1 March 1975, he pulled on the Irish jersey for the 62nd and penultimate time and led his men across the white chalk line at Willie's spiritual home, Lansdowne Road as their captain for the 10th time. Ireland's opponents were France in a Five Nations Championship game. That day he could do no wrong and the big 34-year old Lock not only led his side to a comfortable 25-6 victory but he even managed to score a try himself, his only score for his beloved Ireland. At the final whistle every man, woman and child in the 50,000 audience stood up and applauded as Big Willie John walked off the hallowed Dublin turf, McBride's *Tara*, like Conn Cétchathach, also known as

Legends & Lions

Conn of the Hundred Battles, a semi-legendary High King of Ireland (*Ard-Ri na hEireann*), leaving a battlefield, majestic in victory. Two weeks later, 15 March 1975, he played for and captained Ireland for the last time in an illustrious career, a 32-4 loss to Wales in Cardiff in the 1975 Five Nations Championship.

After retiring from playing the game, he coached the Irish team from 1983-84 and managed the British and Irish Lions on their 1983 Tour of New Zealand. In 1997 he was an inaugural inductee into the International Rugby Board Hall of Fame; in 2004 he was named by *Rugby World* magazine as "*Rugby Personality of the Century*," and he was awarded an MBE in 1971 and a CBE in 2019.

Did You Know That?

Willie John McBride is a leading supporter of the *Wooden Spoon Society*, a Charity which does so much wonderful work for children and young people with disabilities.

KEITH WOOD
It's My Life

KEITH GERARD MALLINSON WOOD was born on 27 January 1972, in Killaloe, County Clare and attended St Munchin's College, Limerick. The motto on the school crest

Is *"Veritas in Caritate"* adapted from Bishop Anthony Wood's own episcopal motto. The text is taken from St Paul's Letter to the Ephesians: *"If we live by the truth and in love, we shall grow in all ways into Christ."* (Eph 4:15)

Killaloe is famous in Irish history. The town, which lies on the River Shannon on the western bank of Lough Derg derived its origin to a sixth-century monastic settlement founded by Saint Molua, also known as Saint Lua, on an island in the Shannon situated less than a mile below Killaloe Bridge although it later moved on to the mainland. In the tenth century it was base for Brian Boru (Brian Bóramha; c. 941 – 23 April 1014), a High King of Ireland (1002-1014), who had his Palace, Kincora (Ceann Coradh), on the high ground where the current Catholic Church stands. Brian Boru brought an end to the Viking Invasions of Ireland. During his reign, Killaloe was the capital of Ireland. In the history of Irish rugby, Keith Wood was not only the captain of his country, he was like a High King. Ironically, these two Irish Legends share a similarity in that they each have five letters in their Christian name and four in their surname.

The young Wood was destined to be a rugby

player. His father, Gordon, played 29 times for Ireland as a Prop between 13 February 1954 and 13 May 1961. Gordon Wood made his Ireland debut in a 14-3 defeat against England at Twickenham Stadium in the 1954 Five Nations Championship. On 27 February 1960, he scored his first and only try for Ireland in a 6-5 loss to Scotland at Lansdowne Road in the 1960 Five Nations Championship. Wood senior made his last full appearance for Ireland on 13 May 1961 in a 24-8 defeat against South Africa at Newlands Stadium, Cape Town. In 1959, Gordon Wood played in 15 of the British and Irish Lions matches when they toured Australia and New Zealand, including two Test Matches against the All Blacks. He scored two tries on the tour, one against New Zealand Universities on 1 July 1959 and another versus Marlborough and Nelson Bays on 29 July 1959.

Aged 16, Keith was a member of the Clare Gaelic Athletic Association hurling side that participated in the inaugural Nenagh Co-Op hurling tournament in 1988. But thankfully for Irish rugby, Keith chose rugby over hurling and took the first step of his rugby career as a hooker with Garryowen who he helped to All Ireland Championship title victories in 1992 and 1994.

When Keith won his second All Ireland Championship winners' medal, Tony Di Bart had his only No.1 success in the UK Music Singles Charts with The Real Thing. Garryowen's 22-year old hooker was The Real Thing.

Between May-June 1994, Ireland embarked on a Tour of Australia which would see them play eight games including two Tests against the Wallabies. It was their second tour of Australia, having previously gone down under in 1979. In 1979, the first Test saw the debut of

Ciaran Fitzgerald whilst it also saw Mike Gibson play his last ever game in the green of Ireland. In 1994, Wood made his debut for Ireland in the first Test alongside fellow debutants, Jonathan Bell, David Corkery and Niall Woods. Ireland won the 1979 Test Series 2-0 and lost the 1994 return by the same score. On their 1994 Tour, Ireland lost the first Test 33-13 at Ballymore Stadium, Brisbane on 5 June 1994, and six days later Keith played in a 32-18 defeat to the Wallabies at Sydney Football Stadium, Sydney.

In 1994, The Lion King was the biggest grossing movie of the year, the same year Keith was an Ireland cub, but he would go on to become a British and Irish Lions' Legend.

In his third outing for Ireland, his first ever game wearing an Ireland jersey at Lansdowne Road, Keith tasted victory when Ireland beat the United States of America 26-15 on 5 November 1994. In 1995, Keith joined Harlequin Football Club (known as Harlequins) after the sport became professional post the 1995 Rugby World Cup hosted by South Africa. A shoulder injury forced him to miss Ireland's 1996 Five Nations Championship campaign and he could only manage to play two games in January 1997, a friendly versus Italy and a Five Nations Championship game against France, both played in Dublin. After having played just 9 games for his country, which included four in the Five Nations Championship, three versus Australia, one versus the USA and one against Japan in the 1995 Rugby World Cup, he was chosen to tour with the 1997 British and Irish Lions side who would take on South Africa in three Test matches. The squad contained three other Irish players: Jeremy Davidson, Eric Miller and Paul Wallace who replaced Peter Clohessy who got injured prior to the players flying over to South Africa.

The Springboks were the reigning Rugby World Cup holders having defeated New Zealand 15-12 after extra-time on home soil in front of the country's new President, Nelson Mandela.

"It always seems impossible until it's done."

Nelson Mandela

When the Lions' touring party arrived in the country they were considered to be huge underdogs by the home sports journalists and an editorial in the South African sports magazine *SA Sports Illustrated* said: *"The British Lions arrived in South Africa rated – by their own media, South African media and supporters – as nothing more than rank underdogs. A nice bunch of blokes who were making a bit of history and, in so doing, winning friends rather than matches."*

If Keith Wood was one thing, he most certainly could never be classed as an underdog. In the 1976 FA Cup final Manchester United were the red hot favourites to beat Southampton at Wembley Stadium, London but the south coast's Jack Russell snarled the Lancashire Alsatian.

In the words of Alicia Keyes' song *Underdog*.
"They said I would never make it
But I was built to break the mold
The only dream that I've been chasing is my own
So I sing a song for the hustlers trading at the bus stop
Single mothers waiting on a check to come
Young teachers, student doctors
Sons on the frontline knowing they don't get to run
This goes out to the underdog
Keep on keeping at what you love

JOHN WHITE
You'll find that someday soon enough
You will rise up, rise up, yeah"

Keith not only broke the mould, he absolutely smashed it into thousands of tiny particles, and played in the first two Tests, a 25-16 win in Cape Town on 21 June 1997 and an 18-5 victory in Durban a week later. And that was it, the underdog had caused an upset and won the Test Series. They were beaten 35-16 at Ellis Park, Johannesburg on 5 July 1997, but Wood returned home as a winning Lion on the back of a 2-1 Test Series success. When the Lions' players ran out on to the pitch for each Test they had to pass under a huge red banner advertising Lion Lager, the sponsors of the Series. The irony of it spoke volumes.

"A leader is like a shepherd. He stays behind the flock, letting the most nimble go out ahead, whereupon the others follow, not realising that all along they are being directed from behind."

From *Long Walk to Freedom*,
The Autobiography of Nelson Mandela

Keith Wood was a born leader and he left The Stoop, Harlequins' home ground, in season 1999-2000 to return to Munster. Munster lost the 2000 Heineken Cup final 9-8 to Northampton Saints at Twickenham Stadium. It wasn't quite the Mark Knoffler *Going Home* return he had hoped for and at the end of the campaign he packed his kit bag and left Munster to re-join Harlequins.

At the 1999 Rugby World Cup in Wales, he scored four tries in Ireland's opening Pool E game versus USA, a 58-13 victory. In doing so, he followed in the footsteps of fellow Irishman Brian Robinson who scored four tries for Ireland in a 55-11 victory over Zimbabwe at Lansdowne

Legends & Lions

Road in the 1991 Rugby World Cup co-hosted by England, Ireland, Scotland and Wales. It was only the second time a forward had netted four tries at a Rugby World Cup finals tournament. Ireland were beaten 28-24 by Argentina in the quarter-finals of the 1999 Rugby World Cup. In 2001, Keith, who was the captain of Ireland, went on his second Lions tour. Martin Johnson (England) was still the captain of the touring party which travelled to Australia. After winning the first of their matches against the Wallabies, 29-13 at the Gabba, Brisbane, a game in which Keith was named Man of the Match, the Lions lost the remaining two games of the Test Series, going down 35-14 in Melbourne and losing 29-23 in Sydney. This was the second time that Australia defeated the Lions in a Test Series (winners in 1930). Keith played in all three Test Matches.

In the year of his birth T-Rex were No.1 in the UK Singles Charts with *Metal Guru*. The title effectively means Metal Teacher, or leader.

But, it wasn't all doom and gloom for the Harlequins' hooker as Keith won the inaugural International Rugby Board World Player of the Year in 2001. He had been nominated for the prestigious award along with some of the sport's biggest names: Australia's George Gregan (scrum-half) and George Smith (flanker), England's Johnny Wilkinson (fly-half) and his Ireland teammate, Brian O'Driscoll (centre). Keith may not have been the most accurate player in a set piece, but time and time again his true strength was in his leadership and open play where he dominated the world XV's hooker position. He was quite simply on a different planet to his peers in the No.2 jersey. No other Irish player won the coveted award until Johnny Sexton scooped it in 2018.

JOHN WHITE

On 22 June 2002, Keith had the honour of winning his 50th cap for Ireland when the tourists played the All Blacks at Eden Park, Auckland. Wood captained his country in their 40-18 loss. Keith said: *'It's great to get this far with my country, but I really don't want to think about that. There'll be plenty of time in the future to look back."*

A year later Keith led Ireland into the 2003 Rugby World Cup hosted by Australia. He played in all five of Ireland's games in the tournament and on 9 November 2003, Keith captained and played for Ireland in his last ever international. France were his final opponents, a Rugby World Cup quarter-final match, and Les Bleus defeated Ireland 43-21 in Melbourne. After the game he confirmed his retirement and passed on the captaincy of Ireland to O'Driscoll.

"It's time to hang up the boots. My desire is still there – I would play for another 10 years if I had the chance. The head is willing and the heart is willing but the body has had enough. The injury to the shoulder is an injury that is waiting to happen and I'm lucky to get out before I make an absolute mess out of it. I knew I was going to retire whenever the end of Ireland's involvement was. It's been a privilege to play for so long."

Keith Wood

Keith Wood played 58 times (3 times from the bench) for Ireland and scored 75 points for his country. In 36 of his appearances for Ireland he captained the side and only Rory Best (38) and O'Driscoll (83) captained Ireland on more occasions. He was also capped 5 times by the British and Irish Lions.

When he was a baby the biggest movie of the year was *The Godfather* starring Marlon Brando in the lead role, Don Vito Corleone, the Godfather. On a rugby pitch, Keith

Legends & Lions

Wood was Ireland's Godfather. Keith was an outstanding, inspirational leader who possessed tremendous power and pace which placed him on the top rung of the ladder of hookers. His ability to run at defenders with the ball tucked under his right arm without losing possession of it was not unlike the legendary Chicago Bears running back, Walter "*Sweetness*" Peyton who helped the Bears to Super Bowl XX glory in 1985. When Keith set off on one of his rampaging runs the Ireland fans inside the stadium rose to their feet. His style was all action hero, he tackled anything that moved and had the knack of being able to rip the ball away from an opponent like a frog's sticky tongue sling shooting from its' mouth to catch an unsuspecting insect.

However, as well as being a weapon of mass destruction, he was also a weapon of mass defence, the first player in green to the ball in a breakdown and unlike other hookers of his generation he was an excellent kicker who on many occasions eased the pressure off his teammates by kicking the ball into touch well away from Ireland's danger zone. Those opponents who were brave enough to attempt a tackle on him literally bounced off him. It was as though he had been carved out of blackthorn wood at birth, a wood renowned for its durability and hardness. Maybe that is why his parents decided to name their son Keith which is a name of Gaelic origin meaning "*wood*" or "*from the battleground.*" How appropriate a name for a player who never left the battleground in an Ireland jersey without giving everything he had in the fight for victory. He was a colossus for Ireland, and a true Legend of Irish rugby.

In 2005, he was inducted into the International Rugby Hall of Fame and in 2014, he took his rightful place in the International Rugby Board Hall of Fame. Keith holds an Honorary Doctorate from the University of Limerick for services to sport. Apart from Philip Dannaher (28 caps for Ireland, 6 points, 1988-95) Wood is the only other player to have captained Garryowen and Ireland.

Keith's birth sign is Aquarius, which is Latin for "*Water Carrier.*" It is also Arabic for "*the lucky stars of the King.*" Keith came from the ancestral birthplace of a King and on many occasions he carried his Ireland teammates to victory.

During his career he had two nicknames, "*The Raging Potato*" as a result of his bald head and "*Uncle Fester*" from The Addams Family as a result of his likeness to that character.

The Bon Jovi song, *It's My Life*, could be used to sum up Keith's rugby journey.

> *"This ain't a song for the broken-hearted*
> *No silent prayer for the faith-departed*
> *I ain't gonna be just a face in the crowd*
> *You're gonna hear my voice*
> *When I shout it out loud*
>
> *It's my life*
> *It's now or never*
> *I ain't gonna live forever*
> *I just want to live while I'm alive*
> *(It's my life)*
> *My heart is like an open highway*
> *Like Frankie said,*
> *"I did it my way."*
> *I just wanna live while I'm alive*

Legends & Lions

It's my life"

Playing rugby for Ireland was Keith Wood's life and he lived it to the full.

Did You Know That?

When he retired Wood's total of 15 full international test tries was the record for a hooker, or indeed any player in the tight five. The previous record for international tries by hookers (or players at any position in the tight five) was 12, scored by New Zealand's Sean Fitzpatrick. Keith's tally has since been bettered with the record now held by Joseph Soosemea Taufete'e (USA).

CIAN HEALY
Ireland's Invictus

CIAN EOIN JAMES HEALY was born on 7 October 1987 in Clontarf, Dublin. He attended Belvedere College, Dublin.

Who's the Boss? was an American sitcom television series which aired on the American Television Channel, *ABC*, from 20 September 1984 to 25 April 1992. Cian's Mum and Dad probably never even seen a single episode of the hit show, they didn't need to, because their son would one day become the Boss of the defence of Ireland's Rugby Union team.

Cían, is a Gaelic name meaning *"Ancient."*

On 5 May 2007, Cian was most certainly not Ancient when he made his debut for Leinster aged 19, coming on for the last sixteen minutes of their 31-0 win over Border Reivers at the RDS Arena. Just a few weeks earlier Take That had reached No.1 in the UK Singles Charts for the tenth time, this time with a song called *Shine*. Healy more than went on to shine for Leinster.

He was named in the Ireland A team that lost 31-13 to England Saxons at Welford Road, Leicester on 1 February 2008. Ireland coach, Eddie O'Sullivan, called him into his squad for the 2008 Six Nations Championship but he never got a run out in any of Ireland's five games in the tournament. He was only one of two uncapped players named in the squad, the other being his Leinster teammate, Johnny Sexton.

"Have patience with all things - but first with yourself. Never

Legends & Lions

confuse your mistakes with your value as a human being. You are perfectly valuable, creative, worthwhile person simply because you exist. And no amount of triumphs or tribulations can ever change that."

Saint Francis de Sales

The young and inexperienced Healy knew he would have to be patient to win his first Ireland cap, he had the quality to become an established international player, but he just had to keep on putting in excellent performances for Leinster and Ireland A. Cian played for Ireland A in the 2009 Churchill Cup when they defeated England Saxons 49-22 in Denver, Colorado, United States of America.

It was in season 2008-09 when Healy established himself as Leinster's first choice Prop and on 23 May 2009, he won the Heineken Cup with Leinster when they beat Leicester Tigers 19-6 at Murrayfield Stadium. It was the first time the Province had reached the final whilst Leicester Tigers were playing in their fifth.

His patience in wearing the Ireland green jersey for the first time finally paid off when he was handed his first cap by coach Declan Kidney. Ireland had won the Grand Slam just eight months earlier. On 15 November 2009, the boy from Clontarf realised his dream when he ran out of the tunnel at Croke Park wearing the No.1 jersey. He was 22-years old at the time when he faced Australia. The Wallabies were on a tour of the Home Nations sides and eight days earlier had beaten England 18-9 at Twickenham Stadium. The gold train rolled into Dublin seeking to claim their first clean sweep over England, Ireland, Scotland and Wales since 1984 (Australia beat Ireland at Lansdowne Road). Cian played well in a 20-20 draw and was praised by Kidney after the game which also marked his Leinster teammate, Brian O'Driscoll's, 100th game for Ireland. Scotland derailed the Australian train winning 9-8 at Murrayfield Stadium although The Wallabies did beat Wales 33-12 in the Principality.

Earlier that year Tinchy went to No.1 in the Music Charts with the song *Number 1*. Some of the lines from the song include:

> *"You lift me off the ground*
> *I always want you around*
> *I ain't gonna let nothing get in the way*
> *I'll never let nothing get in the way"*

Healy was now Ireland's No.1 and thirteen days after the Wallabies Test, Cian retained his place in Kidney's Starting XV when South Africa, the reigning Tri-Nations Champions and Rugby World Cup holders (they beat England in the 2007 final), visited Dublin. Again, the Test was played at Croke Park as Lansdowne Road had been demolished to make way for the Aviva Stadium which was under construction at the time the game was played. Ireland defeated the Springboks 15-10 and remained unbeaten throughout 2009.

Cian made his Six Nations Championship debut versus Italy at Croke Park on 6 February 2010, a game Ireland won 29-11. He missed the Scotland game but played against England, France and Wales. Healy won his second piece of silver when Leinster won a highly dramatic 2011 Heineken Cup final 33-22 against Northampton Saints after trailing 22-6 at half-time. It was a mammoth performance by every player wearing the blue of Leinster at the Millennium Stadium on 21

Legends & Lions

May 2011. A year later he collected a third Heineken Cup winners' medal following Leinster's 42-14 victory over Ulster at Twickenham Stadium.

In Irish Ancestry the Healy's were actively involved in numerous historical events, including resistance against English rule and the struggle for Irish independence in the early 20th Century. Cian had played his part in Ireland's land wars and struggles with the old enemy during their many Rugby Wars against England.

During Ireland's 2013 Six Nations Championship 12-6 loss to England at the Aviva Stadium on 10 February 2013, Healy stamped on Dan Cole. It was his 37th Test Match for Ireland but the incident landed him with a three weeks ban, meaning he missed the games versus Scotland and France. Following the stamping a brawl broke out on the pitch between both sets of players. Healy's trod on Cole's ankle after an Ireland maul had collapsed was missed by referee Jerome Garces, but subsequently investigated by an Independent Disciplinary Committee. Things could have been much worse for Cian, as he could have been given a five weeks suspension. It was a Dr Jeykll and Mr Hyde moment for Cian. Tensions were high during the game and for some reason, the red mist descended on Cian and he lost his composure. However, his previous good behaviour resulted in the three weeks ban. The ban could not have come at a worse time for Ireland or for Cian himself with the British and Irish Lions set to tour Australia later in the year. The Lions head coach, Warren Gatland, had already made it clear that he would select his squad based on a player's performances in the Six Nations Championship.

On 17 May 2013, Cian was a member of the Leinster side that defeated Stade Francais (France) 34-13 at the RDS Arena to win the European Challenge Cup. He scored a try in the game.

Gatland named Cian in his 2013 Lions squad. But, after the Lions' opening game of their 2013 Tour of Australia, a 69-17 win against Western Force in Perth, Cian was accused of biting scrum-half Brett Sheehan on the arm during the encounter. The allegation resulted in Healy having to attend a judicial hearing in Brisbane, and judicial officer Nigel Hampton found insufficient evidence to support the allegation that Healy bit Sheehan. Cian badly hurt his ankle in the game meaning it was the end of his Tour. The Lions won the Test Series 2-1.

In 2014, Cian won the Six Nations Championship with Ireland and continued to be a key player for Leinster, winning a third Pro12 title in 2014, but struggled with a series of injuries, nearly retiring in the summer of 2015 after suffering a serious neck injury. After winning the 2015 Six Nations Championship with Ireland, his second winners' medal in the competition, he underwent surgery on a disc in his neck. He wanted to be fit for Ireland's 2015 Rugby World Cup campaign in England. However, the surgery did not go to plan and resulted in nerve damage that left him without the use of his right arm. His injury was like telling Phil Taylor, who won a record 16 World Professional Darts Championship titles, that his career at the Oche throwing the three arrows was on hold, or worse still, over.

"Don't you dare give up! You are a divine being. A unique expression of the eternal life force. A miracle child. Get up and fight."

Legends & Lions

Anthon St. Maarten

Cian was no quitter. He treated making a comeback as a new challenge to keep his brain focused and his heart ticking. Yes, it was going to be tough, but sometimes for an athlete that's the best part because the greater the obstacle, the more enjoyment in overcoming it. The climb up a mountain is always tough but the view from the top is worth it once you make the summit. No sportsperson has ever achieved anything of significance in their career without overcoming some adversity. Tough situations build character and make them a stronger person.

"Strength does not come from physical capacity. It comes from an indomitable will."

Mahatma Ghandi

And, Cian was as strong as anyone, both physically and mentally. Hardest times often lead to the greatest moments of your life. Cian wasn't one for wallowing in his misfortune, drawing the curtains in his living room and crawling into bed and lying in the foetus position. Strength and growth come only through continuous effort and struggle. He was a fighter, and had he not chosen a career in rugby there is no doubt that he could have been an exceptional boxer or Mixed Martials Arts star. He possessed all of the necessary attributes for either sport: Speed (perhaps not over the first 10 yards, but most definitely in thought during a game): Defence, he was like the *"Great Wall of China,"* and no one was going to breach it: Punching Force, thankfully for his opponents, Cian was not allowed to strike out: Self-Discipline, which he could normally contain: Footwork, he wasn't exactly Muhammad Ali, not capable of floating like a butterfly, but he certainly had a sting like a bee in his tackle; Intelligence, the Gaelic surname Ó hÉalaighthe, meaning *"descendant of Éaladhach,"* a given name likely derived from *ealadhach*, meaning *"Ingenious."*: Grit, in Psychology terms, Grit is a positive, non-cognitive trait based on a person's perseverance of effort combined with their passion for a particular long-term goal or end state. This perseverance of effort helps individuals overcome obstacles or challenges to accomplishment and drives them to achieve: Accuracy, when Cian met an opponent in a one on one tackle he did it with accuracy Phil Taylor would have been proud of if you handed him one dart and asked him to hit the Bullseye with it. But, what would his Cage nickname have been?

Wearing the green jersey of Ireland he was once referred to as Ireland's *"Incredible Hulk"* following a display against South Africa. On 11 November 2017, Ireland played South Africa at the Aviva Stadium. The Springboks were on Tour and faced Ireland first in a four match Test Series which included games against France, Italy and Wales. Cian was up against his opposite No.1, Tendai Mtawarira (117 caps), who won his first international cap in 2008, but nothing fazed Healy despite the fact that when Mtawarira played in South Africa's first Test Match against the British and Irish Lions when the Lions toured the country in 2009, he out scrummaged England's Phil Vickery. Phil made his maiden bow for England in 1998, but he was no match for his less experienced opponent, leading to Vickery being substituted after 45 minutes, and the Man of the Match award was won by Mtawarira after South Africa beat the Lions 26-21 at ABSA Stadium, Durban on 20 June 2009. But, Cian was no Vickery. Ireland ran out 38-3 winners as they recorded their biggest winning margin over South Africa. It was Ireland's highest points total against the Springboks and their fifth win in seven games against them in Dublin. Healy deservedly was named Man of the Match as he bulldozed every Springbok in his way including Mtawarira. In the animal kingdom an adult Springbok is preyed upon by large predators such as lions, cheetahs, leopards, hyenas, wild dogs and caracals. Healy wasn't wearing a red Lions jersey but he roared his way through the game. The Aviva Stadium was his hunting ground and he ripped the Springboks apart like a ravaging lion.

Clontarf, where Cian was born, means "*Meadow of the Bull*." On a rugby pitch, Cian played like a raging bull, charging into anything that stood in his way whether they were wearing red or not. On 31 October 2020, Cian was handed his 100th international cap for Ireland when they faced France in their final game of the 2020 Six Nations Championship campaign. It was a game of mixed emotions for Healy as Ireland lost 35-27 at Stade de France although Cian did score a try in the game.

The Healy family Coat of Arms features a black shield with a silver lion, symbolizing courage, nobility, and strength. Above the lion, there are three gold stars, representing divine quality bestowed from above. This emblem stands testament to the strength and nobility of the Healy lineage.

In his spare time Cian likes to make his own sets of knives. He more than once drove a dagger through the hearts of opposing forwards, stopping them in their tracks before they got anywhere near the Ireland try line.

In 2009, the British Indie Rock band, The Heavy, released a song entitled *How You Like Me Now?* from their

JOHN WHITE

album *The House That Dirt Built*.

"Now there was a time
When you loved me so
I could have been wrong
But now you needed to know
See, I've been a bad, bad, bad, bad man
How You Like Me Now?
So how you like me now?
How you like me now?"

Not too many of the Springboks would have been playing that particular song on their iPods as they sat in their dressing room counting the bruises on their battered bodies after being on the receiving end of a Cian Healy tackle. That night they were in the house that Cian built and they were not welcome guests.

Cian Healy was so much more than the scar his neck injury left on his body. For him, his body belonged to his country. Cian's blood is literally green, he is a Champion, he is a Warrior, he is a Fighter. His passion wearing the green jersey raced through his veins like the Bullet Train on its' way through Tokyo, Japan.

Cian was one of Ireland's star players during the 2018 Six Nations Championship helping them to the Grand Slam, their first since 2009 and only their third ever having won it for the first time in 1948. In 2018, he also won a fourth Pro12 Championship title with Leinster and his fourth Heineken Cup winners' medal to become a member of an elite group of players to have won the Heineken Cup on four occasions along with his Leinster teammates, Isa Nacewa, Johnny Sexton and Devin Toner. Three more Pro12 titles followed in 2019, 2020 and 2021, making it seven for Cian.

Legends & Lions

On 23 September 2022, Cian made his 250th appearance for Leinster as a second half replacement during the Province's 42-10 victory over Benetton at the RDS Arena and when he took to the pitch he was given a standing ovation.

In 2023, Cian won a second Grand Slam with Ireland. However, after making his 125th appearance (60 points) in a green jersey, a 17-13 win over Samoa at Stade Jean-Dauger, Bayonne, France on 26 August 2023, he was ruled out of Ireland's squad for the 2023 Rugby World Cup after suffering a leg injury in the win.

Invictus is a Latin word meaning "to conquer, overcome." It is also the name of a poem written by the British poet, William Ernest Henle, in 1875.

"Out of the night that covers me,
Black as the pit from pole to pole,
I thank whatever gods may be
For my unconquerable soul.
In the fell clutch of circumstance
I have not winced nor cried aloud.
Under the bludgeonings of chance
My head is bloody, but unbowed.
Beyond this place of wrath and tears
Looms but the Horror of the shade,
And yet the menace of the years
Finds and shall find me unafraid.
It matters not how strait the gate,
How charged with punishments the scroll,
I am the master of my fate,
I am the captain of my soul."

Cian Healy was the captain of his soul, he was Ireland's *Invictus*.

JOHN WHITE
Did You Know That?

Cian has painted portraits of fellow rugby players. He is also a DJ, calling himself DJ Church.

DONNCHA O'CALLAGHAN
The King Of Kings

DONNCHADH FINTAN O'CALLAGHAN was born in Cork on 24 March 1979. His rugby schooling began with Highfield Rugby Club, Model Farm Road, Cork. Aged 19, he won a Munster Schools Senior Cup winners' medal with Christian Brothers College Cork defeating Saint Munchin's College, Limerick in the final at Musgrave Park, Cork. The ground is named in honour of Jimmy Musgrave, a former President of the Irish Rugby Football Union from 1930-31. The following season he was a member of Ireland's victorious Under-19 Rugby World Championship winning side.

The movie *Alien* was hugely popular in the cinemas in 1979, and when Ireland faced France in the 1998 Rugby Under-19 World Championship final, the French players were playing on home turf but O'Callaghan must have looked like something from another planet when they confronted him on the pitch. Ireland won the game 18-0 with a certain Brian O'Driscoll on kicking duties for coach Declan Kidney's young band of brothers.

Munster Rugby had a star in the making and Irish Rugby had a Legend in Genesis.

On 4 September 1998, he made his debut for Munster versus Ulster in an Inter-Provincial Championship match. They went down 29-12 at Ravenhill with Killian Keane kicking over four penalties. But, Munster went on to win the 1999 Inter-Provincial

Championship title with Ulster finishing runners-up.

Donncha won the Celtic League with his Province when the men in red saw off the challenge of Neath (Wales), beating them 37-17 on 1 February 2003 at the Millennium Stadium. O'Callaghan did not score in the game, that wasn't part of his impressive armoury, but he was a commanding presence in the Ireland defence that possessed an opposing player, a try scoring machine, in the form of a 25-year old Shane Williams. The Welsh winger, ended his playing career, 1998-2015, with 87 Welsh caps, scoring 290 points, and was capped four times by the British and Irish Lions (2005-13) notching-up 10 points. But, on that day in the Principality, the Land of my Fathers, Donncha was the daddy, and baby Williams was pointless.

Donncha made his international debut for Ireland on 22 March 2003, coming on as a replacement against Wales at the Millennium Stadium in a pulsating 25-24 victory for Ireland in the 2003 Six Nations Championship. Prior to the 2003 Rugby World Cup hosted by Australia, he played in Ireland's warm-up games for the tournament and was on the winning side on each occasion. Ireland defeated Tonga and Samoa away and beat Wales and Italy on home soil. The 61-6 win over Italy on 30 August 2003, was particularly pleasing for the Munster lock as the game was played in his own backyard, Thomond Park.

Eddie O'Sullivan, the Ireland coach, included the 24-year old O'Callaghan in his squad for their trip down under. Just five years after winning the 1998 Under-19 Rugby World Championship final with Ireland, the Cork boy was about to announce himself on the world stage in Rugby Union's most prestigious competition, the Rugby World Cup. In Australia Donncha played in two of Ireland's Pool A matches, a 45-17 win against Romania and a 17-16 loss to the host nation who topped the Pool with Ireland also qualifying for the quarter-final stages having finished second in Pool A. O'Sullivan left Donncha out of the side that were beaten 43-21 by France in the quarter-finals.

O'Callaghan was a key member of O'Sullivan's first choice XV during the 2004 Six Nations Championship playing in four of their five matches. He missed the England game but helped Ireland win the Triple Crown for the first time in 19 years. The 19-13 win over England at Twickenham Stadium was a significant one for Ireland as England were the reigning Rugby World Cup holders and the match against Ireland was their first at home since lifting the Webb Ellis Cup four months earlier. Having tasted action against the Wallabies he looked forward to Ireland's two Test Matches versus the Springboks when Ireland toured South Africa in June 2004.

O'Sullivan was buoyant about Ireland's chances of a first win against the Springboks in 39 years, their only previous win against South Africa came in Dublin in 1965. In the first Test the Cork Constitution's lock was an unused replacement, Ireland lost 31-17 in Bloemfontein. He was a replacement again in the second Test in Cape Town but got a run out in the game which Ireland lost 26-17.

In the 2005 Six Nations Championship he played three times and helped his Province reach the 2004-05 Celtic Cup final with Lansdowne Road the venue for their encounter against Llanelli Scarlets. By now Munster were a ruthless machine of efficiency and this was not lost on Gareth Jenkins, a Legend of Welsh rugby, and now the Director of Rugby for the Scarlets. Speaking before the match he said *"Munster haven't played with that much ambition this year but they are a side who we have always had huge respect for. They haven't got the same kind of stars as Leinster but what they have got is fantastic efficiency. They play limited rugby particularly well. There's also a real honesty within their team. You will never play a Munster team that is not 150 per cent for the cause. They always arrive with total commitment and intensity. So we will need to be spot on in how we approach this game. We are aware that it will be Alan's last game in charge of Munster. Cup finals are often about goodbyes and farewells and his departure is sure to be something Munster will use as motivation. Hopefully it will be a great occasion. We will have supporters making their way over to Dublin by whatever means possible while Munster's fans always travel very well so hopefully there will be a reasonable crowd."*

Donncha started for Munster in the final against the Scarlets on 14 May 2005 in Dublin and they gave their coach, Alan Gaffney, the perfect ending to his time in charge at Thomond Park, winning the game 27–16. By now Donncha, along with his captain, Paul O'Connell, were the bedrock of the Munster defence. Three years earlier the movie *Who's Your Daddy?* was released but O'Callaghan wanted more and set his sights on becoming the Godfather of the Ireland defence.

Nine days after wearing the red of Munster (the Scarlets wore their second kit in the 2005 Celtic League final), Donncha was in red again but this time the three crowns and the stag on the crest of his jersey had been replaced by a shield divided into four with the rose of England top left, the thistle of Scotland top right, the shamrock of Ireland bottom left and the three feathers of Wales bottom right, with a gold lion above the four home nations' symbols. Donncha was about to win his first cap for the British and Irish Lions. In Irish folklore the stag was portrayed as an animal that always defended its own territory, quite apt for the Munster Rugby team. The Lions were managed by Bill Beaumont, a former England and Lions captain, and were coached by Sir Clive Woodward who masterminded England's 2003 Rugby World Cup final success. The side were captained by O'Callaghan's Ireland teammate and captain of Ireland, Brian O'Driscoll.

The Munster Rugby brand embodies the qualities of passion, ambition, excellence and integrity. Woodward recognised all of these when he watched Donncha play, the reason why he selected the Munster lock for his Lions' squad to tour New Zealand. And so on 23 May 2005, Donncha represented the British and Irish Lions for the first time in a warm-up game ahead of their trip to face the All Blacks in three Tests. His first outing in a Lions' shirt was against Argentina with the game ending in a 25-25 draw at the Millennium Stadium.

Donncha did not feature in the Lions' first Test against the All Blacks, a 21-3 loss in Christchurch. He started the 48–18 second Test defeat alongside O'Connell in Wellington and continued with his Munster teammate for the third Test which the Lions lost 38-19 in Auckland.

O'Callaghan played in all three of Ireland's 2005 Autumn Tests, losing to New Zealand and Australia and beating Romania, with all three matches played at Lansdowne Road. The following year he starred in all five of Ireland's games in the 2006 Six Nations Championship, scoring his first and only ever try for Ireland, when they lost 43-31 to France at Stade de France. Ireland won the Triple Crown in 2006. Donncha was a member of the Munster side that won their first Heineken Cup when they defeated Biarritz Olympique 23-19 in the final on 20 May 2006. Further success followed for the Cork native in the green of Ireland and in the red of Munster, another Triple Crown success in 2007 and winning a second Heineken Cup winners' medal in 2008 (beat Toulouse 16-13) and the United Rugby Championship in 2009.

Munster were quickly establishing themselves as not only Ireland's premier team but the best in Europe. They were a driven side with two powerhouses of raging boilers at the heart of their defence, the Limerick born O'Connell and Corkman O'Callaghan.

Interestingly the Limerick Coat of Arms arms depicts a castle with two towers and the portcullis raised. The Cork Coat of Arms features a ship on water between two large red towers. In the 14 years they played alongside one another in Munster red, O'Connell made his debut for the Province on 17 August 2001, they were two red towers of strength and fortitude. They were a partnership not only forged in training but forged from two bars of molten steel.

"A man without courage is a knife without an edge. Courage consists, not in blindly overlooking danger, but in seeing and conquering it. All brave men love; for he only is brave who has affections to fight for. Fortitude is the guard and support of the other virtues."

A Proverb

The motto of the Cork Cost of Arms reads *Statio Bene Fida Carinis* meaning *"A safe harbour for ships."* Cork and

Legends & Lions

Limerick are both port cities but for visiting teams to play Munster, Thomond Park was no safe harbour, more a Sea of Storms welcoming a Ship of Fools with a shipwreck likely to occur.

A few lines from the World Party song, Ship of Fools, should have given sufficient warning to those teams visiting Thomond Park, that they would be sailing against the wind.

"We're setting sail to the place on the map
From which no one has ever returned
Save me, save me from tomorrow
I don't want to sail with this ship of fools, no, no
Oh, save me, save me from tomorrow
I don't want to sail with this ship of fools, no, no
I want to run and hide right now
Avarice and greed are gonna drive you over the endless sea
They will leave you drifting in the shallows
Or drowning in the oceans of history
Traveling the world, you're in search of no good
But I'm sure you'll build your Sodom like you knew you would
Using all the good people for your galley slaves
As you're little boat struggles through the warning waves, but you
don't pay
You will pay tomorrow
You're gonna pay tomorrow, yeah
You're gonna pay tomorrow"

Donncha was a monumental presence in Ireland's historic 2009 Grand Slam winning team. In 2009, Sir Ian McGeechan selected Donncha for the Lions tour of South Africa. He captained the mid-week Lions team to a 28-10 victory over Southern Kings on 16 June 2009, and came off the bench in the first Test which the

Springboks won 26-21 in Durban. He wasn't chosen for the remaining two Tests, a 28-25 loss in Pretoria and a 28-9 win in Johannesburg. However, he didn't let the disappointment of not being able to add to his four caps for the Lions get him down by throwing the toys out of the pram or making a drama of it as that was simply not in his DNA, he was a survivor.

On the day Donncha was brought into the world, Gloria Gaynor was at No.1 in the UK Singles Charts with her massive dance hit, *I Will Survive*. There was no question that when the boy from Cork crossed the white line to enter a rugby pitch, he was a commanding, imposing, massive figure, standing 6 feet, 6 inches tall and weighing 18 stones and would be one of the last survivors of any turf war.

In an interview about his autobiography entitled *Joking Apart*, Donncha spoke about the emotional difference between winning and losing a game.

"Winning is great and there's a glow for a while. But losing is f***ing hell. And it's a burden that sits with you for some time. What's that Lombardi quote? 'If you can accept losing, you can't win.' I'd do anything to avoid that feeling. There's nothing like it. People close to you don't know it. They don't know how much you suffer after a loss. And they never will. People tell you there's another match next week and you play along with that. But we know."

And, O'Callaghan was a real joker, a messer, in the dressing room as his former Munster teammates will testify, especially those that were there the day when he marched a procession of paddling ducks into their sanctuary where the ducks left a few unwanted presents on the floor for the kit man to clean up.

Donncha gave the Munster fans the news they

wanted to hear when he announced on 11 November 2010, that he had committed his future to the club by signing a three-year contract which would end in 2014.

"Munster is all I ever wanted. Playing in front of my family and friends for a team I love and that's the only way I can describe my feelings for Munster. I love it. Granted, I understand you have to make an income and stuff like that but it means a little bit more for me. It's brilliant that I can put bread on the table for my family but I think I'd want to tog out for Munster regardless. It's not a great negotiating tool but I don't ever want to go anywhere else. I'm a Munster man, it means everything to me to play there. But I think it's important that you keep the traditions, like I grew up wanting to play for Munster and Ireland and I think maybe you could be motivated by money but it's not my thing. I want to play well for us and I think it makes me a better player. I can stretch beyond myself when I play for Munster."

Donncha O'Callaghan

And despite his age, 31, he wasn't prepared to rest on his laurels and set his sights on bringing further trophy successes to Thomond Park. And he did just that by helping Munster defeat their most bitterest of rivals, Leinster, 19-9 in the 2011 Magners League Grand final on 28 May 2011 with the game played at Thomond Park.

Aristotle, a Greek Philosopher, once famously remarked that: *"Patience is bitter, but its fruit is sweet."* Losing to their greatest rivals was a bitter pill for O'Driscoll and his band of Leinster teammates to swallow. During a pre-match press conference ahead of a Test match against England in 2009, O'Driscoll was asked what it was like to have played with the England coach, Martin Johnson, during their time together with the British and Irish Lions in 2001, and now to be on opposing sides. The

JOHN WHITE

Ireland captain famously said: *"Knowledge is knowing that a tomato is a fruit; wisdom is knowing not to put it in a fruit salad."*

On 14 April 2012, Donncha became the ninth Munster player to win 200 caps in their league game against Glasgow Warriors. He signed a contract extension with Munster in November 2013, which would see him remain with the Province up until June 2016. When O'Callaghan came off the bench for Munster against Zebre to claim his 241st cap, he made history by surpassing the record for the highest number of appearances for Munster which had been held by a Thomond Park and Ireland Legend, Ronan O'Gara.

He was left out of the Ireland squad for the 2014 Six Nations Championship by coach Joe Schmidt meaning that when he played for Ireland in their 13-13 draw with France in Dublin on 13 March 2013 in the Six Nations Championship, it was his 94th and final game in the green jersey.

In April 2014, Donncha was nominated for the Ireland Rugby Union Players' Association Medal for Excellence award. He missed out on the award which went to Shane Jennings but he did win the inaugural Contribution to Society Award for his work with UNICEF. That same year he played the first of his two matches for the Barbarians.

On 3 September 2015, it was announced that Donncha had been granted an early release from his Munster contract to sign for Worcester Warriors on a two-year contract. He was 36-years old at the time when he moved to the Aviva Premiership club. Quite eerily when he was born one of the cult movies of 1979 was called *The Warriors*. When Donncha left Munster having spent 17 seasons with them, he set the record for the most number of caps which has not been beaten, 268 Titanic games for his Province.

Having made his professional debut some 17 years earlier, he was shown the red card for the first time in his career on 5 December 2015, playing for the Warriors against Leicester Tigers. In his first season at Sixfields Stadium he played in every one of Worcester Warriors Premiership games and was deservedly named the Supporters' Club Player of the Season for 2015-16. In January 2017, he captained the Warriors for the first time in their 2016-17 European Rugby Challenge Cup Pool 3 game versus Russia's Yenisey-STM. A short time later he was handed the captaincy on a permanent basis.

"Donners is a very good captain. Donners is very impressive when he talks and has a wealth of experience. He has many caps for Ireland, been with the British Lions and on winning teams. He knows what a winning team looks like."

David Gold,
Director of Rugby, Worcester Warriors

He then signed a one-year contract extension in April 2017, and ended his career, taking the decision to retire after leading Worcester Warriors to a 44-13 victory against Harlequins on 28 April 2018, a result which guaranteed their place in the Premiership for the following season.

After the game Donncha said: "It's been a rollercoaster year but I'm so proud of how we've performed. I wasn't thinking of it as my last game, I was just thinking that I need to play well because we've got to get a result, so I'm really proud and it's brilliant to see a full stadium. Rugby's a special game and you get out what you put into it, and I've given it my heart."

The stadium announcer would have been applauded

had he played Motörhead's song King of Kings when Donncha walked off the pitch for the last time.

> *"Behold the King*
> *The King of Kings*
> *On your knees dog*
> *Ahahah*
> *All hail*
> *Bow down to the-, bow down to the King*
> *Bow down to the-, bow down to-*
> *The King grinned red as he walked from the place*
> *Where the traitor lost both his name and his face*
> *Through the halls and the corridors stinging in blood*
> *He tasted his grin and it tasted good*
> *The King took his head*
> *Left him broken and dead*
> *Bow down to the-, bow down to the King*
> *Bow down to the-, bow down to the King*
> *Bow down to the-, bow down to-*
> *The King left none living, none able to tell*
> *The King took their heads and he sent them to hell*
> *Their screams echoed loud in the place of their death*
> *Ripped open they died with their final breath*
> *They hailed to the King*
> *The King of Kings*
> *Bow down to the-, bow down to the King*
> *Bow down to the-, bow down to the King*
> *Bow down to the-, bow down to the King"*

Donnchadh is made up of the elements *donn*, meaning *"brown"* or *"dark"* from *Donn*, a Gaelic God, and *chadh*, meaning *"chief"* or *"noble."* The name is also written as Donnchad, Donncha, Donnacha. O'Callaghan is from the Gaelic Ó Ceallacháin meaning *"bright headed."*

Legends & Lions

The name Ó Ceallacháin was that of a 10th century King of Munster from whom many called O'Callaghan claim descent. In 1118, Munster had been divided into the Kingdom of Desmond ruled by the MacCarthy Dynasty, the Kingdom of Ormond under the O'Kennedy's and the Kingdom of Thomond under the O'Brien Dynasty. The three crowns on the Munster crest and on the Munster flag, represent these three Kingdoms.

Donncha O'Callaghan was the King of Munster Rugby from 1998-2015 and a High King of Ireland Rugby from 2003-13. He was Irish Rugby's *King of Kings*.

Did You Know That?

In a television interview with Tommy Tiernan, Donncha was asked to explain what his day job was. Donncha replied: "*Tommy, my job is to put my head between two asses and push, you know what I mean? There are better job specs out there!*"

WILLIE DUGGAN
The People's Champion

WILLIAM PATRICK DUGGAN was born on 31 May 1950, in James's Green, Dunmore, Kilkenny. He went to Christian Brothers Junior School in Kilkenny city, where he played rugby with his cousin, Edward Michael Joseph *"Ned"* Byrne. Aged 8, he was sent to Rockwell College in Tipperary as a boarder and in addition to winning the school's high jump and pole vault championships, he played with the Rockwell senior rugby team which won the Munster Schools Cup in 1967. However, despite his performances for his College, he was not chosen to represent the Munster Provincial Schools XV although seven of his teammates were. Willie began his playing career with Sunday's Well Rugby Football Club, Cork and in 1972, joined Blackrock Rugby Club in Stradbrook, Dublin where later that same year Ned also signed for the team. During his career he also played for Kilkenny Rugby Football Club.

Willie and Ned were also keen hurlers. Duggan hurled as a teenager for Dicksboro Gaelic Athletic Club, losing a Junior A county final to Ballyhale Shamrocks, and he wore the black and amber of Kilkenny in a Leinster Under-21 hurling championship match. Prior to joining Blackrock College, Ned won an All-Ireland title with Kilkenny in 1972, a 3-24 to 5-11 victory over Cork at Croke Park.

On 18 January 1975, Ireland kicked off their 1975 Five Nations Championship campaign and Duggan was given his international debut by Roly Meates, the Ireland coach. It was a winning start to his Test career with Ireland beating England 12-9 at Lansdowne Road. In total, Willie won 41 caps (39 at number eight and two at flanker, all of them from the start) for his country with his final appearance in the green jersey coming against Scotland at Lansdowne Road on 3 March 1984. Willie was made captain of the team by Willie John McBride (Ireland coach 1983-84) for the game but it wasn't quite the farewell that Willie had hoped for as Scotland won their 1984 Five Nations Championship encounter 32-9. In 1982, Willie helped Ireland win the Triple Crown and claim the Five Nations Championship. In between playing for Leinster and Ireland, Willie Duggan worked in the family electrical shop in Kilkenny. He was a truly outstanding number eight for club and country and was also capped four times by the British and Irish Lions, playing in all four Tests during the Lions' tour to New Zealand in 1977 which the All Blacks won 3-1. Willie scored a try in the third Test.

Willie, was often given a *Bad Boy* reputation, perhaps a little unfair on him, because he merely stood up for himself and his teammates and was not exactly one for turning the other cheek. All too often the opposition singled Willie out for special treatment because of his immense reputation on the pitch, which was not out of place at the time, but he was tough as nails and met fire with fire and was still able to enjoy a drink with the opposing players after a game. Former Ireland international Donal Lenihan, who began his international career shortly before Willie's came to an end, described him as: "*The hardest man I ever played with.*" However, on occasion, Willie did overstep the disciplinary code. On 15 January

JOHN WHITE

1977, Ireland faced Wales at Cardiff Arms Park in the 1977 Five Nations Championship. When the rivals met it was always a battle and on this occasion, two players took the battle a little too far. Wales were the reigning Champions and Grand Slam holders. During the match, Geoff Wheel the Welsh Lock, hit Stuart McKinney and Willie then retaliated by taking a swing at Alan Martin. Both infringements happened under the nose of Norman Sanson, the Scottish referee, who instantly sent Wheel and Duggan off thereby becoming the first players to be sent off in the history of the tournament dating back to 1883 and they never even touched one another. Perhaps Willie was exacting his own version of Willie John McBride's famous "*99*" call three years earlier when the British and Irish Lions toured South Africa, when if one Lion was struck by a Springbok then every other Lion on the pitch was expected to smack an opponent regardless of how innocent they were.

Willie was quarried from granite.

Despite protesting his innocence, Wheel was the first of the pair to walk off the pitch. A matter of seconds later Willie ran past him into the tunnel. "*I didn't know what that was about. I wasn't involved with Willie Duggan at all. I didn't even see what he was supposed to have done. We even had a bit of a laugh about it on the side-line. We definitely got the best of it. He was having a really good game at the back of the line-out. Willie was a great character and an exceptionally good player. I don't know what he got sent off for but they ended up losing their best player and we won the game easily enough*," said Wheel. The late Moss Keane, played in the game at Lock for Ireland and sometime later when he was asked about the incident said: "*Duggan always maintained he was never sent off. He said the referee came towards him and asked would he mind*

LEGENDS & LIONS

leaving the field and Duggan replied, 'Sure, not at all, I'm bollixed anyway'." Wales won the match 25-9 whilst Ireland failed to win a single game during the 1977 tournament and ended up with the Wooden Spoon.

On 19 February 1977, Ned won the first of his six caps for Ireland and played alongside Willie when they were beaten 21-18 by Scotland at Murrayfield Stadium in the 1977 Five Nations Championship.

Willie was persuaded to join Blackrock College by the former Ireland rugby selector Dave O'Leary. In Tom English's book *Behind The Green Jersey, Playing Rugby for Ireland*, Willie spoke to the author about a game versus France in his debut Five Nations Championship season. *"Those French packs, they weren't exactly clean. I wouldn't say they were any worse than we were, but there was more of them at it. Before that game a great mentor of mine, Dave O'Leary, phoned me up and said, 'Willie, there's a blondie lad playing for France at the weekend, and the French absolutely love him.' He was talking about Jean-Pierre Rives. Dave says, 'L'Équipe are going to be watching every step this fella takes, and there is going to be 25 photographs of him in their paper. If you're in 18 of the 25 photographs, you've had a great fecking game.' Dave rang me a week later. 'Willie,' he says, 'I've just got L'Équipe. There's 24 photographs of Rives, and you're in 22 of them.' That was Dave's way of measuring how well you played."*

Willie had a brilliant game with Ireland defeating France 25-6 on 1 March 1975 at Lansdowne Road.

The Irish fans adored Willie because he was like so many of them, enjoying the odd pint of Smithwick's or two, a smoker and he was never a great fan of training. But despite all of this, Willie never let himself, his teammates or his country down and was battle fit every time he crossed the white line. He gave 100% to the green jersey every time he was given the honour of wearing it. However, such was his aversion to training that the legendary Willie John McBride once said that he was surprised that Willie won one cap for Ireland, let alone 41. McBride recalled one time when he was the coach of Ireland and Willie was late for training. Willie walked into the dressing room and lit a cigarette. When someone suggested that the players engage in a warm-up before going out to train, Duggan replied: *"Sure, I've had the heater on in the car coming up from Kilkenny. I'm warm enough."* And as Willie Duggan always said himself: *"I could do the warm up, or play the match, but I couldn't do both."*

Willie certainly loved a smoke although he said he only smoked to calm his nerves before a match. After a coach once old him that if he gave up the cigarettes he would be faster around the pitch, Willie replied: *"But then I would spend most of the match offside."*

In 2016, he was selected as Rockwell College Person of the Year for his contribution to the college, where he also excelled in debating, horse riding, snooker and weightlifting. Then in 2010, he was elected to the Guinness Rugby Writers' Hall of Fame.

Willie's Zodiac birth sign was Pisces (Fish) but the boy from Dunmore, Kilkenny was more of a whale on the pitch than a fish. Willie's birthplace was the site of Ireland's earliest recorded witch trial and Willie conducted his own trials on the pitch and condemned many opponents to the stake.

On 28 August 2017, Willie Duggan passed away at his home in Dunmore as a result of a stomach aneurysm. He was 67 years old.

Willie Duggan lit-up a dressing room with his unique wit and vibrant personality. In his death notice, his family said: *"Willie would have wanted a party,"* and asked his many friends to dress colourfully and not in mourning black for the celebration of his life. Willie was a larger than life character, a talisman for club, province and country.

Willie Duggan was the People's Champion.
Ar dheis Dé go raibh a anam dílis.

Did You Know That?

Willie was one of the sport's great characters. During Ireland's successful 1982 Five Nations Championship campaign, he emerged from the tunnel at Twickenham Stadium smoking a cigarette which he gave to the match referee, Scotland's Alan Hosie, and asked him to hold it for him. It was Hosie's first international and the TV cameras caught him attempting to put the cigarette out as he walked out of the tunnel.

CONOR MURRAY
Ireland's Eternal Flame

GERARD CONOR MURRAY was born on 20 April 1989 in Limerick and attended St Munchins College and won the Munster Schools Rugby Senior Cup in 2006 alongside his Ireland teammate, Keith Earls.

When he was born the all-girl American pop rock band, The Bangles, were No.1 in the United Kingdom Music Singles Chart with their hit song, *Eternal Flame*. On 18 April 2010, Conor made his debut for Munster when he came on as a blood replacement in their 18-12 win over Connacht at the Sportsgrounds, Galway in the 2009-10 Celtic League. Conor played in the Munster A team which lost the final of the 2009-10 British and Irish Cup to the Cornish Pirates on 16 May 2010. Six months later, he came off the bench to replace Duncan Williams in Munster's famous 15-6 victory over Australia at Thomond Park on 16 November 2010. Murray made his European debut on 9 April 2011 helping Munster to a thrilling 42-37 win against Brive at Parc Municipal (also known as Stade Amédée-Domenech), Brive-la-Gaillarde in their quarter-final Amlin Challenge Cup encounter. Murray's dedication to training and work ethic paid off when he started at scrum-half versus Leicester Tigers in the 2011 Celtic League Grand final. The 22-year old won his first senior winners' medal when Munster beat the Tigers 19-9 at Thomond Park on 28 May 2011. He rounded his first full season off

Legends & Lions

in a red shirt by winning the John McCarthy Award for being named the Academy Player of the Year. Murray was given a place in the Ireland squad for their 2011 Rugby World Cup warm-up matches. On 13 August 2011, he made his debut for Ireland coming on as a substitute in a 19-12 defeat to France in Bordeaux, France. A fortnight later he ran out for Ireland at Lansdowne Road for the first time to earn his second cap for his country after coming on as a substitute versus England who were on tour. The visitors won 20-9 with his Munster teammate, Ronan O'Gara, scoring all of Ireland's points from three penalties. O'Gara was a huge influence on Murray's career and Murray, who was a capable kicker himself, knew that he would have to wait for his turn to step out of O'Gara's shadow when it came down to being the No.1 choice kicker for his club. But he had done enough in the two warm-up matches to secure a place in Ireland's 30-man squad that flew to New Zealand for the 2011 Rugby World Cup. Down under he played in three of Ireland's Pool C games, including a historic 15-6 win over Australia, and in their 22-10 loss to Wales in the quarter-finals of the tournament.

The famous Irish author, C. S. Lewis, once famously remarked in his novel entitled *The Screwtape Letters*: "*I do not expect old heads on young shoulders.*" The author of famous novels such as *The Lion, The Witch and the Wardrobe* died on 22 November 1963, some 36 years before Conor was born and no doubt had he seen the 22-year old Murray make his debut for Ireland, he may well have had a think about rewording this line from his novel.

On 12 November 2011, Conor made his Heineken Cup debut in a win over the Northampton Saints, a victory which helped Munster top Pool A with six wins from six. However, Munster lost 22-16 to Ulster in the quarter-finals of the competition. During the 2012 Six Nations Championship he played in the home games versus Wales (lost) and Italy (won) and in a draw away to France. A knee injury prevented him from playing in the other two matches. In April 2012, he made his comeback from injury and scored his first try for Munster in a United Rugby Championship league game versus Glasgow Warriors.

In June 2012, he played in all three Tests versus the All Blacks during Ireland's tour of New Zealand. Ireland lost the Test Series 3-0 but there was consolation for Conor in the second Test as he scored his first ever try in the green jersey. Before the end of the year, he played two more times for Ireland, a 16-12 loss to South Africa and a 46-24 win over Argentina, both games being played in Dublin.

In the 2013 Six Nations Championship, he started at scrum-half for Ireland's opening 30–22 win against Wales on 2 February 2013 at the Millennium Stadium, their 12–6 loss to England on 10 February 2013 at Twickenham Stadium and in Ireland's 12–8 loss to Scotland on 24 February 2013. When Ireland drew 13-13 with France at the Aviva Stadium on 9 March 2013, the 23-year old Limerick boy was named Man of the Match despite the fact that he didn't score, Jamie Heaslip scored a try which was converted by Paddy Jackson who also successfully kicked two of the four penalties Ireland were awarded in the game. And, on 16 March 2013, he played in Ireland's 22-15 away defeat at the hands of Italy in Rome. Jackson scored five penalties and missed one in the loss at Stadio Olimpico

Murray's solid performances for club and country

were rewarded when he was chosen to tour Australia with the British and Irish Lions in 2013. Conor was selected by coach Warren Gatland as one of three scrum-halves in the squad. Murray made his Lions' debut on 1 June 2013, coming on as a substitute in their opening game, a 50-18 win versus the Barbarians in Hong Kong when they were en-route to Australia. He started in the 69-17 win against Western Force on 5 June 2013, and in the 64-0 rout of a Combined New South Wales-Queensland Country side on 11 June 2013, a game in which he scored his first try for the Lions. On 29 June 2013, he won his first Test cap for the British and Irish Lions when he replaced England's Ben Youngs in the 53rd minute of the second Test which the Lions narrowly lost 16-15. He also came off the bench in the third Test which the Lions' won 41-16 to give them a 2-1 Series victory. The Lions defeated the Wallabies 23-21 in the first Test.

Conor played in all five of Ireland's fixtures of the 2014 Six Nations Championship to help his country to a title success and on 8 May 2014, he won the 2014 Munster Senior Player of the Year Award. The following year he played in all five of Ireland's Six Nations Championship games, scoring a try against Italy in a 26-3 win in Rome, and won back-to-back winners' medals in the competition as Ireland retained the title. When England hosted the 2015 Rugby World Cup, Conor's name was one of three scrum-halves the Ireland coach, Joe Schmidt, included in his squad. Murray had a firm hold on the No.9 jersey with his main rival for the position being Eoin Reddan, Leinster's 34-year old scrum-half, who Murray usurped midway through the 2011 Rugby World Cup. Conor played in all four of Ireland's Pool D games in the 2015 Rugby World Cup, starting versus Canada (won 50-

7), Italy (won 16-9) and France scoring a try in a 24-9 victory. He was a substitute in the 44-10 victory over Romania. He started in the 43-20 quarter-final loss to Argentina.

Murray played in all of Ireland's 2016 Six Nations Championship games, scoring a try in Ireland's 21–10 defeat against England at Twickenham Stadium, and along with teammate, Johnny Sexton, he was nominated for the Player of the Tournament award, which was won by Scotland's Stuart Hogg. In June 2016, Murray played in Ireland's three Test Series trip to South Africa, with the visitors winning one, a game in which Conor scored a try versus the Springboks, but they lost the other two. Five months later Conor found himself running out on to the gridiron which was Soldier Field, Chicago, USA and the home to the American Football franchise, Chicago Bears.

Ireland's opponents were New Zealand, a side they had never beaten in any of their previous 28 encounters. The best result Ireland walked away from in a game with them was a 10-10 draw at Lansdowne Road on 20 January 1973, a week before Sweet took the United Kingdom's music singles charts by storm with their hit single, *Blockbuster*.

> *"When there's nowhere else to run*
> *Is there room for one more son*
> *One more son*
> *If you can hold on*
> *If you can hold on, hold on*
> *I want to stand up, I want to let go*
> *You know, you know, no you don't, you don't*
> *I want to shine on in the hearts of men*

Legends & Lions

*I want a meaning from the back of my broken hand
I got soul but I'm not a soldier"*

The above are lines from the song by The Killers entitled *All These Things That I Have Done*. In his 50 games for Ireland up to this titanic battle against the All Blacks, Conor had already done a lot of things for his country. And, on 5 November 2016, he showed his soul scoring a try and a penalty and along with fourteen other men in green he became a soldier and left the battlefield victorious after helping Ireland defeat New Zealand 40-29. The All Blacks had no answer to the fight which Ireland brought into the game and left Soldier Field a beaten army. It was a *Blockbuster* performance by the men in green. A fortnight later Ireland lost 21- 9 to the All Blacks in Dublin and then defeated Australia 27-24 in the Irish capital, Conor starred in both games.

Once again Conor was an ever present for Ireland in the 2017 Six Nations Championship, and once again he was nominated for the Player of the Tournament award, which was won for the second year in a row by Stuart Hogg. On 10 May 2017, he won the Rugby Players Ireland Players' Player of the Year award, becoming the third Munster player in a row to win the accolade following in the boots of Paul O'Connell in 2015 and CJ Stander in 2016. Then on 27 May 2017, he won his 100th cap for Munster when he started against Scarlets in the 2017 Pro12 Grand final which the Welsh club won 46-22. In June and July 2017, he played in all three of the British and Irish Lions Test Matches against New Zealand. The tourists returned home with their heads held high after winning one, drawing one and losing one of their tussles with the All Blacks in their own backyard. Conor scored

JOHN WHITE

a try in the Lions' 24-21 victory in the second Test at Wellington Regional Stadium, Wellington. The year proved to be a huge success for the 28-year old when he scooped the Rugby Writers of Ireland Player of the Year award in October 2017, a fitting reward for the imperious scooping he did throughout the year in scrums for club, country and the British and Irish Lions.

"Positive thinkers create large pictures of what they want in their minds and can predict the future from the present."

Israelmore Ayivor

Conor's positive thinking in games gives him the ability to see the bigger picture and allows him the time and space around the back of the scrum to make tactical decisions and set up attacking moves. Being a member of the first ever Ireland side to defeat New Zealand was high up on the curriculum vitae of Murray, but just as a high jumper always sets his sights on raising the bar to reach greater heights, Conor set a new bar on his career by helping Ireland win the 2018 Six Nations Championship, Triple Crown and Grand Slam. It was only the third time in the history of Irish Rugby that they had scaled such great heights (1948 & 2009). He started in every game of the tournament scoring tries against Italy and Scotland, was named Man of the Match in the victory against Italy and scored penalties versus Wales and England. Conor also started in all three Test Matches versus Australia down under in June 2018, when Ireland claimed a historic 2-1 Series win. His 50th Champions Cup cap was claimed on 19 January 2019, a 9-7 win over the Exeter Chiefs meaning Munster had progressed to a record 18th Champions Cup quarter-final game. On 14 May 2021, he was awarded his 150th cap for Munster when they lost at home to Connacht in Round 3 of the Pro14 Rainbow Cup.

In 2021, Conor embarked on his third Lions' tour when they visited South Africa. When the Lions' captain, Alun Wyn Jones (Wales), got injured in a warm-up match against Japan on 26 June 2021, which they won 28-10, Warren Gatland had no hesitation in making Conor his new captain. The coach of the British and Irish Lions spoke about the high regard Murray was held in by his teammates and the fact that he had already been on two previous Tours. Conor described his appointment as an *"unbelievable honour."* But then fate took a twisted course when Jones somehow unbelievably recovered from his injury to assume the captaincy. Despite the respect Gatland held for Conor, much to the surprise of almost everyone, Gatland handed the red No.9 jersey to Scotland's Ali Price for the first Test of a three game Series. However, Murray did come off the bench to help the Lions over the line with a 22-17 victory against the Springboks. The win meant that Conor Murray became one of only 10 players to have won a Test Match with the Lions against Australia, New Zealand and South Africa. Conor started the second Test, a 27-9 defeat to set up a nail biting deciding third Test. Price was again preferred over Conor who came on as a substitute in the game to win his eighth Lions cap but could not help the tourists claim a victory as they lost 19-16 to give the Springboks a 2-1 Series win.

Murray won the Triple Crown with Ireland in the 2022 Six Nations Championship, with France crowned Grand Slam winners. In July 2022, Conor toured New Zealand with Ireland and came off the bench in the 42–19 defeat against the All Blacks in the first Test, and was a substitute again when Ireland claimed their first ever win against the All Blacks on New Zealand soil, a historic 23-12 victory in the second Test. He then played in the third Test which Ireland won 32-22 on 16 July 2022, a first ever Test Series win for Ireland in the *Land of the Long White Cloud*. Conor became an Irish centurion on 5 November 2022, when they beat South Africa 19-16 in Dublin in a 2022 Autumn Series game. However, his 100th cap for his country saw him leave the field of play injured in the first half which ruled him out of Ireland's remaining 2022 Autumn Series matches.

When Ireland claimed their fourth Grand Slam title in 2023, Conor was an integral part of coach Andy Farrell's team, starting three of the games and coming on as a substitute for Craig Casey in the 34-20 win over Italy in Rome and for Jamison Gibson-Park when Ireland beat England 29-16 in Dublin the final game of the tournament.

On 27 May 2023, Conor added yet more silverware to his trophy cabinet starring in Munster's 19-14 victory against Stormers in the final of the 2022-23 United Rugby Championship, played at the Stormers' home stadium, DHL Stadium, Cape Town, South Africa.

Conor was a member of the Ireland squad that were eliminated from the 2023 Rugby World Cup by New Zealand at the quarter-finals stage.

When Conor Murray made his professional debut, Jason Derulo was No.1 in the Singles Chart with the song *In My Head*. More than a decade on and the 34-year old Murray was messing with the heads of his opponents with his control of the scrum as he gently caressed the ball below his foot before reaching down to pick it up and pass to a teammate to begin an attack. He possesses the unique ability of casting his eyes over the sea of players in front of him and be able to see a play develop in his head, some two moves ahead of those around him even knew it was about to happen. It is similar to a Meerkat popping his head up from his hole to see what danger lay in the distance.

Conor Murray is Ireland's *Eternal Flame*.

Did You Know That?

Prior to beginning a professional career with an oval ball, Conor played Gaelic football for Patrickswell and Limerick. He played for Limerick in the Sarsfield Cup and represented Limerick in primary football matches.

PAUL O'CONNELL
The Irish Thor

PAUL JEREMIAH O'CONNELL's birth certificate states he was born in Limerick on 20 October 1979. However, if he had been born when the Vikings plundered Europe from 800–1100, his birth certificate would have read: *Thor, born in North Germanic (modern day Scandinavia), around 999*. Thor is a Prominent God in German paganism and a hammer-wielding God in Norse Mythology associated with Lightning, Protection, Sacredness, Storms, Strength and Thunder.

Paul's first Christmas, aged just 66 days old, was a time when *Pink Floyd* enjoyed their first, and only, No.1 hit in the UK Singles Charts with *Another Brick In The Wall*. POC was not just any old brick in the wall that made up Ireland's defence during his outstanding international career for his country, he was the sand and cement that built it, because he was Ireland's *One Man Brick Wall*.

On a rugby pitch, Paul O'Connell was the epitome of the *Reincarnation of Chaos*. He was the last opposing player you wanted to see standing before you if you had the ball in your hands attacking the Munster, Ireland or British Lions defence. Many players who faced him for the first time on a rugby battlefield must have recalled the scene from the movie, *Gladiator* (2000), when one of the slaves standing in front of Maximus (Russell Crowe's character in the movie) wet himself before the gate leading into Rome's Coliseum were opened. Maximus took two steps back, but POC was a different animal.

245

LEGENDS & LIONS

The words *"Back Down,"* were not in his dictionary. He was prepared to fight fire with fire, but always staying within the Laws of the Game. O'Connell did not need to lower his play to dirty tactics or test the match referee's tolerance of his tackles in a game. He fought hard but fairly. He matched aggression with embattled experience and he swept opponents away like a chef cooking fresh meat on a barbeque would swat flies away from the food with an incisive swoop of a set of tongs.

Anyone who tried to pass him met the equivalent of Thor's Hammer and were instantly brought down before the feet of Ireland's Viking King. Paul O'Connell did not require a noose in his other hand to accompany his hammer body blows, his opponents just accepted the fate of meeting their *Hangman*.

Paul attended the Model School, Limerick and Ardscoil Ris, Limerick. But, for the young O'Connell rugby was not his first choice sport and posters of Ireland rugby union internationals such as Willie Anderson, Keith Crossan, Mick Galwey, Ralph Keyes, Michael Kiernan, Donal Lenihan or Brendan Mullin (all members of Ireland's 1990 Five Nations Championship squad when Paul was aged 11) did not adorn his bedroom walls. Musical artists such as Adamski, Madonna, New Kids on the Block, The Beautiful South and Ireland's very own Sinead O'Connor (so sadly missed following her untimely death on 26 July 2023, aged just 56) were massive in the Music Charts in Ireland in 1990 when Paul was about to enter Secondary School. But, like the Legends who wore the green jersey of Ireland, he was uninterested in these musicians and it was swimming that drew his focus. The young O'Connell was an excellent swimmer and only began playing rugby when he was 16 years old, when he played for his school in the Munster Senior Schools Cup.

No doubt it was the USA's Mark Spitz, who won an incredible seven gold medals, setting seven World Records in swimming at an Olympiad, the 1972 Olympic Games in Munich, West Germany who was the young O'Connell's role model and driving force. Spitz was nicknamed "*Mark The Shark*," and although, and thankfully for Irish rugby fans, POC did not pursue a career over 50 metres in an Olympic swimming pool, every time he crossed the white line to compete in a game, a *Shark Attack* warning was sent to the opposition, similar to those given to swimmers at the beach at Amity Island, USA in the 1975 Blockbuster movie *Jaws*: *Be Afraid, Be Very Afraid*.

In season 1997-98, he represented the Irish Schoolboys side in international junior rugby union, playing in the same team as Gordon D'Arcy. POC also turned out five times for the Ireland Under-21 team playing alongside Donncha O'Callaghan in the second row. Upon leaving school he studied Computer Engineering at the University of Limerick but only completed three of his four year degree course to concentrate on a career playing professional rugby.

On 17 August 2001, aged 21, O'Connell made his debut for Munster in a 25-22 win over Edinburgh at Myreside Stadium (home of Watsonians Rugby Football Club since 1933) in the Scottish capital. POC was given his debut in the Heineken Cup on 29 September 2011, a 28-23 win for Munster over Castres Olympique (France) at Thomond Park. Then on 15 December 2001, Paul played for Munster in the Celtic League final when they lost 24-20 to Leinster at Lansdowne Road. D'Arcy scored

LEGENDS & LIONS

a try for Leinster in the game. Munster also reached the Heineken Cup final in season 2001-02 and once again Paul had to settle for a runners-up medal when they were defeated 15-9 by Leicester Tigers at Millennium Stadium on 25 May 2002.

The 2001-02 season also saw Paul make his international debut for Ireland. On 3 February 2002, Ireland kicked-off their 2002 Six Nations Championship campaign versus Wales in Dublin. The boy from Limerick had a debut to remember scoring a try in his country's 54-10 victory. But, when he was asked how it felt to score on his debut Paul told a reporter: *"I scored a try but I don't remember it. I went to tackle Craig Quinnell and he knocked me clean unconscious with his elbow. I played on for another 25 minutes, scored a try and then, eventually, with seven minutes left in the first half, I came around. I didn't really know what was going on and so I walked off the pitch."*

The following year, 2003, he was a member of the Munster squad that won the Celtic League for the first time. They beat Neath (Wales) 37-17 in the final played at the Millennium Stadium in the Welsh Principality on 1 February 2003. Prior to the 2003 Rugby World Cup hosted by Australia, Ireland played several warm-up matches to give players an opportunity to prove why they should be selected to the Ireland squad for their trip down under. On 16 August 2003, POC cemented his place in the squad after scoring two tries in Ireland's 35-12 win against Wales at Lansdowne Road. Ireland were drawn in Pool A at the 2003 Rugby World Cup with Paul playing in all four of their Pool games: a 45-17 defeat of Romania, followed by another win, 64-7 against Namibia, a 16-15 victory over Argentina and a narrow 17-16 loss to the host nation. Paul also played for Ireland in the quarter-finals when they lost 43-21 to France.

There was no doubt that Paul had made the right choice to swap the swimming pool for the rugby field and his dream of captaining his country came to fruition on 14 February 2004, when he captained Ireland against France. It was their opening game of the 2004 Six Nations Championship and with the regular captain, Brian O'Driscoll injured, POC was the natural choice to stand in for the Leinster man. It was Valentine's Day but there was no love shown to Ireland in the French capital as the home side ran out comfortable winners, 35-17 at Stade de France. It was Ireland's only loss in the 2004 Six Nations Championship, finishing runners-up to Grand Slam winners, France. However, Ireland's wins over England, Scotland and Wales meant they won the Triple Crown, their first since 1985.

In 2005, Paul was a key member of the Munster team that won the last ever edition of the Celtic Cup. On 14 May 2005, they defeated Llanelli Scarlets 27-16 at Lansdowne Road. On 11 April 2005, the British and Irish Lions announced their 44-man squad to tour New Zealand later that year. Eleven Ireland players were chosen with O'Connell's name among them: Leinster's Shane Byrne, Gordon D'Arcy, Denis Hickie, Shane Horgan, Brian O'Driscoll (Tour Captain) and Malcolm O'Kelly; Geordan Murphy from the Leicester Tigers and Paul's Munster teammates: John Hayes, Donncha O'Callaghan and Ronan O'Gara. POC played in all three Tests versus the All Blacks, starting in all three games. The Lions lost the Test Series 3-0.

A man can be an artist in anything. Paul O'Connell's art was War and breaking up the attacks of Ireland's opponents to set-up up victory for his team. Individual accolades and glory did not interest him. He saw the *Bigger Picture*. He knew he was only a small piece of Ireland's canvass, but in 2006, just like Mark Spitz 34 years earlier, he was about to create his own Masterpiece.

The famous Italian artist, Leonardo da Vinci, painted the Masterpiece of his life, the *"Mona Lisa,"* between 1503 and 1506. It was an archetypal Masterpiece of the Italian Renaissance. In 2006, Paul O'Connell put his rugby easel to use and painted his own Masterpiece. The Italian Master put his art on canvas. Paul's canvas was a rugby pitch. Da Vinci was also an Engineer and Inventor who conceived many ideas way ahead of his time on earth (1452-1519), conceptually inventing the parachute and the helicopter. He even drew the first ever plans for a submersible vehicle. Paul, an Irish Master, was also an Inventor, creating many chances for his forwards to score a try he devised in his mind before executing his plans.

In the 2006 Six Nations Championship, POC helped Ireland win a second Triple Crown in just three years, their eighth overall. Paul's name went into the Ireland Rugby Union history book following their 61-17 win over Pacific Islanders at Lansdowne Road, Dublin on 26 November 2006. He scored a try in the game which was the last ever try scored at the old Lansdowne Road ground. Ireland's spiritual rugby home was then demolished to make way for the Aviva Stadium. Paul O'Connell's displays for Ireland and the Lions saw him being shortlisted for the 2006 International Rugby Board Player of the Year, the only one of the five nominees who played his rugby in the northern hemisphere. The other four were Dan Carter (New Zealand), Chris Latham (Australia), Fourie du Preez (South Africa) and the winner, Richie McCaw (New Zealand). McCaw won it.

JOHN WHITE

O'Connell played an integral role for the Munster team that won the 2005-06 Heineken Cup. He was outstanding in all six of Munster's Pool 1 games, winning five and losing one. In the quarter-finals he scored a try in a 19-10 win versus USA Perpignan (France) at Lansdowne Road and followed this up with a steamrollering performance in a 30-6 win against Leinster 30-6 in the semi-finals at Lansdowne Road. On 20 May 2006, Munster defeated Biarritz Olympique 23-19 at the Millennium Stadium to win their first ever Heineken Cup.

On 11 February 2007, Ireland faced France at home on Matchday 2 of the 2007 Six Nations Championship. It was a historic day for Irish rugby as it was the first ever rugby union international to be played at Croke Park. And, once again POC stood in for an injured O'Driscoll as captain. France spoilt the day for everyone wearing green, on and off the pitch, by winning 20-7. But 13 days later Ireland welcomed England to Croke Park with POC being named the Man of the Match in Ireland's 43-13 victory. The 30-point margin surpassed Ireland's all-time record winning margin of 22-0 against England in 1947. England, meanwhile, conceded their highest points tally in Five or Six Nations Championship history, surpassing a 37-12 loss to France at Stade Olympique de Colombes in 1972.

POC travelled to France with Ireland as a member of their 2007 Rugby World Cup squad and played in all four of Ireland's games in France. It was a very disappointing campaign for the boys in green who failed to make it out of Pool D which was won by Argentina whilst the host nation finished runners-up with Ireland third in the table. Anthony Foley (sadly no longer with us, 30 October 1973

Legends & Lions

– 16 October 2016) stood down as captain of Munster at the beginning of the 2007–08 season, making way for POC to succeed him. O'Connell's natural leadership abilities inspired the team to Heineken Cup success when they beat Toulouse (France) 16-13 in the final played at the Millennium Stadium on 24 May 2008. Twelve months later he captained his side to their second Celtic League title with Munster crowned Champions on 30 April 2009.

Words cannot do justice to POC's performances in a green jersey during the 2009 Six Nations Championship. Having beaten France 30-21 at Croke Park, Italy 38-9 in Rome, England 14-13 at Croke Park and Scotland 22-15 at Murrayfield Stadium, Ireland faced Wales at the Millennium Stadium on 21 March 2009 with history standing before them. A victory for Ireland would not only see them crowned 2009 Six Nations Champions and win the Triple Crown, but also claim the Grand Slam for the first time in 61 long years.

"Destiny is not a matter of chance; it is a matter of choice. It is not a thing to be waited for, it is a thing to be achieved."

William Jennings Bryan,
American Lawyer, Orator and Politician

It is in your moments of decision that your destiny is shaped and destiny awaited 15 players wearing green shirts. It was a battle from the start with the home side desperately seeking to stop O'Connell and his teammates from emulating *The Boys of 1948*, Ireland's only Grand Slam win at the time. And the Welsh Dragons almost did it but POC's knack at being able to win the ball at Welsh line-outs, like Oliver Twist picking the pockets of Gentlemen on the streets of Victorian London, proved to be the foundation stone upon which Ireland built their 17-15 win.

Paul featured in all of Ireland's November 2009 Tests at Croke Park which saw them beat Fiji 41-6, defeat South Africa 15-10 and draw 20-20 with Australia. Ireland were now a moving force in world rugby, a team to be feared with an immovable object at the heart of their engine room in the shape of Paul O'Connell. At times Paul looked like he could start a row in an empty house, but false impressions are too easy to assume.

The *Green Monster* is a popular nickname for the 37-foot-2-inch-high (11.33m) left field wall at Fenway Park, the home of the Major League Baseball team, the Boston Red Sox. The wall stands 310 feet (94 m) from the home plate and is a popular target for right-handed hitters. The wall was part of the original ballpark construction in 1912 along Fenway's north side facing Lansdowne Street. When it was first built it was an all wood structure before being given a covering of concrete and tin in 1934. Then in 1976, it was encased in hard plastic. In its' early years it was simply known as "*The Wall.*" There must have been many times when opposing players stood before POC, creaking their necks to look upwards at this 6 feet, 6 inches tall giant of a man weighing almost 18 stone, and thinking to themselves that the Irish lock was a *Green Monster*, carved from Irish oak trees. The biggest grossing movie at the Box Offices in 1979, when Paul was just a baby, was *Apocalypse Now*. So many teams that played Ireland knew that when they saw Paul O'Connell standing in the tunnel, with his barrelled chest sticking out, legs like tree trunks, shoulders so wide that players behind him were standing in the shade, arms that could crush rocks and a neck as tough as that of a

Legends & Lions

Rhinoceros, they feared their own Apocalypse.

Nobody in any of the four home nations disagreed with Ian McGeechan, the 2009 coach of the British and Irish Lions, when on 21 April 2009, he named Paul his captain for the Lions' forthcoming tour to South Africa. In Paul, he had a Big Game Hunter to snare the Springboks in the three Test Matches they would play. When asked about being appointed captain of the 2009 Lions' squad, POC said: *"I looked at the squad last night and it will be a privilege to lead them. It's a great honour considering the captains that have gone before me, some of them legends of the game."*

"Leadership and learning are indispensable to each other."

John F. Kennedy,
President of the United States of America, 1961-63

Paul was always willing to learn never assuming that he knew all there was to know about the game. But, despite his dynamism, his natural protective but warrior like style of play, his ability to unify teammates in search of a common goal and his superb leadership qualities, Paul was not able to lead the Lions to a Test Series victory against South Africa. The Springboks won the first Test 26-21 at King's Park, Durban with Alun Wyn Jones (Wales) playing alongside O'Connell: South Africa beat the Lions 28-25 at Loftus Versfeld Stadium, Pretoria in the second Test meaning they won the Test Series. In Pretoria, Ian McGeechan gave Paul a new second row partner, England's Simon Shaw. Thankfully for Paul and the Lions, including his Munster teammates (Keith Earls, Jerry Flannery, John Hayes, Donncha O'Callaghan, Ronan O'Gara, Tomas O'Leary, Alan Quinlan and David Wallace), the Lions beat the Springboks in the third Test to avoid the first whitewash by South Africa over a touring Lions party in 118 years. Hindsight is wonderful and it remains a mystery why McGeechan, a Master Tactician, did not partner O'Callaghan with O'Connell in the Tests. They were a tried and trusted pairing for Munster and Ireland and both played on the Lions' tour to New Zealand four years earlier. O'Callaghan came off the bench in the first Test defeat, his only Test appearance on the 2009 tour.

In 2010 and 2011, Paul suffered a few niggling injuries but none were serious enough to keep him out of action for too long. POC was a member of Ireland's squad at the 2011 Rugby World Cup where they reached the quarter-finals of the competition in New Zealand losing 22-10 to Wales at Regional Stadium, Wellington. In the absence of Brian O'Driscoll, Paul captained Ireland during the 2012 Six Nations Championship. Paul hurt his back in 2012 which forced him to miss the start of the 2012-13 season, but made his Munster comeback in October 2012. It proved to be a false dawn in terms of his return to fitness as he had to undergo surgery to his back which ruled him out of action until April 2013, missing all five of 2013 Ireland's Six Nations Championship matches. Following another comeback for Munster, he was selected for his third British and Irish Lions Tour, this time to Australia. In the absence of an injured Sam Warburton (Wales) he captained the Lions in their opening tour fixture against the Barbarians on 1 June 2013, scoring a try in the 59–8 victory. POC started in the Lions' first Test on 22 June 2013, a 23-21 win against the Wallabies, but after he fractured his arm in the game that spelt the end of his tour down under. Always the fighter, instead of flying home, which a lot of players would have done, Paul stayed in Australia and took on a coaching role for the Lions' head coach, Warren Gatland. The Lions won the Test Series 2-1 to become *Wizards of Oz*.

The following two years were like a rollercoaster of ups and downs for Paul. The downs were further injuries but in between them there were the highs. On 27 January 2014, he was named in Ireland's 34-man squad for the 2014 Six Nations Championship and captained them to the title. However, he did miss the opening game of the tournament against Scotland with a chest infection. He was Ireland's captain for their 2014 Tour of Argentina and on 22 November 2014, he received the Man of the Match award in Ireland's 26-23 win versus Australia in Dublin. During the 2015 Six Nations Championship he won his 100th cap for Ireland in a 23-16 loss to Wales on 14 March 2015 at the Millennium Stadium, meaning Ireland could not win the Grand Slam. However, under his leadership they were crowned back-to-back Champions for the first time since winning the Five Nations Championship in 1948 and 1949. And to top it off, Paul was named the Player of the Championship, not bad for someone who had been written off by some sports journalists less than a year earlier. Maybe those old bones of his were not that rickety after all. In May 2015, he won the Irish Rugby Union Players' Association Player of the Year award, but the following month it was announced that O'Connell had been granted an early release from his contract with Munster and the IRFU. His contract with the IRFU was scheduled to expire in June 2016, but it was brought forward meaning that the curtain would be closed on his international career after the 2015 Rugby World Cup finals hosted by England.

He just did not know when to give up even though his tired and aching body was sending him reminders. On 16 June 2015, he left this beloved Munster and signed for Toulon (France) on a two-year contract. It was almost like an old Grizzly Bear plodding along and taking one last swipe of his giant paw before going into hibernation for the final time. Paul's mantra throughout his career was to never give up, never willingly accept defeat and always show courage and leadership to those around him even when adversity was on the horizon. If POC got knocked down six times, he would get up seven. What drove him was that no matter how hard the past had been, you can always begin again. Winston Churchill once famously said: "*If you're going through Hell, keep going.*" Paul dragged his body through Hell for Munster, Ireland and the Lions. In the novel, *The Wonderful Wizard of Oz*, written by L. Frank Baum and first published in 1900, the Scarecrow tells Dorothy that he wants a brain, the Tin Woodman wanted a heart and the Lion wanted courage. Very few players were as intelligent as Paul at set plays; his heart belonged to Munster and Ireland and there were not many players as courageous as Paul on the battlefield of international rugby union.

O'Connell won the 2015 Guinness Rugby Writers Player of the Year award. On 29 August 2015, Paul captained Ireland for the last time which also marked his last ever game before home fans, a 19-10 loss to Wales at the Aviva Stadium. It was an emotional day for Paul, and for his family in attendance, with a rousing and upbeat rendition of *The Soldier's Song* followed by the playing of *Ireland's Call*. Ireland had called Paul O'Connell for one final game in the Irish capital and everyone inside the stadium paid tribute to one of the sport's biggest Icons.

Dorothy took her dog, *Toto*, the Scarecrow, the Tin Woodman and the Lion to the Emerald City by following the Yellow Brick Road. Paul O'Connell said farewell to Ireland's Emerald City having led his teammates along a path to unprecedented glory during his 13 years wearing a green jersey.

At the 2015 Rugby World Cup, he started the opening Pool D game against Canada which Ireland won 50-7, was a substitute in their 44-10 victory over Romania, played in the 16-9 win against Italy and helped Ireland defeat France 24-9. Ireland topped Pool D and faced Argentina in the quarter-finals, but POC played no further part for Ireland when he had to be replaced at half-time in the France game having suffered a hamstring injury. He needed surgery meaning he had played his 108th and last ever game for Ireland (2002-15). Paul also won 7 caps for the British and Irish Lions. Argentina beat Ireland 43-20 to end their 2015 Rugby World Cup ambitions.

On 9 February 2016, Paul O'Connell announced that he had to retire from all professional rugby based on medical advice, following the injury he suffered during the 2015 Rugby World Cup. The 36-year old never played for Toulon and accepted an offer from Munster in an advisory role with the club's Academy.

In total he won the Six Nations Championship three times, while collecting two European Cups and three United Rugby Championships with Munster. He scored 8 tries for Ireland, captained his country 28 times and led the British and Irish Lions in 3 Tests. But more importantly, he earned the respect of the entire rugby fraternity.

JOHN WHITE

"It is with deep regret that I have decided to retire from professional rugby following medical advice. I would like to take this opportunity to thank all at Rugby Club Toulonnais for their understanding and support over the past few months. Since sustaining the injury at the World Cup I have been fully focused on returning to fitness and starting an exciting new chapter for both myself and my family in Toulon. Unfortunately this will no longer be possible.

I have been blessed to be a professional rugby player for over 14 years and to be part of Munster and Ireland teams that have experienced success. I have played with some of the best players to ever line out in the red of Munster and the green of Ireland and have had the privilege of captaining my country. I would like to thank those at Young Munster RFC, Munster Rugby, the IRFU and Lions Rugby who have supported me over the course of my playing career. Special thanks must go to my wife Emily for her unwavering support through the good and the bad and to my parents Michael and Shelagh. Lastly I would like to thank everyone who has supported the teams I have been a part of. The support you have shown me is humbling and an immense source of pride for both myself and my family."

Paul O'Connell

And the tributes to Paul flooded in:

"He is probably the best I have ever played against."

Victor Matfield

"Tough old goat Paul O'Connell. Wonderful player, outstanding man. Rugby hasn't seen the last of him."

Will Greenwood

"For those that followed, Paul O'Connell raised the bar for second rows."

Legends & Lions

Fabien Pelous

"Sad to see Paul retire. But what a Legend on and off the field."

Gethin Jenkins

"Sensational career in Red and Green. Simply irreplaceable."

Brian O'Driscoll

"The jersey he has left behind is going to be incredibly difficult to fill."

Joe Schmidt

"Just because we come from a small island doesn't mean we can't beat anybody. That's Paul's Legacy."

Rory Best

Like Thor, Paul O'Connell will forever be remembered as a Legend, a player famous for protecting his players, a player who possessed the ability to cause a storm on the pitch in an instant, a player of immense physical attributes who harnessed his power and strength to send claps of thunder down the line-out. Norse Mythology praised Thor but the Irish fans idolised their Thor, and his name was Paul Jeremiah O'Connell.

Did You Know That?

On the 8 November 2014, Paul O'Connell captained Ireland in their Test Match versus South Africa at the Aviva Stadium. Sean Cronin started the match as hooker and in the 73rd minute of play, Dave Kilcoyne came on as a replacement for Mike Ross. Ireland won the game 29-15. It was the first and only time that three past pupils of Ardscoil Ris won an international cap for Ireland in the same game. The school, all of Munster

JOHN WHITE

and the entire population of Ireland owe a great deal of thanks to Paul Jeremiah O'Connell.

PETER O'MAHONY
Ireland's Firestarter

P ETER JAMES O'MAHONY was born on 17 September 1989, in Cork. He went to Presentation Brothers College, a fee-paying Roman Catholic school for boys in Cork, ranked among the best educational establishments in Ireland. Aged 18, Peter was accepted into the Munster Academy after starring for his School's XV side where their Number 8 was regarded as a player with prodigious talent, a future Ireland international. The Academy was formed in 2004 "to prepare young players for life in and beyond professional rugby." The initial crop of 22 players included Keith Earls, Billy Holland, Duncan Williams, Donnacha Ryan and Tomás O'Leary, the latter was the inaugural winner of the Academy Player of the Year award. In 2009, Peter captained the Ireland Under-20 team in the 2009 Six Nations Under-20's Championship with Ireland finishing runners-up to France. Both teams won four of their five games, Ireland beat France 9-6 at Dubarry Park, Athlone but were beaten 35-20 by Scotland at McDiarmid Park, Perth, Scotland. France were crowned Champions on points scored difference, +97 to Ireland's minus 2. Later that same year he captained the Ireland Under-20's at the 2009 **IRB** Junior Rugby World Cup where they finished in eighth place in Japan. In season 2009-10, he won the All-Ireland Cup with Cork Constitution and was named Man of the Match in the final, a 15-11 victory over Garryowen and helped his team to glory in the 2009-10 All-Ireland League.

Peter made his debut (as a replacement) for Munster in a 15-10 defeat to Ulster at Ravenhill in the United League on 2 January 2010. In season 2009-10, he captained Munster A to the final of the inaugural British and Irish Cup, losing 23-14 to the Cornish Pirates at the Recreation Ground, Camborne, Cornwall. He played like a one man demolition team of the opposition which earned him a full development contract with Munster for season 2010-11. In November 2010, still aged only 21, he was not selected for any of Ireland's November Test Matches. The Ireland squad included some of his Cork Constitution and Munster teammates - Denis Leamy, Donncha O'Callaghan and Ronan O'Gara - plus John Hayes (Bruff/Munster) and Peter Stringer (Shannon/Munster). But, as the saying goes, one man's absence is another man's opportunity and O'Mahony was not one for missing an opportunity. On 16 November 2010, Munster welcomed a touring Australia side to Thomond Park. Munster were without 17 Irish internationals although Keith Earls was made available for the contest. Australia did not field their first choice starting XV for the encounter which on paper looked like a straight forward victory for the Wallabies whose second string comprised 11 Test players. However, rugby isn't played on paper as Munster famously proved in 1978 when they defeated New Zealand 12-0 at Thomond Park on 31 October 1978.

Peter O'Mahony was handed his first start for Munster in the game and played a pivotal role in his side's under-strength team which beat the visitors 15-6, **all** 15 points scored by the Irish province's fly-half Paul Warwick, three penalties and two drop goals. It was **Munster's** fourth straight victory against touring Australia teams. The Australian players must have felt like the Wallaby on the crest of their badge confronted by an Irish version of a *Tasmanian Devil,* a famous carnivorous marsupial from Tasmania, an island state of Australia. The animal is coyote/hyena-like in its' features, instantly recognisable by its' muscular and stocky build, a very loud and quite off-putting screech, possesses a keen sense of smell and a ferocity, almost savagery, when feeding. The wild animal's distinctively large head and neck allows it to generate among the strongest bites per unit body mass of any extant predatory land mammal. It hunts prey and scavenges on carrion which begins to decay as soon as an animal dies. Here before their eyes the Australian players were faced by O'Mahony who was ready to spill blood in a red shirt to rip them apart. Peter was like a *Dog of War* and held nothing back forcing turnovers and flattening anything in a gold jersey that stood in his path like a wrecking ball demolishing a condemned tower block of flats. It was as though every part of the pitch he marauded was strewn with the carrion of dead bodies or to quote an extract of literature from Act 3, Scene 1 of William Shakespeare's play *Julius Caesar*:

> *"Cry 'Havoc,' and let slip the dogs of war;*
> *That this foul deed shall smell above the earth*
> *With carrion men, groaning for burial."*

Peter was given the honour of captaining Munster in their opening Pro12 game during season 2011-12. His Munster international teammates, including his captain Paul O'Connell, were preparing for the 2011 **Rugby World Cup** hosted by New Zealand. The stand-in captain helped his side to a 20-12 win versus Newport Gwent Dragons at Musgrave Park, Cork on 3 September 2011. On 12 November 2011, he captained Munster in his debut Heineken Cup game, winning the Man of the Match award in his team's 22-20 victory over Northampton Saints at Thomond Park. A week later he scored his maiden try for Munster in their 27-24 defeat of Castres at Stade Ernest-Wallon, Toulouse, France in the Heineken Cup. In season 2011-12, he won the Munster Young Player of the Year award after helping the team to a third place finish in the Pro12 table and the quarter-finals of the Heineken Cup.

Peter wore his heart on his sleeve for Munster but when he played for Ireland, his entire body was on display. When the Selection Committee at the IRFU chose the Ireland squad for the 2012 Six Nations Championship, it was impossible for them to overlook **POM** after witnessing his performances for his province, when time and time again he was a disturbing nuisance to the opposition who were incapable of containing his destructive ability of regularly being able to force the ball to be turned over. On 25 February 2012, the boy from Presentation Brothers College was given his international bow by Ireland coach Declan Kidney, coming on in the 58th minute for Sean O'Brien versus Italy. Ireland ran out 42-10 victors at the Aviva Stadium. He was 22 years old when he pulled on the Ireland jersey to win his first cap, a game of marked contrast for another player wearing green that afternoon as Ronan O'Gara came off the bench in the 69th minute to replace Gordon D'Arcy, to overtake Brian O'Driscoll as the most-capped Irish player with 118 caps. On 10 March 2012, he made his first start in a green jersey wearing the No.7 when

Legends & Lions

Ireland beat Scotland 32-14 in Dublin in the Six Nations Championship, standing in for an injured Sean O'Brien.

From the moment he represented his country it was evident to all those watching that he was a Legend in Genesis, a player who would become one of the greatest Irish players of all-time. In the snooker world Alex Higgins earned the nickname of *"The Hurricane"* and Jimmy White was known as *"The Whirlwind."* In the world of international rugby union the sport had a new meteorological phenomenon because POM dominated opponents blowing them away as if they were smoke in a Tornado.

In the year of Peter's birth, 1989, the most devastating Tornado in history occurred on 26 April 1989, in the Manikganj District of central Bangladesh, resulting in the loss of almost 1,300 inhabitants. Four years later the USA searched in vain for *Weapons of Mass Destruction* in the war against Iraq. Unbeknown to the US Military's specialist spy network, a young boy was about to start school in Cork, who went on to become a *Weapon of Mass Destruction* at rugby stadiums all over the world. He wasn't on America's radar until 8 June 2013, when Ireland played the USA on their Tour of Canada and the United States of America. POM, aged 23, captained Ireland when they beat the USA 15-12 at BBVA Compass Stadium, Houston, Texas. Ian Madigan scored all of Ireland's points in the game, five from seven penalty attempts, in the city which has a Space Science Museum in homage to the country's National Aeronautics and Space Administration (NASA). In POM, Ireland had found their very own Rocket Man, a player who would go on to reach limits only the sky above could match.

JOHN WHITE

Peter O'Mahony was fearless, reaching deep down into a sea of bodies during a ruck to win the ball, putting his head where most players dared not even to place their boot. At 6 foot, 3 inches and weighing 16 stones he is a brute force who has the knack of sniffing out a ball like a Truffle Hog, a natural forager. When the scrum collapsed he was the first person rummaging for the ball, staying on his feet and bending over to reach deep down among a mass of bodies strewn on top of each other in search of the player who had the prize he was seeking, the ball. It was if his arms were the gripping claw inside a glass box full of stuffed toys which you can find in most Shopping Malls. The claw became active whenever the requisite fee was inserted in the machine, setting it in motion, moving it forward, then changing the direction of it to move left or right before the operator hit the snatch button meaning the open claw descended among the toys and closed. More times than enough the claw returned to its home location empty leaving the operator frustrated and out of pocket. If you owned a Shopping Mall with one of these machines in it, you would hastily arrange for an "*Out of Order*" sign to be stuck on the glass if Peter O'Mahony entered the building. The Ireland star would have emptied its' bed of toys and handed them out to any child who stood at the side of one of the four glass panels watching in awe this "*really big man*" pick up toy after toy as if they were just sitting on a shelf in a toy store before him. You can just envisage the owner of a "*Dunking for Apples*" stall at a Fairground in Cork banning a young O'Mahony from emptying his barrel of apples.

And, it came as no surprise to Irish sportswriters when he scooped up the Irish Rugby Union Players'

Legends & Lions

Association Young Player of the Year award for the 2011–12 season. He played in all three of Ireland's Tests versus the All Blacks when they toured New Zealand in June 2012, losing all three including a humiliating record defeat when they were beaten 60-0 at Waikato Stadium, Hamilton on 23 June 2012. By the end of the Tour he had played in all three back-row positions in his seven appearances for his country, which included four games in the 2012 Six Nations Championship. In November 2012, he won cap numbers eight and nine when Ireland lost 16-12 to South Africa in Dublin and a 46-22 defeat of Argentina in the Irish capital.

POM played in all five of Ireland's games in the 2013 Six Nations Championship, finishing in fifth place, and when Rory Best was included in the British and Irish Lions squad to tour Australia in June 2013, Peter was appointed captain of Ireland for their Tour of Canada and the USA. On 9 November 2013, Peter scored his first international try for Ireland when they beat Samoa 40-9 in Dublin. He was a catalyst for Ireland during the 2014 Six Nations Championship helping them to win the title which they then retained the following year. When the 31-man Ireland squad was named for the 2015 Rugby World Cup in England, his name stood out like a beacon in the list. However, after injuring his knee in a Pool D match versus France, he was ruled out of the rest of the tournament.

Over the next two seasons he recovered to full fitness and in 2018, he was a member of the Ireland team that won the 2018 Six Nations Championship, their fourteenth title, a Triple Crown for an eleventh time and the Mount Everest of the tournament, the Grand Slam. Ireland defeated England 24-15 at Twickenham

Stadium on Matchday 5 to seal the Grand Slam and straight after he was given his winners' medal, the kind hearted Cork man gave it to a young female Irish fan with Down Syndrome.

POM's regular Man of the Match displays for his club, province and country did not go under the radar of the coach of the 2017 British and Irish Lions, Warren Gatland, and his assembled team of trusted coaches, including his defensive coach, Andy Farrell, who was an assistant to the Ireland coach, Joe Schmidt, at the time. All of these men were charged with the responsibility of selecting the best players the home four nations had to offer to take on the might of New Zealand. The All Blacks were the reigning Rugby World Cup holders having successfully defended the Webb Ellis Cup they won in 2011 (defeating France 8-7 on home soil) by defeating Australia 34-17 at Twickenham Stadium in the 2015 final. In April 2017, Gatland, selected POM in his 41-man squad for their Tour of New Zealand. On 7 June 2017, Peter wore the famous Lions shirt for a first time coming off the bench in a 22-16 win over the **Blues** (also known as the Auckland Blues) at Eden Park, Auckland. Three days later he was in the starting line-up that defeated Crusaders 12-3 at Rugby League Park, Christchurch. Peter's dream of captaining the famous touring side came true on 17 June 2017 at Rotorua International Stadium, Rotorua when he was asked to lead the team. POM led the Lions to a record 32-10 win over the **Māori** All Blacks. A week later, although Sam Warburton (Wales) was the nominated Lions' captain, Peter looked to be Gatland's new first choice captain when he led the team out at Eden Park for the first of three Test Matches versus the All Blacks. New Zealand won 30-15 with O'Mahony replaced in the 53rd minute by Warburton and little did he know it at the time, but it was the first and last Test cap he won for the British and Irish Lions. He was controversially dropped from the squad after the defeat and therefore, did not even get a place on the bench for the second (the Lions won 24-21) or third Tests (drew 15-15). When quizzed about his decision to drop the Munster man, Gatland, a former coach of Ireland from 1998-2001, simply said: "*There has to be someone to point the finger at in defeat.*" A similar fate befell Brian O'Driscoll who Gatland dropped from the squad before the Lions' third Test match in Australia four years earlier.

"Real leadership is leaders recognising that they serve the people that they lead."

Pete Hoekstra,
Dutch-American politician

Most ordinary players would have thrown the toys out of the pram had they been treated the way O'Mahony was. However, POM was a galaxy away from being an ordinary player and decided to put what happened to him in New Zealand firmly behind him and move on to the next step in his rise to rugby stardom. New Zealand may be feted across the globe as a leading exporter of lamb, but Cork's Peter O'Mahony would soon play a major part in the slaughter of what New Zealand had the best to offer, not on the dinner plate, but on the field of play.

When Ireland toured Australia in June 2018, POM was selected as team captain in the absence of Rory Best. Ireland played three Tests against the Wallabies and when they lost the first Test 18-9 at Lang Park, Brisbane on 9 June 2018, it brought to an end Ireland's 12 match winning run dating back to March 2017. First Blood to the Wallabies. But O'Mahony led Ireland to a historic 2-1 Test Series victory after they defeated the Wallabies 26-21 at AAMI Park, Melbourne a week later and then won 20-16 at Sydney Football Stadium, Sydney on 23 June 2018. It was the first time since 1979 that Ireland claimed a Test Series success over Australia, which was so much more sweeter for their captain who won his 50th cap in the third Test.

O'Mahony was starting to help shape a new rugby union history for Ireland and was outstanding in the 2018 Autumn Tests. Ireland beat Argentina 28-17 at the Aviva Stadium on 10 November 2018 and then claimed a first ever home win over the All Blacks in Dublin, with POM being named Man of the Match in Ireland's 16-9 victory. In 2019, he attended his second Rugby World Cup and played in all four of Ireland's Pool A matches: their opening 27–3 win against Scotland, a shock 19–12 loss to the host nation, Japan, the 35–0 defeat of Russia and a 47-5 victory over Samoa. Alas, New Zealand sent Ireland home after beating them 46-14 in the quarter-finals.

Peter's fiery temper went a few degrees too high in Ireland's first game of the 2021 Six Nations Championship when he was sent off in the 14th minute of play versus Wales at the Millennium Stadium on 7 February 2021. Wales won the encounter 21-16. It was the first red card given to an Ireland player in a Five/Six Nations Championship match since Willie Duggan's dismissal versus Wales at Cardiff Arms Park in the first game of the 1977 Five Nations Championship (Ireland lost 25-9). The red mist cost POM a ban until 14 March

Legends & Lions

2021.

"The ultimate measure of a man is not where he stands in moments of comfort, but where he stands at times of challenge and controversy."

Martin Luther King Jr.

O'Mahony was selected in the squad for Ireland's 2022 Tour of New Zealand and played in all three Tests. They lost the first Test 42-19 to the All Blacks at Eden Park, Auckland; won the second Test 23-12 at Forsyth Barr Stadium, Dunedin and claimed a historic 2-1 Test Series victory over New Zealand with a 32-22 victory at Sky Stadium, Wellington. It was the first time Ireland had won a Test Series in New Zealand. POM had lived up to Martin Luther King Jr's immortal words. But much more importantly in his psychic, he laid the embarrassment of the Lions' 2017 Tour to New Zealand firmly to rest, a bad dream as it where, a minor bump on the path to glory, because he was the man in charge of Ireland's abattoir, a slaughterhouse of a team, that cut the All Blacks into pieces that were barely unrecognisable.

When Ireland set-up for a scrum the **IRB** should consider asking **POM** to place a sign around his neck saying "*Beware of the Dog.*" And, as an extra precautionary health warning, the following small print could be added: "*Ireland's No.8 does not bite, but he has the striking prowess of a Sidewinder snake.*" This breed of snake is the fastest in the world thanks to its' ability to move in a different, quite unique way to other snakes. Rather than adopting the standard wavy movement, a Sidewinder carves indents into the sand to use the ridges this creates to push against, resulting in explosive power. The Sidewinder, like O'Mahony on the field of play, is instantly recognisable, very easily identified by the unique horns on the top of their head which it uses to prevent anything from getting into their eyes whilst it is submerged in the sand waiting patiently to pounce on their targeted prey.

In 2023, Peter O'Mahony won a second Grand Slam title with Ireland and helped to establish his country as the No.1 ranked side in the world. Totally unheard of before in the upper echelons of rugby union in the Northern Hemisphere, let alone the world. World Rankings are based on the performance of each nation, with their most recent results and wins in significant Test Matches being more heavily weighted to help reflect the current competitive state of a country. The men's ranking system was introduced in September 2003, the month before the fifth edition of the Rugby World Cup, hosted by Australia. The IRB, the governing body of the Rugby World Cup, instigated the inaugural IRB Rugby World Cup 1987, which was won by New Zealand on home soil. The first official rankings were published on 8 September 2003, when they were called the "*IRB Rankings*," and when England defeated Australia in the 2003 Rugby World Cup final, they were the No.1 ranked team in the world.

At the end of the 2023 Six Nations Championship, Peter had made 77 appearances for Ireland, 38 of them in the tournament and 8 in the Rugby World Cup as well as winning a solitary British and Irish Lions cap. He rounded his 2022-23 season off by winning the United Rugby Championship with Munster, the pvince's fourth success in the competition (2003, 2009 & 2011), defeating South Africa's Stormers 19-14 in the final at DHL Stadium, Cape Town, South Africa.

Ireland kicked-off their 2023 Rugby World Cup

campaign against Romania in Bordeaux, France on 9 September 2023. Ireland won the Pool B game very comfortably at Noveau Stade de Bordeaux, 82-8, with POM being named Man of the Match. Ireland then defeated Tonga 59-16 a week later at Stade de la Beaujoire, Nantes despite the Munster No.8 being sin binned in added on time at the end of the first half. Peter won his 100th international Test cap on 23 September 2023, when Ireland beat South Africa, the reigning Rugby World Cup holders, 13-8 at Stade de France having played 99 times for Ireland and once for the British and Irish Lions.

When Ireland defeated Scotland 36-14 in their final Pool B match at the 2023 Rugby World Cup, the match marked POM's 100th international cap. Peter also played in Ireland's 28-24 loss to New Zealand at Stade de France in the quarter-finals of the tournament.

The word *Pyrokinesis* (Greek language: pyr=fire, kinesis=movement) was popularised by Stephen King, an American horror novelist, in his 1980 novel called *Firestarter*. The book was about a young boy's ability to create and control fire with the mind. Some Irish fans would not disagree with the claim that Peter had Pyrokinesis, the purported Psychic ability which allows a person to create and control fire solely with the mind because he was like a *Man on Fire* in a green jersey.

Peter O'Mahony could set fire to the rain and to use the words from 'Firestarter', a song by The Prodigy, Peter O'Mahony's fiery displays makes him Ireland's Firestarter.

"I'm the trouble starter, punkin' instigator
I'm the fear addicted, a danger illustrated

JOHN WHITE

I'm a firestarter, twisted firestarter

I'm the bitch you hated, filth infatuated, yeah
I'm the pain you tasted, fell intoxicated
I'm a firestarter, twisted firestarter

I'm the self-inflicted, mind detonator, yeah
I'm the one infected, twisted animator
I'm a firestarter, twisted Firestarter"

Did You Know That?

Peter O'Mahony was the first Munster player since Paul O'Connell in 2013 to captain a British and Irish Lions team. He became the 11th Irishman to captain a British & Irish Lions Test team and the first Cork Constitution player to do so since Tom Kiernan in 1968 on the Lions' tour of South Africa.

THE BIG IRELAND RUGBY QUIZ

1. Ireland won the Triple Crown and Five Nations Championship in 1985, but can you name the Irish boxer who won the WBA World Featherweight boxing title in the same year, 8 June 1985, when he defeated the reigning World Champion, Panama's Eusebio Pedroza, at Loftus Road, London, the home of Queens Park Rangers Football Club?

2. Going into the 2023 six Nations Championship, Ireland were ranked the No.1 team in the world. Name any 3 of the 5 nations ranked No.2 to No.6.

3. On 5 November 2016, Ireland recorded their first ever victory over New Zealand in 28 attempts since 1905, a 40-29 win. In which city in the United States of America was the game played?

4. Despite the Ireland captain's famous three B's remark "Boot, Bollock and Bite" to his players before Ireland beat Wales 6-3 at Ravenhill, Belfast to win the Grand Slam in 1948, a former teammate, wing forward James McCarthy, described his captain as: "A quiet sort of man." Name this legendary Irish captain.

5. On 17 October 1959, an England and Wales XV beat an Ireland and Scotland XV at Twickenham Stadium, London. The game was

played to celebrate a 50th anniversary but can you name the anniversary the match was played for?

6. Ireland won the wooden spoon in the Five Nations Championship, coached by Brian Ashton. Dublin's Ken Doherty beat Stephen Hendry (Scotland) 18-12 in the final of the World Professional Snooker Championship. U2 had their third UK No.1 hit with "*Discotheque*." *Titanic* was one of the year's blockbuster movies. Malcolm O'Kelly made his international debut for Ireland. Guess the Year.

7. This Irish fly-half also played Association Football for Shamrock Rovers (1973-75) and Limerick United (1971-82) in the Football of Association's (FAI) League of Ireland. In season 1974-75, he scored six goals for the Rovers and in season 1981-82, he played for Limerick United in the UEFA Cup. He won an FAI Cup winners' medal playing for Limerick United in the 1982 final when they beat Bohemians 1-0 at Dalymount Park, Dublin. Can you name him?

8. During the 2020 Six Nations Championship, Johnny Sexton captained Ireland in a home international match for the first time. Who were the opposition?

9. Can you name the Belfast-born flanker whose career came to an end following the injuries he sustained when an IRA Bomb exploded on 25 April 1987 and who went on to work as a Sports Reporter for Ulster Television?

10. Six Ireland players were named in the World Rugby Men's 15s Dream Team of the Year for 2022. However, can you name any two the six?

11. On 13 April 2023, President Joe Biden was in the Windsor Pub, Dundalk, on the first day of his three day visit to Ireland. Biden was paying tribute to Rob Kearney who won 95 caps, scoring 82 points for Ireland from 2007-19, and who is a distant fifth cousin of the US President. By what term did President Biden mistakenly refer to the All Blacks?

12. Ireland has never played host to a Rugby World Cup but it has played host to three Pool games in the competition as well as a quarter-final and semi-final match. In what year did this Rugby World Cup take place?

13. Since their first meeting on 28 January 1882, Ireland and Wales have played each other more than 130 times with both nations using different stadiums to host the games. Can you name any four of the seven grounds Ireland used?

14. In their opening match of the 1973 Five Nations Championship Ireland beat this nation 18-9, the famous game when the Irish fans cheered the opposing players out on to the pitch at Lansdowne Road, Dublin. Who were Ireland's opponents?

15. Can you name any one of Ireland's opponents for their three warm-up games prior to the 2013 Rugby World Cup?

Legends & Lions

16. What is Ireland's lowest ever ranking in the International Rugby Board's World Rankings system?

17. Coached by Andy Farrell, and captained by Johnny Sexton, Ireland could only manage three victories in the 2020 Six Nations Championship, all at home. Name any two of the sides they defeated.

18. On how many occasions has Ireland met and defeated Russia in an international match?

19. In the 2021 Six Nations Championship Ireland met a nation for the 100th time in a Test Match. Name them.

20. Name the Ireland Legend who became the first substitute in a Test Match when he came on for Barry John during the British and Irish Lions Tour of South Africa in 1968.

21. *"He encourages, criticises, and demands more from everyone on every play. He's hard on people but it makes us so much better. At the end of training, he was smashing into guys, trying to counter-ruck in a non-contact session. It is so encouraging when our out-half is on the edge like that. Everyone can follow."* Who was Paul O'Connell describing in his autobiography entitled "The Battle"?

22. Four players made their debut for Ireland versus Italy in the 2020 Six Nations Championship. Name one of the quartet.

23. In January 2022, Rugby Dome published who they believe to be the five best blindside or open-side flankers to play for Ireland. Can you

identify any two of the Famous Five?

24. In 1888, the British & Irish Lions began their Touring tradition when a party of 22 players from England, Ireland, Scotland and Wales, captained by Robert Lionel "*Bob*" Seddon (England). Since Robert Seddon, only 12 Irish players have been afforded the unique honour of captaining a British & Irish Lions touring side. Can you name any one of the six Irish Legends who were given this honour from 1888-1959?

25. During the 1950's Ireland appointed seven new captains of the national team but can you name two of them?

26. On 2 March 1985, Ireland played France at Lansdowne Road in the Five Nations Championship, a match that ended 15-15 which prevented Ireland from claiming a feat that would have won the country a second Grand Slam following their first in 1948. The TV cameras spanned the crowd and spotted a banner which an Irish fan had made for the game. The banner read: "*Our Willie's bigger than your Condom!*" Name the Irish Willie.

27. Name any one of the two countries who refused to play against Ireland in 1972 in the Five Nations Championship as a result of escalating political tensions in the wake of "*Bloody Sunday*."

28. Ireland got their 2022 Six Nations Championship campaign off to the best possible start, defeating the reigning Champions, and Triple Crown holders, 29-7 at the Aviva Stadium,

Legends & Lions

Dublin. Who did they beat?

29. In 2015, the British and Irish Lions toured New Zealand, playing 11 games which included three Test matches against the All Blacks. The first Test was played on 25 June 2015, at Lancaster Park, Christchurch and will forever be remembered for one of the ugliest incidents that has ever happened in a game of international rugby. Name the Ireland player who was subjected to a vicious tackle which injured him and ruled him out of playing any further part on the tour.

30. When Ireland defeated the All Blacks for the first time, a 40-29 win on 5 November 2016, the game was played in Chicago, United States of America. But, can you name the stadium the match was played in and the name of the American Football team play their home games in?

31. *"I watched a game of beach volleyball between the Lions and four local girls, two of whom had represented Australia at the London Olympics. With Paulie involved, it became ridiculously competitive. He was up front with Geoff Parling and nearly killed one of the poor girls with a spike."* Name the Ireland international who was recalling the time during the British and Irish Lions 2013 tour of Australia when he went to the beach with Paul O'Connell and England lock, Geoff Parling.

32. Ireland's head coach Andy Farrell was on the list of nominees for the 2022 World Rugby Coach of the year but missed out on the award to the New Zealand Black Ferns' World Cup-winning head coach. Who did Farrell lose out to?

33. In 1982, the Irish Rugby Football Union agreed a contract with an Irish sports manufacturing company to make the Ireland kit. The deal lasted until 1985, but can you name the company?

34. Following his retirement after the 1954 Five Nations Championship this former Ireland captain concentrated on his second love in sport and participated in the Irish Senior Cup with his local Club. But, can you name the player or the sport?

35. Who became the first Irish player to be shown a red card in a Six Nations Championship match when he was given his marching orders against Wales in the 2021 tournament?

36. Since the inaugural Rugby World Cup in 1987, only 11 countries will have contested every tournament including the 2023 Rugby World Cup. Apart from Ireland, can you identify any 7 of the remaining 10 nations?

37. On 21 October 1978, he famously coached Munster to a historic victory over a touring New Zealand side at Thomond Park, Limerick. It was the first time any Irish side, including the international team, had defeated the all-conquering All Blacks. He played for Ireland against the All Blacks in 1963 and 1973 and was capped 54 times by Ireland. But, who is he?

38. What has been incorporated into the emblem on every Ireland shirt since the side played their first Test Match against England in 1875?

Legends & Lions

39. In what year was Lansdowne Road, Dublin demolished to make way for the Aviva Stadium?

40. He played for North of Ireland Football Club, Howe of Fife (Scotland), Ballymena and Ulster, winning 10 caps for Ireland from 1991-92. He only scored one try for Ireland but it almost put Ireland into the semi-finals of the Rugby World Cup. On 20 October 1991, Ireland faced Australia at Lansdowne Road, Dublin in the quarter-finals of the 1991 Rugby World Cup. With only a few minutes remaining, he scored a try, converted by Ralph Keyes, which gave Ireland the lead, 18-12. But, Michael Lynagh broke the hearts of the 54,000 Irish fans inside the stadium when he scored a try down the other end and made the conversion to give the Wallabies a 19-18 victory. Name this Irish player.

41. Founded in 1879, the Irish Rugby Football Union is the third-oldest rugby union in the world after which other two rugby playing countries?

42. Re-arrange the Anagram to reveal the player's name – Jackboots Laced.

43. Who in 2008, became the first Ireland player to be inducted into the International Rugby Board Hall of Fame?

44. How many new caps did Ireland award in 2022 (January to December)?

45. *"Willie John McBride will always be synonymous with the great game of rugby and in particular with the British and Irish Lions. It's been a pleasure to have played*

alongside him, it's been a great pleasure to have known him. Without question, he's not only a fine rugby player, he's a great gentleman." Name the Welsh Legend who said this, a teammate of Willie on the 1971 (New Zealand) & 1974 (South Africa) British & Irish Lions Tours.

46. Since their first meeting on 20 March 1909, Ireland and France have played each other over 100 times with both nations using different stadiums to host the games. Name any two of the four grounds the French used to stage a home game against the Irish.

47. While playing rugby for Ireland (1978-87) this fly-half was a Geography and Physical Education teacher at Saint Andrews Secondary School, Booterstown, Dun Laoghaire, Ireland. In 1993, his biography was published and entitled: *The Good, the Bad and the Rugby - The Biography of ….. …..* Who is he?

48. In what year during the early 1970's did the Five Nations Championship end in a 5-way tie, the first and only time in the competition's history the Championship was shared by all of the nations that had participated?

49. Can you name the future captain of Ireland who was arrested in 1980 for stealing an Argentina flag from a Government Building in Buenos Aires, Argentina and was placed in jail?

50. Ireland, coached by Eddie O'Sullivan, finished in third place in the Six Nations Championship as France claimed the Grand Slam. South

LEGENDS & LIONS

Korea hosted the FIFA World Cup finals which were won by Brazil who beat Germany 2-0 in the final. Westlife enjoyed their tenth UK No.1 hit single with "*World of our Own*." Lennox Lewis retained his WBC World Heavyweight Boxing Championship title following an eighth round knockout win over Mike Tyson. *Ice Age* was a popular film for young movie goers. Paul O'Connell made his international debut for Ireland. Guess the Year.

51. A smallpox epidemic broke out in this country in March and April 1962, causing the postponement of Ireland's home Five Nations Championship game against this nation, moving it from March until 17 November 1962. Name the country.

52. Ireland's first ever game at a Rugby World Cup final was played on 25 May 1987 at Athletic Park, Wellington, New Zealand. It was the inaugural Rugby World Cup and was co-hosted by Australia and New Zealand. Wales won the encounter 13-6. The game was noteworthy for the national anthems. The Welsh team listened to a rendition of *Land of our Fathers* sung by the massed Welsh Choirs which was recorded at Cardiff Arms Park, Wales. When it came to the Irish national anthem the team lined-up to hear a recording of a song performed by James Last and his Orchestra from a concert held at Austin Stack Park, Tralee. Can you name the song played?

53. *"He was one of the finest players of his generation,*

JOHN WHITE

one of the finest players ever to represent Ireland and the British & Irish Lions and a man who epitomised the very ethos of the game and its values." Syd Millar speaking about a former teammate, after his teammate was inducted to the IRB Hall of Fame in May 2011. Name the *"Mike"* he was referring to.

54. Can you name the English sports equipment manufacturer who made the Ireland kit from 1991-93?

55. During the 1999 Five Nations Championship, Wales used an English ground to host their home matches as the Millennium Stadium, Cardiff was still being built. Ireland beat Wales 29-23 at their temporary home but where was the match played?

56. After finishing fourth in the 1954 Five Nations Championship, James McCarthy, who was the Ireland captain at the time, informed a senior official at the Irish Rugby Football Union that several of the team would no longer be standing for what?

57. On 24 August 2007, Ireland played a warm-up match for the 2007 Rugby World Cup finals in Northern Ireland, defeating Italy 23-20. At what stadium was the international played?

58. Ireland went into the 1950 Five Nations Championship as the holders having defended the crown they won in 1948 as Grand Slam Champions and in 1949, when they narrowly missed out on winning back-to-back Grand Slam titles.

Legends & Lions

However, the 1950 tournament was a disappointing campaign for Ireland. Can you name either their captain or the only side they defeated, winning just one of their four games, drawing one and tasting defeat in two?

59. Re-arrange the Anagram to reveal the player's name – Lions Arcade.

60. Name any three of the Ireland players who scored eight tries in their 59-16 win versus *The Sea Eagles*, Tonga's nickname, at the 2023 Rugby World Cup.

61. In season 1951-52, this side were on a Tour of Europe and on 8 December 1951, they were in the Irish capital, Dublin. It was the sixteenth game of their Tour, having won 14 and losing just one and it was the fourth occasion they had faced Ireland. They beat Ireland 17-5 at Lansdowne Road to maintain a 100% winning record versus Ireland but who are they?

62. In 1959, two players became the first players from University College Dublin to represent the British and Irish Lions (then known as the British Lions) during their 1959 Tour to Australia and New Zealand. Can you name the William (Bill) or Niall?

63. *"I don't know whose game plan that was out there but it wasn't mine." This remark was made by the Ireland coach when replying to journalists questions* about Ireland's tactics in a 17-16 loss to Scotland at Lansdowne Road, Dublin on 7 February 1998 in the first game of the 1998 Five Nations Championship. The jour-

nalists were inferring that the Irish players were running around like headless chickens. Who was the Ireland coach?

64. At the 1991 Rugby World Cup, Ireland hosted three Pool 2 games plus a quarter-final and a semi-final. Apart from Ireland, name any one of the sides who played a Pool 2 match at an Irish ground.

65. Ireland played Wales on 18 January 1992 at Lansdowne Road, Dublin. It was both team's opening game of the 1992 Five Nations Championship. To the amazement of the fans inside the stadium and those watching on television, the referee allowed Tony Copsey, who was making his Welsh debut, to stay on the field despite the fact that the 6 foot seven inches lock landed a punch on the left cheekbone of an Irish player. Can you name the player who was on the receiving end of the punch?

66. On 5 August 2023, Ireland beat Italy 33-17 in Dublin in a 2023 Rugby World Cup warm-up game. Name any one of the three players who made their debut for Ireland in the game.

67. Ireland have met Western Samoa/Samoa on seven occasions, but how many of these Tests did Ireland win?

68. Who was Ireland's coach from 1984-87 and guided them to the Five Nations Championship and Triple Crown in 1985?

69. When Mick Doyle played his last game for

Ireland on 26 October 1968, a 10-3 victory over Australia at Lansdowne Road, he lined out alongside his brother. Can you identify his brother?

70. On 18 November 1989, Ireland played New Zealand in an international friendly at Lansdowne Road, Dublin. Name the player who was handed the honour of captaining the side for the first time in his career and marched his teammates, arms inter-linked, into the All Blacks' half when they were performing the Haka.

71. Only four Ireland Rugby Union players have been named RTÉ Sports Person of the Year. Name three of them.

72. When Ireland won the 1949 Five Nations Championship, this player scored 26 of his country's total of 41 points, a record for an Irish player in the history of a single tournament. This *George* shares the same surname as a former heavyweight boxing *Ken* who fought Muhammad Ali, George Foreman and Larry Holmes but never won the World Boxing Heavyweight Championship. What is the surname of the Irish player and the boxer?

73. Only Brian O'Driscoll (2006, 2007 & 2009) and one other player have won the Six Nations Player of the Championship award three times. O'Driscoll was also runner-up on three occasions (2005, 2013 & 2014) whilst the other player was runner-up in 2021. Name this other

player.

74. Can you name the American sports manufacturer of footwear, apparel, equipment and accessories who made the Ireland kit from 1994-2000?

75. In 2009, Ireland embarked on a Tour of North America and played four games, two of which were Test Matches. On 30 August 1989, Ireland kicked off their tour with a game versus British Colombia who they beat 21-18 at a Stadium in British Colombia, Canada which shares the same name of a British science fiction television series created by Gerry and Sylvia Anderson which was made between 1964 and 1966 using a form of electronic marionette puppetry (dubbed "*Supermarionation*"). Name the Stadium or TV series.

76. Can you name any one of the four Ireland players who were inducted into the International Rugby Board Hall of Fame in 2014?

77. "*The main difference between captaining your country and captaining the Lions is of course that the Lions captain has to unite four different sets of players. To do that, he has to be a motivator and leader of men. The captain has to develop that pride in the Lions. I made Willie John McBride Irish captain and I made him Lions captain too. He was my choice because I knew how he thought and he knew how I thought, so it wouldn't take long to get us working together.*" Name the Ireland & British & Irish Lions coach who said this about an Irish Legend.

78. In 1888, the British & Irish Lions began their

Legends & Lions

Touring tradition when a party of 22 players from England, Ireland, Scotland and Wales, captained by Robert Lionel *"Bob"* Seddon (England). Since Robert Seddon, only 12 Irish players have been afforded the unique honour of captaining a British & Irish Lions touring side. Can you name any three of the six Irish Legends who were given this honour from 1960 to 2023?

79. Re-arrange the Anagram to reveal the player's name – Cell Mop Liable.

80. With four tries each to their name, these two players were Ireland's top try scorers in 2022. Name either of them.

81. Name any 2 of the 7 players who won their first cap for Ireland in 2022.

82. What is the nickname of the Ireland team?

83. Name the Ireland player who scored the famous *"Hand of Back"* try against England in 2001.

84. Which country performs the *"Sipi Tau"* before a match versus Ireland?

85. Who in 2017 became the first Munster player since Paul O'Connell in 2013 to captain a British and Irish Lions team?

86. When Ireland won back-to-back Five Nations Championship titles in 1948 and 1949, it was the only the fifth time in history a team had successfully defended its' crown. Name the only other two teams to have achieved this feat.

JOHN WHITE

87. The England versus Ireland Five Nations Championship match scheduled to be played at Twickenham Stadium, London on Saturday 9 February 1952, was postponed as a mark of respect for someone who died on 6 February 1952. Who died?

88. Can you name the *Barry* who scored 28 points in four appearances for Ireland in 1973, including 6 points in Ireland's 10-10 draw with New Zealand at Lansdowne Road, Dublin on 20 January 1973?

89. In 1987, the Ireland squad flew to New Zealand ten days before their first ever game at a Rugby World Cup finals. The day after they arrived the Irish team and all participating nations attended a pre-tournament dinner. The Ireland coach collapsed at the dinner with a suspected heart attack and was confined to hospital for a few days before being given the all-clear by the medical team to re-join his players in time for Ireland's opening game versus Wales. Who was the Ireland coach?

90. Ireland ended the Six Nations Championship as runners-up to France who claimed the Grand Slam. Ireland won the Triple Crown for a seventh time whilst Gordon D'Arcy was named Player of the Tournament. Todd Hamilton won the British Open Golf Championship. The movie *Shrek 2* was released. Ireland's Best Mate won the Cheltenham Gold Cup for the third year in a row. Athens, Greece hosted the Olympic Games. LMC vs U2 enjoyed their only UK No.1 hit single with *Take Me To The Clouds*

Legends & Lions

Above. Tommy Bowe made his international debut for Ireland. Guess the Year.

91. On 25 January 1969, he became the first substitute to be used by Ireland in an international match (excluding official trial games and international representative matches). Ireland beat France 17-9 at Lansdowne Road, Dublin in their opening game of the 1969 Five Nations Championship. Who came on for an injured Noel Murphy?

92. What was the score of the game when Ireland beat South Africa in their third Pool game on 23 September 2023 at Stade de France in the 2023 Rugby World Cup?

93. *"I do not think that players today practice individual skills. Perhaps skills come naturally, but you can improve these things. I used to practise sidestepping past a line of flagpoles. Likewise I could never kick with my left foot until an accident to my right ankle made me use the left foot all the time. By the time my right ankle had recovered, I was a better kicker with my left foot than with my right."* Name the player who said this who has a kick to his nickname.

94. This *Tom* has scored more Test points for the British and Irish Lions than any other Irish player. He is seventh in the all-time Points Table having scored 25 points in his 5 Lions Tests from 1962-68. Can you identify him?

95. Re-arrange the Anagram to reveal the player's name – Graying Errors.

96. Can you name any one of the three Queen's University Rugby Football Club players who were capped by the 1950 British and Irish Lions on their tour of Australia and New Zealand?

97. In March 1968, the International Rugby Board announced that substitutions would be permitted to replace an injured player in official trial games and international representative matches. This Ireland player with the initials BB, became the sport's first replacement when he came on for an injured Mike Gibson during the British and Irish Lions opening game of their 1968 Tour of South Africa. Name the player.

98. During the three years, 2007-10, when the Aviva Stadium was being built, at what ground did Ireland play their home Six Nations Championship matches?

99. Since the inaugural Six Nations Championship in 2000, only Ireland and one other country have never finished bottom of the table and awarded the infamous and much unwanted Wooden Spoon. Name this country.

100. Edward J "Ned" Walsh was born in 1861 in Graiguenahown, Abbeyleix, County Laois and won seven Ireland caps. He was also an outstanding athlete. In 1885, he was the joint-holder of an Irish Amateur Athletic Association (IAAA) title and that same year he won an "unofficial" World Championship title when he beat the American Champion, William Fordan. The Irish Athletic team were touring the United

LEGENDS & LIONS

States of America. In what track and field event did he excel?

101. When the Irish team ran out of the tunnel at Lansdowne Road, Dublin on 13 February 1926, they wore numbers on the back of their jerseys for the first time. Ireland won the 1926 Five Nations Championship match 19-15 but who did they play?

102. *"Rugby is a game for big buggers. If you're not a big bugger, you get hurt. I wasn't a big bugger but I was a fast bugger and therefore I avoided the big buggers."* Name the Irish actor, comedian, writer, musician, poet, playwright and was the co-creator, main writer, and a principal cast member of the British radio comedy programme *The Goon Show* who said this about the sport.

103. *"Stringer may as well be looking for a Mars bar in a bucket of s**t."* Name the Ireland coach, 2001-08, who said this when he was watching his players train.

104. The inaugural World Rugby Player of the Year award was presented in 2001 and was won by Ireland's hooker and captain. Can you name this Irish Legend?

105. Name any three of Ireland's Top 5 appearance makers in the Six Nations Championship, 2000-23.

106. Paul O'Connell shares the same middle name of the name of one of the major Prophets from the Holy Bible nicknamed *"The Weeping Prophet."*

JOHN WHITE

What is his name?

107. Ireland finished third in the Six Nations Championship which was won by Wales who also claimed an 11th Grand Slam. Declan Kidney was the Ireland coach with Rory Best and Paul O'Connell sharing the captaincy. Italy moved their home games to Stadio Olimpico, Rome. The movie *Django Unchained* starring Jamie Foxx and Miami Vice star, Don Johnson, was a big attraction in the cinemas. London, England hosted the Olympic Games. Peter O'Mahony made his international debut for Ireland. Guess the Year.

108. Re-arrange the Anagram to reveal the player's name – Like Hearts.

109. Since their first meeting on 19 February 1877, Ireland and Scotland have played each other 140 times with both nations using different stadiums to host the games. Name any two of the five grounds used by Scotland to host a match against Ireland, three of which are in Edinburgh and two in Glasgow.

110. Since the appointment of Ronnie Dawson as Ireland's first coach in 1969, how many men have followed him in the role, excluding caretaker coaches or interim coaches, and can you name any eight of them?

111. For the first time in the history of the competition, the 22nd Six Nations Championship, the 127th edition of the competition overall, something unusual occurred which affected all six

teams. What occurred?

112. Ireland went into the 2015 Six Nations Championship as the reigning Champions and after the five rounds of the tournament the Irish held on to the trophy for another year. It was the 121st edition of the competition including all of its previous formats and marked Ireland's 13th triumph, the first time the Irish had retained the title outright since what year?

113. The construction work for this Stadium began in 1927. During its' early years the stadium was called Stadio dei Cipressi. It was designed and constructed within the larger project of the *Foro Mussolini* (Mussolini Forum) which was renamed *Foro Italico* after the Second World War. Name this Stadium where Ireland have played numerous Six Nations Championship matches.

114. Can you name the Ireland winger who won 6 caps from 1960-65, and whose surname is the same as an American city which is the most populous in Texas and have sports teams called Astros, Rockets and Texans?

115. How many times was Mike Gibson capped by Ireland from 1964 to 1979 - 59, 69 or 79?

116. *"Where's your f*****g pride?"* Name the famous Irish captain who delivered this line to his forwards during a game in 1985 against England that Ireland won to win their sixth Triple Crown and their tenth overall victory in the Home Nations/Five Nations Championship.

117. Re-arrange the Anagram to reveal the player's name – Achy Alien.

118. When Ireland played Italy in the 2021 Six Nations Championship, a player won his 50th Test cap for Ireland and two others were awarded their first cap. Name any one of these three players.

119. In 2013, Ireland toured Canada and the United States of America and played both nations. Prior to the start of the tour and not long after the 2013 Six Nations Championship had ended, which saw Ireland finish second from bottom, Ireland sacked their coach, Declan Kidney, on 2 April 2013. Who was appointed as interim coach for the tour and whose surname would be well received by a male or a female?

120. Can you name any one of the two Ireland players, one also a former Ireland coach, who were inducted into the International Rugby Board Hall of Fame in 2009?

121. I was a member of the British and Irish Lions' Tours in 1964, 1968, 1971, 1974 & 1977, winning 12 caps having played for Ireland for 15 years. Who am I?

122. In the 2010 Six Nations Championship, two Ireland players shared the title of top try scorers along with the Welsh pair of James Hook and Shane Williams, scoring three tries each. Name either one of the Irish duo.

123. Name Ireland's coach and their captain in the

LEGENDS & LIONS

2018 Six Nations Championship.

124. He was born in Currow, Kerry on 8 October 1966 and won the first of his 41 caps for Ireland (4 times as captain, scored 15 points) in a 21-13 loss to France at Lansdowne Road, Dublin on 2 February 1991 in a Five Nations Championship game. Prior to commencing his rugby union career, he won an All-Ireland Senior Football Championship title with Kerry in 1986. He was only 19-years old when *The Kingdom* beat Tyrone, who were playing in their first final, 2-15 to 1-10 at Croke Park, Dublin. Who is he?

125. *"Oh good God, yeah. In fairness, he had a New Zealand passport and if you had one of those at that stage it was enough. As well as being poor, he was unpleasant. You put that mixture together and it's hard to stomach."* Name the Ireland coach Nick Poppelwell (Ireland 1989-98) was speaking about.

126. He played out-half for Ireland from 1958 to 1963, his career sandwiched between two of the greatest ever players to wear a green jersey, Jack Kyle and Mike Gibson. He won 16 caps and scored 9 points (all from drop goals). When he made his Irish debut on 15 March 1958, he replaced Kyle in the team. In 1959, he was a member of the British and Irish Lions side that toured Australia and New Zealand, playing twice before he had to go home early through injury. Can you name him?

127. This player was named 1979 European Rugby Player of the Year when he had an outstand-

ing season for Ireland in the 1979 Five Nations Championship. Ireland finished in third place and he scored 8 penalties, 3 conversions and a drop goal (33 points). In total, he won 19 caps for his country and scored 113 points comprising 29 penalties, 7 conversions and 4 drop goals. He brought the curtain down on his international career on 3 June 1987, a 32-9 victory against Tonga in the 1987 Rugby World Cup. Who is he?

128. I made my 125th appearance for Ireland in a 17-13 win over Samoa in Bayonne, France in a warm-up game for the 2023 Rugby World Cup. However, I injured my leg in the win which meant I missed the 2023 Rugby World Cup. Name me.

129. In 2017, Peter O'Mahony became the 11th Irishman to captain a British & Irish Lions Test team and the first Cork Constitution player to do so since which player in 1968 on their Tour of South Africa?

130. In 1996, this bank/financial institution became the first company to have their name emblazoned on the front of the Irish jersey. Can you name them?

131. Ireland's first ever game at a Rugby World Cup final was played on 25 May 1987 at Athletic Park, Wellington, New Zealand. It was the inaugural Rugby World Cup and was co-hosted by Australia and New Zealand. Wales won the encounter 13-6, but who scored two penalties in

the game for Ireland thereby becoming the first Irish player to score in the tournament?

132. Ireland finished in fifth place the Six Nations Championship which was won by Wales. Jamie Heaslip was the Ireland captain. France won the wooden spoon. *The Wolf of Wall Street* was one of the biggest grossing movies of the year. Andy Murray defeated Novak Djokovic 6–4, 7–5, 6–4 in the final of the Men's Singles Championship at Wimbledon to become the first British winner of the Gentlemen's Singles title at Wimbledon since Fred Perry won it in 1948. Robbie Henshaw made his international debut for Ireland. Guess the Year.

133. Since their first meeting on 31 December 1988, Ireland and Italy have played each other 35 times with both nations using different stadiums to host the games. Ireland have used five grounds for these games but can you name any four of them?

134. During England's game against Ireland at Twickenham Stadium, London in the 1988 Five Nations Championship, the English fans inside the ground burst into song after Chris Oti (only the second black player, and the first for 80 years, to be capped by England) scored a hat-trick of tries in England's emphatic 35-3 victory. But, can you name the song?

135. *"The heart is willing, the head is willing but the body has had enough."* The words of an emotional Ireland captain after playing his final game in

the green shirt, a 43-21 loss to France in the quarter-finals of the 2003 Rugby World Cup at Telstra Dome, Melbourne, Australia. Name this Irish Legend.

136. Name the Ireland player who won the IRB Player of the Year award in 2009.

137. On 12 October 2019, this player was sent off during Ireland's 47-5 win against Samoa at Fukuoka Hakatanomori Stadium, Fukuoka, Japan in the 2019 Rugby World Cup. He became the first Irish player to be given a red card in a Rugby World Cup match after he made a dangerous tackle on fly-half Ulupano Seuteni. Name him.

138. When Ireland won the Five Nations Championship, Triple Crown and Grand Slam in 1948, can you name the team they beat 13-6 away on New Year's Day?

139. On 13 February 1954, he became the first Munster man to captain Ireland, a 14-13 loss to England at Twickenham Stadium, London in the 1954 Five Nations Championship. He was one of the sport's great characters, instantly recognisable on the pitch with his flowing red hair, and did not like having to stand to "God Save The Queen," prior to an international match at Ravenhill, Belfast. Who is he?

140. He was born on 3 December 1942 in Belfast, Northern Ireland and was educated at Campbell College, Belfast, and went on to study law at Queen's College, Cambridge, England. He

played for the Cambridge University XV and helped them win the Varsity Match v Oxford in December 1963. He also won Varsity Blues in 1964 when Oxford were the victors and in their 1965 drawn game, captaining the team in 1965. The IRFU Selection Committee awarded him the first of his 69 international caps for his country on 8 February 1964. Name this Irish Legend.

141. *"They came to me and said, you're a big guy. If you play we'll have 15. I hadn't a clue about this game, but I was big and it wasn't a problem to me, I could shake people off,"* recalled this Ireland and British and Irish Lions captain and Legend about the time the rugby coaches at Ballymena Academy asked him to play for the school's First XV rugby team. But, do you know his name?

142. First up for Ireland in the 1985 Five Nations Championship was an away trip. According to most rugby pundits at the time, Ireland had no chance of winning the game. They were merely there as cannon fodder to their opponents who were not only defending the Triple Crown they won the previous year (they mauled Ireland 32-9 at Lansdowne Road, Dublin), they were also the reigning Grand Slam Champions having beaten France 21-12 at home in their last game. It was their 12th Home/Five Nations Championship title and only their second Grand Slam having first won it in 1925. Name this nation.

143. When Ireland beat Tonga 59-16 Tonga on 16 September 2023 at Stade de la Beaujoire,

Nantes, France in their 2023 Rugby World Cup Pool B game, Johnny Sexton became Ireland's all-time record points scorer. The Ireland captain scored his 1,088th point for his country. However, can you recall if his record was achieved with a conversion, a drop goal, a penalty or a try?

144. The 1990's did not get off to a dream start for Ireland as they finished one place above the Wooden Spoon winners. Wales, in the table. Can you name the former Ireland captain who helped the team to a Five Nations Championship success in 1985, and who replaced Jimmy Davidson as Ireland coach before the completion began?

145. On 19 February 2000, this Irish Legend was handed his first Ireland cap as one of five debutants in the green jersey when they played Scotland in the newly created Six Nations Championship. The 23-year old had a great game converting two conversions and scoring two penalties in Ireland's 44-22 victory at Lansdowne Road, Dublin. Can you name him and any one of the other four debutants?

146. On 8 June 2103, Ireland beat the USA 15-12 at BBVA Compass Stadium, Houston, USA. A Leinster fly-half scored all of Ireland's points, successfully scoring five of the seven penalties he took. Who is he?

147. Name all four of Ireland's Grand Slam winning captains and the year in which Ireland were in-

Legends & Lions

vincible in the Five/Six Nations Championship.

148. This Ireland international player, a famous Horticulturist, was the first Wanderers player to become the President of the Irish Rugby Football Union (1889-90) and during the time the four Home Nations were disputing the Regulations of the game, he proposed establishing an International Board which became a reality in 1886 and became the ruling authority for rugby union. Name him.

149. On 13 March 1948, 33,000 fans poured into Ravenhill Stadium, Belfast, Northern Ireland to see Ireland play their final game in the 1948 Five Nations Championship although reports at the time suggested 100,000 fans would have been inside the ground had it been big enough to accommodate the demand for a match ticket. Ireland won the encounter 6-3 to claim their first ever Grand Slam title but who were the opposition that day?

150. In the 1982 Five Nations Championship Tom Kiernan was still the Ireland coach, but the captaincy had switched to two players, Ciaran Fitzgerald and a "*Willie.*" Can you recall the dual captain's name?

ANSWERS

1. Barry McGuigan - McGuigan had never been beyond 10 rounds but the fight went the distance, 10 Rounds, with the man from Clones, County Monaghan crowned the new Champion of the World on a unanimous points verdict

2. France, New Zealand, South Africa, Scotland & England

3. Chicago

4. Karl Mullen

5. 50 years of Rugby Union at Twickenham Stadium, London. England and Wales won 26-17. The first international was played at Twickenham Stadium on 15 January 1910, England beat Wales 11-6, although the first match there was played on 2 October 1959, Harlequins versus Richmond (Harlequins won 14-0).

6. 1997

7. Tony Ward

8. Scotland

9. Nigel Carr

10. 15. Freddie Steward (England), 14. Will Jordan (New Zealand), 13. Lukhanyo Am (South Africa), 12. Damian de Allende (South Africa), 11. Marika Koroibete (Australia), 10. Johnny Sexton (Ireland), 9. Antoine Dupont (France), 1. Ellis Genge (England) 2. Malcolm Marx (South Afri-

ca) 3. Tadhg Furlong (Ireland) 4. Tadhg Beirne (Ireland) 5. Sam Whitelock (New Zealand) 6. Pablo Matera (Argentina) 7. Josh van der Flier (Ireland) 8. Gregory Alldritt (France)

11. The Black & Tans

12. 1991 - England, Ireland, Scotland, Wales and France were co-hosts of rugby union's most prized tournament

13. Lansdowne Road, Dublin - Ulster Cricket Ground, Belfast - Thomond Park, Limerick - Balmoral Showgrounds, Belfast - Ravenhill, Belfast - Croke Park, Dublin -Aviva Stadium, Dublin

14. England

15. Italy (won 33-17), England (won 29-10) & Samoa (won 17-13)

16. No.9 – in 2013

17. They beat Scotland 19-12 at the Aviva Stadium Dublin, Wales 24-14 and battered Italy 50-17. England defeated Ireland 24-12 at Twickenham Stadium, London and they lost 35-27 to France at Stade de France, Paris

18. Three - 21 September 2002 – Rugby World Cup Qualifier: Russia 3 Ireland 35 - Central Stadium, Krasnoyarsk, Russia; 15 September 2011 – Rugby World Cup Pool C: Ireland 62 Russia 12 - International Stadium, Rotorua, New Zealand; 3 October 2019 – Rugby World Cup Pool A: Ireland 35 Russia 0 –Noevir Stadium, Kobe, Japan

JOHN WHITE

19. France – Ireland lost 15-13 at the Aviva Stadium, Dublin

20. Mike Gibson – Barry John, the Welsh fly-half, started the game at Loftus Versfeld, Pretoria on 8 June 1968, but broke his collar bone fifteen minutes into it. When John was lying on the pitch injured, Gibson was sitting in the stands wearing his tour blazer as substitutes could not change into their kit until a doctor had authorised the need for a replacement.

21. Johnny Sexton

22. Ed Byrne, Will Connors, Jamison Gibson-Park and Hugo Keenan

23. Sean O'Brien, Fergus Slattery, David Wallace, Stephen Ferris & Gordon Hamilton

24. 1896 - Tom Crean (Lion #53, Ireland) v South Africa; 1910 - Tommy Smyth (Lion #183, Ireland) v South Africa; 1938 - Sam Walker (Lion #311, Ireland) v South Africa; 1950 - Karl Mullen (Lion #333, Ireland) v Australia & New Zealand - 1955; Robin Thompson (Lion #367, Ireland) v South Africa 1959 & Ronnie Dawson (Lion #388, Ireland) v New Zealand and Australia

25. Des O'Brien v South Africa, 08/12/1951, Jack Kyle v France, 24/01/1953, Jim McCarthy v England, 13/02/1954, Robin Thompson v France, 22/01/1955, James Ritchie v France, 28/01/1956, Noel Henderson v Scotland, 25/02/1956 & Ronnie Dawson v England,

Legends & Lions

14/02/1959

26. Willie Anderson - Jean Condom played in the game and won 61 caps for France from 1982-90

27. Scotland and Wales. On Sunday 30 January 1972, British soldiers shot 26 unarmed civilians during a protest march in the Bogside area of Derry, Northern Ireland resulting in 14 people losing their lives.

28. Wales

29. Brian O'Driscoll – the captain of the British & Irish Lions. At a ruck, Tana Umaga, the New Zealand captain, and Kevin Mealumu each grabbed one of O'Driscoll's legs and drove him into the ground. To protect his head from hitting the hard surface first, he twisted his body meaning that his shoulder took the full force of the landing. His shoulder was instantly dislocated, his tour was over.

30. Soldier Field – home to the Chicago Bears

31. Johnny Sexton - – *from his autobiography "Becoming A Lion"*

32. Wayne Smith - in 2021, Smith led the Black Ferns to their sixth Rugby World Cup success (1998, 2002, 2006, 2010, 2017 and 2021). Smith became the first coach to win both the men's and the women's Rugby World Cup having been an assistant coach of the All Blacks team which won the Webb Ellis Cup in 2011 and 2015.

33. O'Neill's

34. Peter O'Mahony

35. James McCarthy – Golf, he played for Cork Golf Club

36. Argentina, Australia, England, France, Italy, Japan, New Zealand, Romania, Scotland and Wales. South Africa were banned from participating in the 1987 and 1991 Rugby World Cups because of the country's apartheid system. Canada played in every Rugby World Cup from 1987 to 2019, but failed to qualify for the 2023 tournament after losing a two-leg qualifying tie to Chile 54-46 on aggregate. Canada beat Chile 22-21 in the first leg at Starlight Stadium, Langford, British Colombia but were beaten 33-24 at Estadio Elías Figueroa Brander, Valparaíso.

37. Tom Kiernan

38. A Shamrock

39. 2006

40. Gordon Hamilton

41. England (1871) and Scotland (1873) - Ireland was formed two years before the Welsh Rugby Union (1881)

42. Jacob Stockdale

43. Jack Kyle

44. Seven

45. Gareth Edwards

46. Parc des Princes, Paris - Stade Olympique de

Colombes, Paris - Stade de France, Paris & Stade Chaban-Delmas, Bordeaux

47. Tony Ward

48. 1973

49. Willie Anderson

50. 2002

51. Wales - the match ended in a 3-3 draw at Lansdowne Road, Dublin

52. *The Rose of Tralee*

53. Mike Gibson

54. Umbro

55. Wembley Stadium, London

56. The playing of the national anthem, *God Save The Queen*, prior to an international match at Ravenhill, Belfast. On 27 February 1954, Ireland beat Scotland 6-0 at Ravenhill which was the last occasion they played a Test Match in Belfast. Since then Ireland have played the vast majority of their home games in Dublin.

57. Ravenhill Stadium, Belfast – home to Ulster

58. Karl Mullen was captain and Ireland defeated Scotland 21-0 at Lansdowne Road, Dublin. They lost 3-0 to England at Twickenham Stadium, London and 6-3 to Wales at Ravenhill, Belfast. The draw (3-3) was versus France at Stade Olympique de Colombes, Paris

59. Caelan Doris

60. Bundee Aki (2), Tadhg Beirne, Caelan Doris, Mack Hansen, Johnny Sexton, James Lowe and Rob Herring

61. South Africa – they won 30 of their 31 games on their Tour including wins over England (8-3 at Twickenham Stadium), France (25-3 at Stade Olympique de Colombes, Paris), Scotland (44-0 at Murrayfield, Edinburgh) and Wales (6-3 at the Arms Park, Cardiff) and a 17-3 win over the Barbarians at the Arms Park.

62. William Albert Mulcahy & Niall Brophy

63. *Brian Ashton* resigned on 20 February 1998, and was replaced by Warren Gatland four days later

64. Pool 2 Games: Ireland 55 Zimbabwe 11 at Lansdowne Road, Dublin; Ireland 32 Japan 16 at Lansdowne Road and Japan 52 Zimbabwe 18 at Ravenhill, Belfast

65. Neil Francis

66. Ciaran Frawley, Calvin Nash & Tom Stewart

67. Ireland won six and lost one whilst Western Samoa became Samoa in 1997.

68. Mick Doyle - only a draw with France, 15-15 at Lansdowne Road, Dublin prevented his side from emulating *The Boys of '48* and clinching the Holy Grail of northern hemisphere ruby, the Grand Slam.

69. Thomas Doyle

70. Willie Anderson

LEGENDS & LIONS

71. 1991 – Ralph Keyes – Top points scorer at the 1991 Rugby World Cup, 68 points; 2004 – Ronan O'Gara – Won the Triple Crown in 2004; 2009 – Brian O'Driscoll – Captained Ireland to the 2009 Six Nations Grand Slam and won the Heineken Cup with Leinster in 2008-09; 2018 – Johnny Sexton – Won the 2018 Six Nations Grand Slam and a Pro14-Champions Cup double with Leinster as well as being named World Rugby Player of the Year in 2018.

72. Norton

73. Antoine Dupont (Scrum-half, France in 2022, 2022 & 2023)

74. Nike

75. Thunderbird Stadium – the TV series was *Thunderbirds* which is about the Tracy family, Jeff a retired astronaut, and his five sons who all pilot a vehicle for *International Rescue*. Thunderbird 2 is a huge green supersonic aircraft carrier that transports various supporting rescue vehicles and equipment in detachable capsules called "*Pods*." International Rescue's kicked into action with the words *Thunderbirds Are Go!*"

76. Tom Kiernan, Basil Maclear, Fergus Slattery, Keith Wood

77. Syd Millar

78. 1968 - Tom Kiernan (Lion #428, Ireland) v South Africa; 1974 - Willie John McBride (Lion #433, Ireland) v South Africa; 1983 - Ciaran Fitzgerald (Lion #579, Ireland) v New Zealand;

JOHN WHITE

2005 - Brian O'Driscoll (Lion #697, Ireland) v New Zealand; 2009 - Paul O'Connell (Lion #738, Ireland) v South Africa & 2017 - Peter O'Mahony (Lion #832, Ireland) v New Zealand

79. Ollie Campbell

80. Bundee Aki and Josh van der Flier

81. Jack Crowley, Mack Hansen, Jeremy Loughman, Mike Lowry, Joe McCarthy, Jimmy O'Brien & Cian Prendergast

82. The Boys in Green – some refer to them as *The Shamrocks*

83. Peter Stringer

84. Tonga

85. Peter O'Mahony

86. England were the first nation to it winning the Home Nations Championship in 1883 and 1884, then Wales did it by winning the Home Nations Championship titles in 1908 and 1909 followed by England in 1913 & 1914 (Five Nations Championship) and again by England in 1923 & 1924 (Five Nations Championship).

87. King George VI - the game was played on 29 March 1952, England won 3-0.

88. Barry McGann

89. Mick Doyle

90. 2004

91. Michael Hipwell

Legends & Lions

92. Ireland 13-8 South Africa

93. Michael English, nicknamed *"Mick the Kick"*

94. Tom Kiernan

95. Gary Ringrose

96. Noel Henderson, Jackie Kyle & Bill McKay

97. Barry Bresnihan

98. Croke Park, Dublin

99. England

100. High Jump

101. England. The Wales versus England game at Cardiff Arms Park, Cardiff, Wales on 21 January 1922, was the first time players wore numbers in the Five Nations Championship. Wales beat England 28-6.

102. Terence Alan *"Spike"* Milligan

103. Eddie O'Sullivan - After one play he was angry about how they were protecting rucks and presenting the ball to the scrumhalf (Peter Stringer). O'Sullivan let the pack know exactly what he was thinking.

104. Keith Wood. At the time the award was known as the IRB International Player of the Year.

105. Brian O'Driscoll 65 Caps, Rory Best 64 Caps, Ronan O'Gara 63 Caps, Cian Healey 60 Caps & Johnny Sexton 60 Caps

106. Jeremiah

107. 2012

108. Keith Earls

109. Hamilton Crescent, Glasgow, Raeburn Place, Edinburgh, Powderhall Stadium, Edinburgh, Inverleith, Glasgow & Murrayfield Stadium, Edinburgh

110. Seventeen - Ronnie Dawson 1969-72; Syd Millar -1973-75; Roly Meates -1975-77; Noel Murphy -1977-80; Tom Kiernan -1980-83; Willie John McBride - 1983-84, Mick Doyle -1984-87; Jim Davidson -1987-90; Ciaran Fitzgerald - 1990-92; Gerry Murphy - 1993-95; Murray Kidd -1995-97; Brian Ashton -1997-98; Warren Gatland - 1998-2001; Eddie O'Sullivan - 2001-08; Declan Kidney - 2008-13; Joe Schmidt -2013-19; Andy Farrell -2019-

111. All ten games were played behind closed doors. No spectators were permitted into the stadiums because of the COVID-19 pandemic.

112. 1949

113. Stadio Olimpico

114. Kenneth Houston

115. 69 plus 12 British & Irish Lions caps

116. Ciaran Fitzgerald

117. Cian Healy

118. Robbie Henshaw won his 50th Test cap for Ireland. Ryan Baird and Craig Casey made their international debuts for Ireland. The Ireland coach, Andy Farrell, selected an all-Leinster starting backline, the first time this had occurred

LEGENDS & LIONS

since 1931 and the third time in history.

119. Les Kiss
120. Syd Millar (Coach and player), Tony O'Reilly
121. Mike Gibson (69 caps for Ireland, 1964-79)
122. Tommy Bowe and Keith Earls -Bowe was named Player of the Tournament pulling almost 50% of the fans' votes
123. Ireland were coached by Joe Schmidt and captained by Ulster's Rory Best
124. Michael Joseph Galwey
125. Murray Kidd (Ireland coach 1995-97)
126. Michael English
127. Anthony Joseph "*Tony*" Ward
128. Cian Healy
129. Tom Kiernan
130. Irish Permanent
131. Michael Kiernan
132. 2013
133. Lansdowne Road, Dublin - Thomond Park, Limerick - Ravenhill, Belfast - Croke Park, Dublin - Aviva Stadium, Dublin
134. *Swing Low, Sweet Chariot.* The song later was adopted as the unofficial rugby anthem for the England Rugby Union team.
135. Keith Wood
136. Brian O'Driscoll

137. Bundee Aki

138. France at Stade Olympique de Colombes, Paris

139. James McCarthy

140. Cameron Michael Henderson Gibson

141. Willie John McBride

142. Scotland – Ireland won 18-15 at Murrayfield Stadium, Edinburgh

143. Johnny had already equalled Ronan O'Gara's record of 1,083 points before he scored try in the 38th minute running between the posts, quite apt as he was 38-years old

144. Ciaran Fitzgerald

145. Ronan O'Gara - Simon Easterby, John Hayes, Shane Horgan (scored a try) and Peter Stringer made-up the new pack of five who played in the game

146. Ian Madigan

147. 1948 – Karl Mullen, 2009 – Brian O'Driscoll, 2018 – Rory Best, 2023 – Johnny Sexton

148. Frederick Moore

149. Wales

150. Willie Duggan

BIBLIOGRAPHY

Belfast Telegraph; Limerick Leader; New York Times; The Guardian; The Independent; The Irish Examiner; The Irish Independent; The Irish News; The Irish Times; The News Letter

BOOKS

A Miscellany of Rugby's World Cup by John White – Pitch Publishing

The Story of Irish Rugby by Edmund Van Esbeck – Stanley Paul & Co. Ltd

Crossing the Line by Brendan Fanning - Reach Sports

Behind The Green Jersey, Playing Rugby for Ireland by Tom English – Arena Sport

Reggie Corrigan – Leinster In The Beginning by Reggie Corrigan – Hero Books, Dublin

Joking Apart, My Autobiography by Donncha O'Callaghan – Penguin Books

POEMS

The Sperrin Mountains by Aine MacAodha

AND THANKS TO...

To Gerry and Geraldine McCollum for their advices.

Printed in Great Britain
by Amazon